C000126396

# LITERACY, LEADING *
# ~ ~G

How might educational leaders and teachers improve literacy achievement in schools serving communities experiencing high levels of poverty? This question is the focus of this book. Drawing on long-term case studies of four primary schools located in these communities, this book describes the difference between what is commonly practised and those practices that have a greater chance of supporting young people's literacy learning.

In this multilayered analysis of the effects of policy on practice, the authors: discuss global concerns with literacy policy and testing in view of the growing gaps between rich and poor; examine the effects of the intensification of inequality and entrenched poverty, and the implications for schools; illustrate how deficit discourses pertaining to communities living in poverty are contested in schools; and describe the complexities of sustaining pedagogical and curriculum change to address the problem of unequal educational outcomes in literacy.

This book grapples with some of the most debated questions regarding educational disadvantage, school change, leadership and literacy pedagogy that face educational researchers, policy-makers and practitioners internationally. As well as providing a critique of the risks of current policy rationales, it conveys some hopeful accounts of practice that provide leads for further development.

**Debra Hayes** is an Associate Professor in the Faculty of Education and Social Work at the University of Sydney, Australia.

**Robert Hattam** is an Associate Professor in the School of Education at the University of South Australia, Australia.

**Barbara Comber** is a Research Professor in the School of Education at the University of South Australia.

**Lyn Kerkham** is a research associate and teacher in the School of Education, University of South Australia.

**Ruth Lupton** is a Professor of Education at the Manchester Institute of Education, University of Manchester, UK.

**Pat Thomson** is a Professor of Education in the School of Education, the University of Nottingham, UK.

# Local/Global Issues in Education

**Greg Thompson**, *Murdoch University, Australia*
**Peter Renshaw**, *University of Queensland, Australia*
**Nicole Mockler**, *University of Sydney, Australia*

This series investigates the interplay between the local and the global in contemporary education policy and practice. While globalisation is transforming local education systems, the local cannot be conceived as homogeneous or passive. Local policy advocates, educators and researchers mediate globalisation by adapting, resisting and amplifying its effects and influences. In this book series, the local perspective taken is from Australia, whose geographical and cultural positioning provides a unique analytical lens through which processes of globalisation in education can be explored and understood. Published in association with the Australian Association for Research in Education, this series includes high-quality empirical, theoretical and conceptual work that uses a range of qualitative and quantitative methods to address contemporary challenges in education.

**National Testing in Schools: An Australian Assessment**
*Bob Lingard, Greg Thompson and Sam Sellar*

**Literacy, Leading and Learning: Beyond Pedagogies of Poverty**
*Debra Hayes, Robert Hattam, Barbara Comber, Lyn Kerkham,*
*Ruth Lupton and Pat Thomson*

# LITERACY, LEADING AND LEARNING

## Beyond Pedagogies of Poverty

*Debra Hayes, Robert Hattam,*
*Barbara Comber, Lyn Kerkham,*
*Ruth Lupton and Pat Thomson*

First published 2017
by Routledge
2 Park Square, Milton Park, Abingdon, Oxon OX14 4RN

and by Routledge
711 Third Avenue, New York, NY 10017

*Routledge is an imprint of the Taylor & Francis Group, an informa business*

© 2017 Debra Hayes, Robert Hattam, Barbara Comber, Lyn Kerkham, Ruth Lupton & Pat Thomson

*British Library Cataloguing in Publication Data*
A catalogue record for this book is available from the British Library

*Library of Congress Cataloging in Publication Data*
Names: Hayes, Debra N. A., 1960- author.
Title: Literacy, leading and learning: beyond pedagogies of poverty / Debra Hayes, Robert Hattam, Barbara Comber, Lyn Kerkham, Ruth Lipton & Pat Thompson.
Description: Abingdon, Oxon; New York, NY: Routledge, 2017. |
Series: Local/global issues in education | Includes bibliographical references.
Identifiers: LCCN 2016054713 | ISBN 9781138893436 (hardback) |
ISBN 9781138893559 (pbk.) | ISBN 9781315180014 (ebook)
Subjects: LCSH: Literacy–Australia–Adelaide (S.A.) | Reading (Primary)
–Australia–Adelaide (S.A.) | Language arts (Primary)–Australia–Adelaide (S.A.) |
Children with social disabilities–Education (Primary)–Australia–Adelaide (S.A.) |
Academic achievement–Australia–Adelaide (S.A.)
Classification: LCC LC159.3.A44 H38 2017 | DDC 372.6/044–dc23
LC record available at https://lccn.loc.gov/2016054713

ISBN: 978-1-138-89343-6 (hbk)
ISBN: 978-1-138-89355-9 (pbk)
ISBN: 978-1-315-18001-4 (ebk)

Typeset in Bembo
by Deanta Global Publishing Services, Chennai, India

*We dedicate this book to our former friend and colleague Professor Annette Patterson, who was a compassionate and supportive educational leader, generous mentor, and visionary editor of the journal of the Australian Association for Research in Education.*

# CONTENTS

# ILLUSTRATIONS

**Figures**

**Tables**

# SERIES EDITORS' PREFACE

The series *Local/Global Issues in Education (LGIE)*, a partnership between Routledge and the Australian Association for Research in Education (AARE), investigates contemporary issues in education policy and practice. The series is particularly interested in the interplay between local and global forces in education. While processes of globalisation are transforming local education systems and practices, the series refuses a reductive notion of the *local* as either homogeneous or passive. Rather, conceptions of the local and global are mutually implicated in each other, and these implications reverberate within policy, practice, education values and systemic structures. For example, local policy advocates, educators and researchers mediate processes of globalisation by adapting, resisting and amplifying its effects and influences. Conversely, global moves are informed by specific local histories, values and approaches to education.

Relevance to the Australian context is important, however, as the title of the series suggests. Each volume will include multiple perspectives, global interpretations and international voices. So, while the series welcomes proposals directly relevant to the Australian context, as editors we also welcome proposals that are more broadly focused on global trends and directions in education from researchers working outside the Australian context.

*LGIE* publishes high-quality empirical, theoretical and methodological work that deepens our understanding of the fluid contexts, policies and practices of education. Particular *LGIE* volumes may focus on issues of theory, or methodology or empirical inquiry, or may consider theoretical, methodological and empirical analyses directed to a specific topic or issue. Importantly, *LGIE* is not bound by theoretical or paradigmatic affiliations. The series aims to publish scholarship arising from diverse theoretical paradigms and research approaches, because deeper and richer understanding of education issues arise when diverse scholarly approaches engage in dialogue, debate and open communication within the scholarly and broader community.

*Literacy, Leading and Learning: Beyond pedagogies of poverty* is the second in the series, and the first co-authored volume to appear in *LGIE*. The book exemplifies our commitment in the *LGIE* series to publish high-quality empirical work that deepens our understanding of the fluid contexts, policies and practices of education. The focus on literacy learning, and particularly on the lived consequences of poverty for students, teachers and school leaders, highlights how contemporary educational practice is shaped by both the local and the global, and examines how the attendant forces work in the minute practices that constitute schooling.

It reports on the authors' collective histories in researching in high-poverty contexts in South Australia, with a particular focus on literacy learning and leadership. The research on which the book draws was close and sustained ethnographic research, and has resulted in a series of beautifully drawn, extended portraits of leadership and literacy learning practices enacted in high-poverty contexts. Portraits of 'uncommon pedagogies', grounded in detailed empirical evidence, provide aspirational exemplars of practice useful for the work of teachers, teacher educators and educational researchers. Perhaps more powerful, however, are the portraits of more common and challenging practices, and the authors 'pull no punches' in representing these.

*Literacy, Leading and Learning: Beyond pedagogies of poverty* presents a compelling and optimistic vision for education, albeit tempered by an honest engagement with the actualities, challenges and intractable difficulties that abound. Readers, whether educational researchers, teachers or policy-makers, can expect to take away from this volume a broad and contextualised understanding of the issues that confront us in leading literacy learning in schools characterised by high levels of poverty, as well as a sense of the possible in enacting change at the local level. We are pleased to commend this book to all interested in educational research, literacy and the politics of educational change.

Peter Renshaw
Nicole Mockler
Greg Thompson

# ACKNOWLEDGEMENTS

Most of the original research upon which this book is based was conducted during the period 2012–14, but members of the research team were still conducting follow-up visits in some sites during 2016. During this period, we came into contact with many school leaders, teachers, parents and students, as well as other workers and community members. Some were directly involved in the research, participating in ongoing interviews and giving us access to their offices and classrooms, while others simply made us welcome during our many visits. We are grateful to all these people, particularly the principals and other school leaders who scheduled our visits and made time available for us in their busy working days.

We acknowledge that working in schools where there are high levels of poverty is not for the faint-hearted, and we recognise the constant challenges and demands of leading, teaching and learning in these places. We have attempted to honour the contributions of participants by portraying what we heard and observed without exaggeration, and without censoring the stories that are hard to tell. This kind of gritty tale is only made possible by the willingness of our participants to open up to us, again and again. To them we say: We are deeply grateful for your trust, and hope that you will feel we have done our job adequately, if not well.

The original research proposal was led by Rob Hattam and funded under the Australian Research Council's Linkage programme [LP120100714]. This programme is intended to support collaborations with industry. Our industry partner was the South Australian Department of Education and Children, and the contributing universities were the University of South Australia, Queensland University of Technology and the University of Sydney.

The fieldwork was undertaken by Barbara Comber, Rob Hattam, Debra Hayes and Lyn Kerkham (senior research associate).

We are grateful to the AARE/Routledge Series Editors, Peter Renshaw, Nicole Mockler and Greg Thompson, for accepting the proposal in their series and for their constructive and detailed feedback throughout the writing process. The Series Editors encouraged us to seek the involvement of colleagues based outside Australia to strengthen the relevance of the book to an international audience. It was at this point in the project that Pat Thomson and Ruth Lupton joined the team. They added immensely to the process of analysing and writing up our research.

We are grateful to our colleague Helen Nixon for taking on the task of editing a multi-authored manuscript.

Finally, we collectively express our gratitude to our families, friends and colleagues for their ongoing support and interest in our project.

# LIST OF ABBREVIATIONS

| | |
|---|---|
| ABS | Australian Bureau of Statistics |
| ACARA | Australian Curriculum, Assessment & Reporting Authority |
| ACEO | Aboriginal Community Education Officer |
| ACER | Australian Council for Educational Research |
| AL | Accelerated Literacy |
| CAASR | Concepts about literacy; Attitudes to writing and reading; Aspects of written products and reading comprehension; Strategies for writing and reading; Range of writing and reading purposes and forms |
| CLS | Critical Leadership Studies |
| DECD | Department for Education and Child Development |
| DEEWR | Department of Education, Employment and Workplace Relations |
| DSP | Disadvantaged Schools Program |
| EALD | English as an additional language or dialect |
| ICT | Information and communication technologies |
| IED | Index of Educational Disadvantage |
| IRSD | Index of Relative Socioeconomic Disadvantage |
| ITLED | Information Technology, Literacy and Educational Disadvantage |
| NAPLAN | National Assessment Program – Literacy and Numeracy |
| NCPs | Negotiated Curriculum Plans |
| NIT | Non-instructional time |
| OECD | Organisation for Economic Cooperation and Development |
| PAT-Maths | Progressive Achievement Test in Mathematics |
| PAT-R | Progressive Achievement Test in Reading |
| PISA | Programme for International Student Assessment |
| PLC | Professional learning communities |

| | |
|---|---|
| RES | Resource Entitlement Scheme |
| RPiN | Redesigning Pedagogies in the North |
| SILA | Supporting Improved Literacy Achievement |
| SPA | Screen of Phonological Awareness |
| SSOs | School Support Officers |
| TROLL | Teacher-Rating Oral Language and Literacy |

# ABOUT THE AUTHORS

**Barbara Comber** BA, GradDip(Teaching), GradDip(Reading Education), MEd(Hons), PhD, is a Research Professor in the School of Education at the University of South Australia. Her research interests include teachers' work, critical literacy and social justice. She has conducted longitudinal ethnographic case studies and collaborative action research with teachers working in high poverty and culturally diverse communities. Her research examines the kinds of teaching that make a difference to young people's literacy learning trajectories and what gets in the way. She recently published *Literacy, Place and Pedagogies of Possibility* (Comber, 2016).

**Robert Hattam** BSc, GradDip(Teaching), PhD, is an Associate Professor in the School of Education at the University of South Australia. He has been involved in book projects with others that include: *Schooling for a Fair Go*, *Teachers' Work in a Globalising Economy*, *Dropping Out, Drifting Off, Being Excluded: Becoming somebody without school*, *Connecting Lives and Learning* and *Pedagogies for Reconciliation*.

**Debra Hayes** BSc, DipEd, MA, PhD, is an Associate Professor in the Faculty of Education and Social Work at the University of Sydney. Her mainly ethnographic research is located in contexts where there are high levels of poverty and difference. Her research aims to shed light on how schools work in ways that generally limit the educational participation and achievement of young people who live in these places. She is a former teacher of science in secondary schools.

**Lyn Kerkham** B.Ed, M.Ed, PhD, is a former primary school teacher in regional and suburban disadvantaged schools. Currently a research associate and teacher in the School of Education, University of South Australia, she teaches in the undergraduate core literacy courses for pre-service teachers. Her research interests include teacher identity, literacy and place, eco-social justice and critical literacies.

**Ruth Lupton** DMS, MA, MPhil, PhD, is a Professor of Education at the Manchester Institute of Education, University of Manchester, England. She researches poverty and educational inequalities, with a particular focus on urban dynamics and low-income neighbourhoods, and she teaches about these on undergraduate and postgraduate courses. Books include *Poverty Street: The dynamics of neighbourhood decline and renewal* (2003) and *Responding to Poverty and Disadvantage in Schools: A reader for teachers*, with Tamara Bibby and Carlo Raffo (in press, 2017).

**Pat Thomson** PSM, PhD, FRSA, is a former school principal in disadvantaged schools in South Australia. Now in England, her research focuses on arts, creativity and school and community change, academic writing and doctoral education. Her most recent books are *Educational Leadership and Pierre Bourdieu* (Routledge, November 2016), *Place-based Methods for Researching Schools*, with Christine Hall (Bloomsbury, November 2016) and *Detox Your Writing: Strategies for doctoral researchers*, with Barbara Kamler (Routledge, 2016). She blogs at patthomson.net.

# INTRODUCTION: THE PROBLEM OF LITERACY

## Long-running debates and new concerns

Learning to read and write is universally considered to be an important outcome of schooling, but there are differing views about how this might best be achieved. Our understanding is informed by the New Literacy Studies (Barton, Hamilton & Ivanic, 2000), and also by the theory of multiliteracies (Cope & Kalantzis, 2000; New London Group, 1996). These theories take account of political and socio-cultural contexts, the relational nature of pedagogy and the lives of diverse student populations when conceptualising literacy. In other words, these approaches to literacy foreground the actual semiotic work of learning to communicate in academic English. Moreover, they theorise learning literacy as an integral part of schooling and learner trajectories. Hence, the location of our research within these fields is due to their relevance to the literacy pedagogies of teachers and school leaders working in linguistically and culturally diverse communities living with poverty. In contrast to psychologically informed models of literacy, New Literacy Studies take into account the negotiation of power relations in the context in which learning takes place. However, such approaches have not, as far as we are aware, been applied to the study of leadership, literacy and poverty in schooling. This is the contribution this book seeks to make.

Different theorisations of literacy each have different implications concerning how best to teach literacy. For example, early arguments concerned whether children should learn to memorise whole words, or sound words out phonetically. Later, debates raged about whether children would best learn to read and write through being immersed in meaningful engagements with literature, or whether they needed to be explicitly taught using basal readers. Other debates focused on the centrality of phonics training as an essential first step in learning to read. Similar debates occurred about children learning to write. Could we assume that children would transfer their knowledge from producing one genre to another or did they need to be shown? Clearly, such polarised alternatives are problematic, particularly for children who face putting together all these elements to acquire strategies and repertoires of complex practices over time. Further, such contrastive approaches also require different resourcing in the way of professional development, resources and materials; hence, schools make significant financial investments in literacy programmes and the various associated paraphernalia marketed as part of the packages.

Freebody and Luke (1990) developed a powerful unifying framework, known as the 'four resources model of literacy' (Freebody, 1992), to convey that readers (and writers) need to know how to crack the code,. make meaning and use and analyse texts. It is not about either/or. From the very start, children need to engage all aspects of the practice. Their approach was influential in many states of Australia (and beyond) during the nineties. However, conservative educational commentators, e.g. Donnelly (2012, 2013, 2014), and indeed politicians (see Snyder, 2008), continued to argue that teachers had erred in following what they claimed was trendy left-wing advice, which had failed to provide children with the basics. Such rhetoric was inflamed by the results of international tests that purported to show that Australian children were falling behind their peers in other nations in terms of reading, science and mathematics.

In recent years, the success of schooling systems in improving literacy achievement has become an issue of global significance, due largely to the growth of international comparative testing, such as the Programme for International Student Assessment (PISA) (e.g. OECD, 2012). This triennial survey aims to evaluate and compare education systems by testing the skills and knowledge of 15-year-old students. Australia and a growing number of other countries, approximately 70, participate in PISA. Importantly, PISA is not directly linked to the curriculum outcomes of schooling. Instead, it is intended to assess the degree to which students are able to apply their knowledge to real-life situations and are equipped to fully participate in society once they have completed compulsory schooling. PISA results have intensified concern about low levels of literacy achievement by children from low socioeconomic backgrounds.

When Julia Gillard became federal education minister in Australia in 2007, she actively supported national testing of literacy and numeracy, and the public tabling of the results for each school in Australia on the *My School* website (ACARA, 2016). In many respects, the focus on annual national census testing of literacy (reading comprehension, writing, spelling and grammar) and numeracy redefined in practical terms what was to count as basic school literacy. The advent of testing and the display of results on *My School* supported comparison of school performance by handing to parents a new metric by which they could assess and select schools for their children. Consequently, school leaders and teachers began to attend to the demands of the tests (Comber, 2012).

This emphasis on literacy was not new. Primary school teachers, in particular, had long appreciated that being able to read is crucial to accessing school learning. However, the emphasis on literacy as measured on standardised tests, combined with the demand of governments for schools to produce a workforce that could compete in a knowledge economy – another important driver of the national testing in Australia – regularly places literacy at the forefront of public discourse, resulting in a kind of 'literacisation' (Hill & Comber, 2000) that has made educational success a matter of literacy and, to a lesser extent, numeracy. One danger in making literacy so prominent is that when limited versions of literacy become dominant, other important practices can become marginalised (Comber, 2012). Recently, Sellar and Lingard (2015) have argued persuasively that there is a 'new literacisation' occurring, through the emphasis in PISA on valuable knowledge that is applicable in everyday life.

> All the literacies measured by PISA are linked to an instrumental rationale for schooling to prepare young people for new workplaces, new economies and new spaces of civic and personal life.
>
> *(Sellar & Lingard, 2015, p. 28)*

The instrumental rationale for improving literacy contrasts with the rather traditional, narrow approach to literacy testing in National Assessment Program – Literacy and Numeracy (NAPLAN). Yet neither emphasis is likely to adequately prepare young people for imagined future workplaces, or deliver governments with measurable evidence of a return on their investments, since what is measured is limited to what can be assessed by a standardised test. There is a very good chance that it is these limited versions of literacy that get prioritised in teachers' classroom practices. In the case of PISA, its lack of connection to the school curriculum can contribute to vague definitions of literacy. Although what constitutes literacy is no longer clear, the concept has been put to work to measure a range of instrumental skills and knowledges prioritised internationally, and this has an impact at national, state and local levels. School literacy can become domesticated and simply part of a regime of training for compliance (Luke, 1992). To summarise, at least two key dangers come with the proliferation of literacy testing:

1.  that the literacy tested may be limited to the basics, and associated with schools offering a narrow curriculum; and
2.  that literacy becomes another word for utilitarian capacities to apply unquestioned knowledge.

An impetus for conducting our research was a concern that an emphasis on the functional uses of literacy might weaken other types of literacy learning, particularly those intended to develop the critical skills of contestation and new thinking. In such an overwhelmingly evaluative educational context, we wanted to investigate if it might be difficult for teachers to make space for critical, creative and collaborative forms of literate practices. How literate practices can allow people to exercise power, accomplish identity work, respect different linguistic and cultural practices and codesign new genres might be lost in the insistence on individual displays of dominant normative standards. Literate practices, as they are emerging with respect to the ever-changing range of information technologies, mean the capacities to understand and make meaning using print, paper, digital, visual and oral communications. Learners are seen as assembling a dynamic repertoire of such practices.

## Redesigning school literate practices: pedagogies of possibility

Up until now, we have situated our interest in writing this book within the recent growth of standardising testing, and the effects of comparison of literacy achievement. However, there is a long history of concern about the provision of limited forms of literacy learning for children from communities that are marginalised within societies. We have chosen to provide a brief introduction to literacy research by summarising two studies: a concise review of decades of research that contests conclusions based upon deficit judgement of 'difference'; and a study that demonstrates that these deficit judgements can be challenged in ways that make a positive impact on literacy learning. Our intention here is to introduce key ideas from the literature to readers of this book, in order to provide background knowledge for nonexpert readers, and make explicit for those familiar with the literature our orientation and approach. Where relevant, reference is made later in the book to prior research studies, thus providing a timely and comprehensive introduction to the literature.

### Challenging deficit assumptions: A meta-analysis

Kris Gutiérrez, Zitlali Morales and Danny Martinez (2009) described the ubiquitous and limited versions of literacy that are often made available to children of families who live in poverty, or who are marginalised in other ways, as *autonomous models of literacy*. These forms of literacy are underpinned by deficit and normative stereotypes of these children and their families that perpetuate hierarchical differences. For example, these forms of literacy strongly distinguish between home and school, everyday and school-based literacies, and informal and formal practices. The latter part of each pair is considered the concern of schooling. These forms of literacy are frequently associated with reductive and essentialised notions of culture and thought.

When translated into policy and practice, autonomous models of literacy translate into remedial education for 'at risk' students that overemphasise basic skills, and hence 'technical dimensions of literacy', with little connection to content or the practices of literacy. Instead Gutiérrez and colleagues frame their 'critique and normative program' in terms of New Literacy Studies.

From a new literacies perspective, 'literacies are always embedded in social practices', and hence, to understand literacy learning, we need to give account of the social organisation of schooling and its effects. When literacy is conceived as social practice, this demands that researchers capture the socially mediated nature of literacy and literacy learning *in situ*, and understand the sociocultural history of the development of literacy. Such a view requires detailed, in-depth accounts of the actual practices of people in different cultural settings. New Literacy Studies focus on producing more complex understandings of literacy, particularly in terms of power relations and the social nature of literacy activity, through ethnographies of literacy that document the situated literacy practices that constitute everyday life in particular ecologies (Gutiérrez *et al.*, 2009, p. 215). For us, this means investigating how literacy gets done in primary schools, and with what effects.

Against studying literacy as an autonomous skill, or as 'being static, unchanging, and immune from influences of local practices or the process of hybridisation resulting from local–global contact' (p. 215), new literacy research aims to understand how 'repertoires of literate practice come into being' (p. 215). Borrowing from Cole (1998), Gutiérrez *et al.* (2009) state that there are two ways to deal with diversity: 'make it go away or make use of it as a resource' (p. 216). They identify theories of culture and cultural difference as a key terrain of struggle for educators and for driving the rationale for what schools might do about 'differential performance in literacy learning for students from nondominant communities' (p. 216). They highlight the rationale of a 'culture of poverty' (Lewis, 1966) that 'posits that students who fail in school do so because of internal deficits or deficiencies rather than external attributions of school failure' (Gutiérrez *et al.*, 2009, p. 218). A culture-of-poverty thesis explains difference in performance by invoking concepts such as cultural mismatch, cultural deprivation and cultural deficit that assume some form of nonalignment of cultural practices (including literacy) of the home and school. These mismatches and deficits are often rendered using 'medical or pathological' theories that assert that the students are problematic, 'rather than a population who are experiencing problems with the educational system' (Gutiérrez *et al.*, 2009, p. 218). Assuming a culture-of-poverty thesis has traditionally informed school practices, and especially sustained forms of remediation, as the 'default strategy and the preferred pedagogical arrangement' (p. 227). This position assumes that the mainstream classroom actually does not work for students diagnosed with a cultural mismatch, and that therefore they need some form of intervention to fix them up, enabling them to be successful in mainstream classrooms.

According to Gutiérrez *et al.* (2009), remedial interventions informed by these kinds of arguments are problematic because they 'develop unproductive and weak strategies for literacy learning'; and there is 'an overemphasis on basic skills with little connection to content or the practices of literacy' (p. 225). In addition, they often employ 'moralistic and deficit-oriented perspectives to justify their need and implementation' (p. 227).

They argue for a shift from *remediation* to *re-mediation*, which at first reading sounds like a simple play on words. However, they make the case for a fundamental reframing of the problem, away from fixing up deficiencies (*curing* student deficits), to an approach that emphasises literacy learning as fundamentally a cultural practice that mediates human life. The interventions required are not about a cure, but concerned with strengthening the mediation or reconciling the differences in our relations with others. Remedial programmes laminate over cultural differences and re-mediation understands cultural differences as a learning asset.

Instead of emphasising basic skills – problems of the individual – re-mediation involves a reorganisation of the entire ecology for learning: 'The concept of re-mediation constitutes a framework for the development of rich learning ecologies in which all students can expand their repertoires of [literate] practices[s] through conscious and strategic use of a range of theoretical and material tools' (Gutiérrez et al., 2009, p. 227).

A re-mediating approach for Gutiérrez et al. (2009) invokes a 'dynamic and processual view' (p. 230) of culture. A processual view of culture not only 'attempts to bridge home and school, as well as nondominant and dominant cultural practices', it also explores 'genuine connections that students can make with school-based learning' (p. 230), in which cases curriculum for mainstream classrooms actively works with 'important cultural resources for students' home and community experiences' (p. 231). Importantly for re-mediation, students are 'socialised into academic discourse [school-based literate repertoires] as they learn more about their familiar tools and practices, as well as about unfamiliar and even canonical texts' (p. 231). This approach:

- provides 'opportunity for educators [and researchers] to examine their assumptions' (p. 232).
- 'makes links between what [students] learn in homes and what they know at school' (p. 232).
- 'recognises students' repertoires of [literate] practice' (p. 232).
- designs 'new learning ecologies in which new forms of collective [literacy learning] activity can occur' (p. 234).

## Overcoming deficit assumptions: turn-around pedagogies

The second study that we introduce here is an Australian research project by Barbara Comber and Barbara Kamler, which documents how teachers were supported to overcome deficit views of young people from nondominant groups, by paying attention to their lives and interests (such as popular culture), and including their resources in classroom practices rather than seeing them as problems to be overcome.

Comber and Kamler (2004) worked with teacher–researchers, both early- and late-career, to investigate the problem of unequal literacy outcomes with respect to the young people in their classrooms. In focusing on students who were experiencing difficulties with the demands of school literacy, they encouraged teachers to (re)examine their students and their families, and to engage with related research and theories. They redesigned aspects of their pedagogy in order to help students make connections between their lives and school literacy lessons. The process involved (re)learning about students' lives, and considering implications for changes to curriculum and pedagogy that were described as *turn-around pedagogies*. Teachers learned about students' strengths and interests beyond their school lives, and were often surprised to find out about shared family practices and passions, where previously they had seen only deficits. For example, an early-career early childhood teacher learned about an Aboriginal family's active engagement with supporting refugees in detention. Another learned about a year nine student's ambition to join the army, and his capacities for understanding computers and software. On a home visit, another teacher was delighted to see, beside the student's bed, a stack of books about his favourite football team.

Teachers found children, young people and families actively involved in a range of cultural, linguistic and literate practices that dispelled their assumptions about students' and families' lack of interest in, and capacities for, learning. Student commitments to sports (e.g. football or netball), social issues, regular family pastimes such as fishing and camping, part-time work, voluntary pursuits (e.g. army cadets) and exploring a range of communication devices (such as computers, etc.) indicated that the young people in their classrooms were active and successful learners across a range of contexts. When teachers observed children and young people in these positive contexts for learning beyond the literacy classroom, they began to see potential and capabilities that had not been evident in the individualised spaces of school literacy. They began to see that the request for display of school-sanctioned literacy could position students as having nothing to contribute, since they were unable or unwilling to deliver on cue. Yet teachers witnessed these same students leading their peers, going out of their way to develop desired skills and sharing knowledge with others.

The challenge was to find ways to enable these learners to make sense of, and learn at, school, in order to assemble additional repertoires of language and literate practices. In order to do this, teachers redesigned their curriculum and pedagogies to reposition these students. The starting point was to turn to the students and actively recognise their capabilities as knowers, learners and communicators. Students' interests and knowledge about television, for example, could be mobilised in making films for younger peers. Working together on a documentary about netball entailed learning a range of specific literate practices, and negotiating ways of representing information. That study produced a range of co-authored accounts from the teacher–researchers and the team, about how they had learned to design turn-around pedagogies (Boyer & Maney, with Kamler & Comber, 2004; Comber & Kamler, 2005; Fuller & Hood, 2005; Kerkham & Hutchison, 2005; Peterson, 2005).

In initiating the project on which we report here, we provided interested teachers and school leaders with copies of the edited book *Turn-Around Pedagogies: Literacy Interventions for At-Risk Students* (Comber & Kamler, 2005). We had made the assumption that because these schools had demonstrated signs of improvement in literacy, positive and productive pedagogies for literacy were already somewhat in place. We had also assumed to some degree that, because the school leaders had agreed to participate in a three-year ethnographic research project, they were open to further extending and sustaining their pedagogical approaches to literacy. Generally speaking, these assumptions were unfounded, as we shall show. This is not to discount the long-term commitment of educators in each of the four schools towards improving students' literacy. However, it is important to recognise that what is actually accomplished in schools and specific classrooms is contingent on a range of forces – the mix of students, the actual classroom and school spaces and resources, teachers' preferred approaches, school and departmental policies, what is going on in families and the neighbourhood, the media and political spin on education, literacy and teacher quality, and so on.

The notion of turn-around pedagogies, or at least the recognition that young people bring useful resources into the classroom from their lives beyond it, was largely absent in our conversations with teachers, but a range of contemporary and often eclectic strategies, theories and practices were evident in each of the school sites, enacted in different ways in different classrooms. Yet, as we argue later, in this complex mix we tended to see and hear more about discrete literacy skills than anything else.

## Educational leadership and turn-around literacy pedagogies

The research that underpins this book is best described as ethnographically informed, because it involved at least one researcher developing and maintaining a long-term connection with one school through regular visits over three years. We observed and participated in the routines of the four schools that were visible in classrooms, offices, playgrounds, hallways, and so on. Our choice of schools is not intended to canvass a wide range of approaches to literacy, or to illustrate 'best practice', but to describe and to theorise how some school leaders and teachers in contexts where there are high levels of poverty are (1) interpreting the problem of improving literacy, and (2) creating pedagogical and leadership practices designed to address the problem, as they see it.

The researchers who conducted the fieldwork are all former teachers of school-aged children. While we were able to make basic sense of what we experienced in each of the four schools, we worked to access the local meanings that a range of people, including school leaders, teachers, children and their parents, assigned to what we observed. All of these people assisted us in developing the means by which to collect and interpret information that would enable us to document and analyse the local conditions and dilemmas of schooling.

We are writing this book for all these people as a record, albeit partial, of their efforts, and the challenges that confront them daily. We hope that it will support and inform other school leaders and teachers, the parents of school-aged children, educators working in non-school-based settings, community workers supporting young people and their families, and those elected to government who have a responsibility for the provision of schooling and the well-being of young people. We also want to contribute to ongoing debates and analysis engaged in by our colleagues in educational research and schooling systems, by documenting how education policies are taken up, contested, mediated and have a range of effects at the local level, both intended and unintended.

Our project is situated within a tradition of educational research into inequalities in schooling that dates back to the mid-twentieth century in Australia, and in other countries. We draw upon literature produced elsewhere with similar economies, systems of government and language, including the United Kingdom, United States, Canada, South Africa and New Zealand. While not being an historical project, we describe briefly the shifting nature of this research, particularly in the Australian state of South Australia, where we conducted our research. We trace changes in how the problem of educational inequality has been conceptualised and measured, and changes in the socioeconomic, political and policy contexts of schooling.

We are interested in the ways that questions related to inequality in education are understood as problems for policy and practice. Our collective interest in these questions arises from our longstanding individual research programmes related to the persistent problem of inequality in education. We acknowledge that an emphasis on literacy is the dominant current form of this enduring issue in education – how to support young people raised in families who live in poverty to do well at school.

We each draw upon a range of conceptual frameworks to assist us in making sense of our experiences, and we share an understanding of schooling practices as being shaped by knowledge and relationships of power. Furthermore, we see knowledge as something that is socially constructed by individuals and groups in ways that reflect their interests, their cultural values and norms, and, most importantly, relationships of power. While schooling practices are universally identifiable, it is easy to fall into the trap of taking for granted the common sense understandings of these places that often prevail in research accounts, or to take up an overdetermined position regarding the effects of policies and their associated logics on what goes on in schools. Researching and describing the complex practices of schooling presents serious challenges to all educational researchers. Since these practices take place in schools, in this book we can only describe and analyse ideas about practice – our ideas about both its material and discursive forms. The familiar form and function of schooling means that we can easily forget that we make it up, again and again. The taken-for-granted nature of its material form has been described using concepts such as educational ground rules (Mercer & Edwards, 1981), and grammars of schooling (Tyack & Tobin, 1994), while the taken-for-granted nature of its discursive form has been described using concepts such as default modes of schooling (Johnson & Hayes, 2007).

While schooling practices might appear predictable, stable and complete, they operate in ways that demonstrate their contingent, temporal and partial nature. This is perhaps most powerfully illustrated through *telling cases* that afford us the opportunity to describe the practices of school leaders and teachers who demonstrated uncommon practices by working 'against the grain' (Cochran-Smith, 1991). We draw upon Bloome, Sheridan and Street (1993, p. 18, cited in Lankshear & Knobel, 2004, p. 369) to distinguish between *typical* cases, intended to be generalised to all cases everywhere, and *telling* cases, used to investigate theoretical propositions and social relationships through specific cases, and from a particular theoretical stance.

One application of researching telling cases is to provide counter-examples to the dominant, mainly deficit, assumptions about young people and their families that are prevalent in schools serving communities where there are high levels of poverty. In subsequent chapters we claim that such deficit assumptions misrepresent the children and families they are intended to describe. In short for now, these assumptions inform how educational practices are tailored in particular ways. Alarmingly, for some children the resultant practices do not support the kind of learning that will lead to their success at school and beyond.

In contrast to some recent attempts to foreground the individual teacher as the site for change and the problem for policy makers and politicians, we propose *the school* as the site for reform. This is evident in our methodology – a *multisited school ethnography* (Smyth, 2003) – and the location of our work within Critical Leadership Studies in Education (discussed in Chapter 3). Theorising the school requires specific conceptual resources, which we borrow from Foucault (1972, 1977, 1991), from Institutional Ethnography (Smith, 2006), and from ethnomethodology in education (Freebody & Freiberg, 2011). These resources frame our engagement with some of the most debated questions regarding educational disadvantage, school change, leadership and literacy pedagogy, including:

- What can school-based educators do to make a difference to the educational outcomes of students disadvantaged by poverty?
- To what extent is literacy pedagogy central to this process and how might it be understood and practised in ways that enable complex learning by all students?
- How can these schools avoid the pitfalls of narrowed curriculum associated with standardisation?
- How can educational leadership make a difference to what is accomplished in classrooms?
- What is the impact on pedagogy of the commercialisation of teaching resources, and professional learning?

Through this book, we hope to contribute to international conversations about these questions, including the particular perspectives and practices of educational leaders for improving literacy learning for students living in high-poverty communities. We were alerted to emerging forms of 'educational leadership' in primary schools in disadvantaged communities in South Australia by a three-year State Government intervention project – *Supporting Improved Literacy Achievement* (SILA) pilot project. Importantly, the term 'educational leadership' here refers to leadership in schools that focuses on teaching and learning processes. The international literature uses a variety of terms, including 'instructional leadership', 'leading learning', 'curriculum leadership' and 'pedagogical leadership'. During the SILA project, many of the participating school principals shifted their leadership practices towards being leaders of learning and away from the managerialist versions of leadership that were being promoted at that time. Below we explain the connections between this prior study and our research into educational leadership that is attempting to effect changes on school culture, pedagogy and student learning.

## Supporting Improved Literacy Achievement (SILA) pilot project

During the first term of the Rudd/Gillard Federal Labor Government, there was renewed impetus in federal schooling policy on improving learning outcomes for students living in high-poverty contexts. For example, the Australian Department of Education, Employment and Workplace Relations (DEEWR) funded a range of projects such as *Literacy and Numeracy Pilots in Low SES Communities* and *The National Partnerships for Low SES School Communities* (Commonwealth of Australia, Department of Education and Training, 2015). In addition, the Rudd/Gillard Labor Government supported recommendations from the *Bradley Review* into higher education (Commonwealth of Australia, 2008), which in the context of this research is important because of the renewed commitment to increasing the participation of low SES students in university.

In South Australia, the *Literacy and Numeracy Pilots in Low SES Communities* project funded the *Supporting Improved Literacy Achievement* (SILA) pilot project, which was also being used to inform project development for the South Australian version of *The National Partnerships for Low SES School Communities* (see Lingard, 2011). The SILA pilot project was developed in 2008–9, as a significant departure from common practice in the State's Department of Education and Children's Services (DECS), to deliver improved literacy outcomes for learners in schools serving high-poverty communities.

The SILA project was conducted in 32 primary schools that were chosen on the basis of their low scores on the initial NAPLAN tests and being either Category 1 or 2 on the Index of Disadvantage (see, for example, Government of South Australia, DECD, 2012). As such, the SILA schools served communities with a range of complexities, including some or all of the following characteristics: high levels of public housing, unemployment and families classified as being 'at risk'; significant community change as a result of growing cultural diversity and complexity; and high levels of transience. In some instances, there were additional specific challenges, such as being involved in urban renewal, or experiencing significant levels of regional unemployment. Many of the schools were situated in suburbs experiencing an influx of refugee families, most recently from African countries. A small number of the SILA schools had high proportions of Indigenous students. In terms of staffing, many SILA schools had high levels of staff turnover, whilst in others there had been little staff turnover in recent years. Some schools thus had a mixture of new and highly experienced staff, but mostly the SILA schools had many staff who were in their first five years of teaching, and a significant number of teachers who were in their first permanent or long-term-contract appointment. This profile was more prevalent in the county schools.

The SILA project involved: a diagnostic review that included mandatory reporting by all schools on system-determined targets, strategies and evaluation measures; the development of clear, sustained whole-school approaches to lifting literacy levels; leadership coaching support to achieve recommendations and build an effective culture; specialist literacy and early-years coaches working with teachers and in networks; high-quality and targeted in-school professional learning for teachers; ongoing evaluation, with a significant focus on using student outcomes data; and strengthened preschool–school–community partnerships.

The SILA project thus attempted to make a difference to literacy achievement in some of the most 'educationally disadvantaged' schools in South Australia, and hence to take seriously what has been an intractable policy and practice problem for many decades. One of us led the evaluation of the SILA Project (Hattam *et al.*, 2011), in which we argued that SILA made profound changes in some schools, including significant turnarounds in school culture, leadership practices, pedagogy and student learning, and revealed a number of interconnected trends that were worthy of further investigation. These included:

1. the development of school improvement plans that provide focus and engage the school community in substantial reforms;
2. the significance of emerging forms of 'educational leadership' in whole-school change processes that improve literacy outcomes in these schools;
3. the need to fill a serious knowledge gap in the profession about language and literacy teaching; and
4. the nature of turn-around pedagogy.

The research we undertook for this book provided an opportunity to investigate these trends in more depth in terms of how they actually played out in particular locations over time. We were particularly keen to look for and describe the forms of 'educational leadership' that emerged in SILA schools and that seemed to be driving the substantial turnaround in school culture, leadership practices, pedagogy and student literacy learning. We were especially interested in the sustainability of such practices. In these challenging circumstances, school cultures can quickly revert to default forms when key personnel leave or other supportive conditions change. Such is the fragile and tenuous nature of whole-school reform in places where it is needed most. It is difficult to study fleeting formations, and consequently the first stage of many research projects is taken up finding highly functioning school cultures.

In our case, we checked the conditions in schools identified by the SILA project as associated with significant turnaround. This also provided us with an opportunity to conduct reconnaissance for site selection for the ethnographic phase of our study, in the hope that we might identify schools in which the positive outcomes reported in the SILA review had been sustained. Three of the four schools selected were SILA schools, and the fourth school was selected on the basis of school reviews demonstrating the beginnings of changes in school cultures and practices with regard to literacy.

Perhaps one of the main contributions of the SILA project to the research reported in this book is that key members of the research team were familiar to leaders of the schools who had participated in SILA. These researchers had also established working relationships with system-based personnel, who subsequently became partners in the research we report on. The prior research of other members of the team, particularly in the area of literacy, also helped to establish and sustain the relationships across the years in which we conducted our research. These relationships are significant. Without the trust and respect between school-based educators and university-based researchers, it is not possible to conduct such research. We acknowledge the school leaders and the teachers who embarked on this risky and, at times, confronting journey with us. We note that many of them are still working on the front line, while we have the luxury of making sense of this collective experience over time and in hindsight.

Throughout this book, we attempt to make explicit our approach to the research, and to the ideas and concepts we have drawn upon to make sense of the four schools that we maintained close contact with over three to four years. As previously discussed, our observations are the result of ethnographically informed approaches, the traces of which are still evident in our presentation of interviews and observations. It is possible for readers of this book to draw different conclusions to us by critically engaging with our analysis and interpretations.

We have attempted to show how literacy, as it is enacted and practised, becomes a site of negotiation with varying effects, characterised by enabling relationships full of potential on the one hand, and missed opportunities on the other. The same might be said of our research project. Where we have missed opportunities to explore the potential and draw out the lessons from the participants in our schools, we hope at least that we have enabled the conditions that will support readers to do so.

## Overview of the book

In brief, the following seven chapters of the book fall into two sections. Chapters 1–3 operate at the level of the school and beyond. They are about the wider material conditions of everyday life for families, educational leaders and systems of schooling. Chapters 4–6 take us into the classrooms, and illustrate the work of the teachers and children engaged in the processes of learning and doing school, and what hinders and helps. In all of this, traces of embodied poverty and educational discursive practices are in tension.

In Chapter 1, we describe the material and discursive conditions of schooling that shape the experiences of young people attending the schools in our study. We divide our analysis of the conditions of poverty now into three sections, associated with place, policy and people. In the section on place, we trace the histories of the schools and their neighbourhoods. The neighbourhoods are those surrounding the three schools on the northwestern fringe of Adelaide, centred around the suburb of Elizabeth, and those of a regional 'port' town of South Australia. In both sets of schools, their histories have been integrally linked with industry, particularly manufacturing. Our research is the latest in a series of studies that have shared an interest in schools in the north of Adelaide. We outline these studies and recount the key messages from each one.

In Chapter 2, we provide a description of each of the four schools in terms of enrolments and other information that affords opportunities to illustrate the similarities and differences between these sites. These descriptions add to the histories of each school and their neighbourhoods that are featured in Chapter 1. Our purpose in this chapter is to continue to build up a picture of each school, thus making them more familiar, while also contributing towards making them strange by challenging commonly held assumptions about the kinds of places they are, the kinds of students and communities they serve, and the kinds of teachers who work in them. We also make explicit in this chapter our approach to the research, which has been informed by our backgrounds in these sites, as well as other similar locations that have been investigated in the literature on inequality in education, involving mainly longitudinal and ethnographically informed research.

In Chapter 3, we begin to make available the data we collected during our fieldwork in each of the schools. One approach we adopted to accessing the work of educational leaders was by shadowing them over a period of three to five days. These opportunities to observe were supplemented by extended dialogue with each leader, sometimes during formal interviews and sometimes during incidental conversations as we accompanied them around the school, sat in on meetings, and so on. We draw upon the earlier work of Berlak and Berlak (1981), who developed a set of concepts that they described as dilemmas, to represent the complexity of the everyday realities of schooling that they encountered in their ethnographic research in schools. We draw upon our work shadowing educational leaders to illustrate a series of dilemmas that we have developed for this purpose. We also discuss some of the ways in which these educational leaders are responding to the increasing assessment of their work in terms of standards and performance measures.

In Chapter 4, we describe six teachers from across the schools in our study whose pedagogies stood out. Their practices were unusual, not because of what they were doing, but because of how they went about their work. On the surface, they adopted similar pedagogies to their colleagues, but the nature of their interactions with students, and for some with families, was substantially different. In this chapter, we attempt to describe what it was about their pedagogical practices that was uncommon and palpably different from the majority of their peers. These practices were made visible in what they noticed about their students' learning and how they commented on it, how they arranged resources and made them available in their classrooms, and how they related to knowledge and worked with it. There was also an absence of deficit assumptions in their descriptions of their students and their families.

In Chapter 5, we describe the practices of three teachers to illustrate the pedagogical practices that we mainly observed during our fieldwork. These common pedagogies are contrasted with those described in Chapter 4. Common pedagogies are not limited to rote learning and low-level tasks that require students to fill in missing words or letters, colour-code letter–sound relationships and match words and pictures. They also include tasks designed in the name of differentiation, genre pedagogy, explicit teaching, accelerated literacy, and so on. We claim that these common pedagogies suggest that teachers understand literacy as a set of autonomous skills to be learnt, rather than as a meaning-making communicative social practice.

In Chapter 6, we trace the schooling experiences of three children and explore how the adults in their lives understand and attempt to support their learning needs. This chapter deploys a discursive analysis to examine what is said, as well as what is not said, about three young people who struggle to succeed at school. The relationships of power and knowledge associated with these discourses have enabling and constraining effects. In high-poverty contexts, discourses on schooling generally locate the problem of underperformance and underachievement with young people and their families, and these groups also bear the lion's share of responsibility for improving their situation.

In Chapter 7, we summarise the key findings of our research, emphasising the relevance and impact of poverty on the conditions of schooling in our study schools. We provide an overview of the ways in which their educational leaders worked to mediate the impact of policy at the level of the school by optimising potential benefits and limiting unintended negative consequences. We return to the dilemmas we introduced in Chapter 3 to render accessible the insights from our research. We conclude by considering the implications of our findings for practice, policy and further research.

The research at the heart of these seven chapters is most certainly Australian in nature. However, as we have demonstrated in this Introduction, we attempt to make explicit its location within prior research, both in Australia and overseas, as well as prior and current educational policies, both in Australia and overseas. The impact of global testing regimes, and globalisation more generally, suggest that much can be learnt from how educational policies and practices travel from place to place, are taken up and modified in diverse settings, and produce a range of outcomes. In this regard, we hope to provide international readers with some insight into the situation in our study schools, and our UK-based co-authors make explicit connections with the UK context.

Our interests are focused on the impact of educational policies and practices on communities where there are high levels of poverty. While this is a relative term, it signals our concern for the educational outcomes of young people who are the least served by public systems of schooling. We know that we share this concern with the educational leaders and teachers whose practices are described in this book. Their willingness to work with us afforded us opportunities to observe their leadership and pedagogical practices first-hand over an extended period of time. They also assisted us to make sense of what we saw. It is our hope that our representation of their work in the following chapters will contribute to improving the education outcomes of young people who live in poverty.

## References

Australian Curriculum, Assessment and Reporting Authority (ACARA) (2016). *My School®*. Retrieved 16 July 2016 from https://www.myschool.edu.au/.

Barton, D., Hamilton, M., & Ivanic, R. (2000). *Situated Literacies: Reading and writing in context*. London: Psychology Press.

Berlak, A., & Berlak, H. (1981). *The Dilemmas of Schooling: Teaching and social change*. London: Methuen & Co., Ltd.

Boyer, I., & Maney, B., with Kamler, B., & Comber, B. (2004). 'Reciprocal mentoring across generations: Sustaining professional development for English teachers'. *English Teaching: Practice and Critique, 3*(2), 139–150.

Cochran-Smith, M. (1991). 'Learning to teach against the grain'. *Harvard Educational Review, 61*(3), 279–311.

Cole, M. (1998). 'Can cultural psychology help us think about diversity?' *Mind, Culture, and Activity, 5*(4), 291–304.

Comber, B. (2012). 'Mandated literacy assessment and the reorganisation of teachers' work: Federal policy, local effects'. *Critical Studies in Education, 53*(2), 119–136.

Comber, B., & Kamler, B. (2004). 'Getting out of deficit: Pedagogies of reconnection'. *Teaching Education, 15*(3), 293–310.

Comber, B., & Kamler, B. (eds.) (2005). *Turn-around Pedagogies: Literacy interventions for at-risk students.* Newtown: Primary English Teaching Association.

Commonwealth of Australia, Department of Education, Employment and Workplace Relations (2008). *Review of Australian Higher Education: Final Report.* (The Bradley Review). Retrieved 16 July 2016 from https://www.ssc.gov.au/decommissioned/deewr-gov-au.

Commonwealth of Australia, Department of Education and Training (2015). *National Partnerships for Low SES Schools: Literacy and numeracy, and improving teacher quality.* Retrieved 16 July 2016 from https://www.education.gov.au/national-partnerships-low-ses-schools-literacy-and-numeracy-and-improving-teacher-quality.

Cope, B., & Kalantzis, M. (eds.) (2000). *Multiliteracies: Literacy learning and the design of social futures.* Melbourne: Victoria: Macmillan.

Donnelly, K. (2012). 'The equality myth: What really drives success at school'. *Australian Broadcasting Commission, ABC News.* Retrieved 16 July 2016 from http://www.abc.net.au/news/2012-07-16/donnelly-school-disadvantage/4132814.

Donnelly, K. (2013). 'School debate not left or right'. *The Australian.* Retrieved 16 July 2016 from http://www.theaustralian.com.au.

Donnelly, K. (2014). 'Social class affects school achievement less than you think'. *The Conversation.* Retrieved 16 July 2016 from https://theconversation.com/social-class-affects-school-achievement-less-than-you-think-23973.

Foucault, M. (1972). *The Archaeology of Knowledge.* New York: Random House.

Foucault, M. (1977). *Discipline and Punish: The birth of the prison.* London: Penguin.

Foucault, M. (1991). 'Governmentality'. In G. Burchell, C. Gordon & P. Miller (eds.) *The Foucault Effect: Studies in governmentality.* (pp. 87–104). London: Harvester WheatSheaf.

Freebody, P. (1992). 'A socio-cultural approach: Resourcing the four roles as a literacy learner'. In A. Watson & A. Badenhope (eds.), *Prevention of Reading Failure* (pp. 48–60). Sydney: Ashton Scholastic.

Freebody, P., & Freiberg, J. (2011). 'Ethnomethodological research in education and the social sciences: Studying "the business, identities and cultures" of classrooms'. In L. Markauskaite, P. Freebody & J. Irwin (eds.), *Methodological Choice and Design: Scholarship, policy and practice in social and educational research* (pp. 79–98). Dordrecht; London: Springer.

Freebody, P., & Luke, A. (1990). 'Literacies programs: Debates and demands in cultural context'. *Prospect: Australian Journal of TESOL, 5*(7), 7–16.

Fuller, R., & Hood, D. (2005). 'Utilising community funds of knowledge as resources for school literacy learning'. In B. Comber & B. Kamler (eds.), *Turn-Around Pedagogies: Literacy interventions for at-risk students* (pp. 63–76). Newtown: Primary English Teaching Association.

Government of South Australia, Department for Education and Child Development (DECD) (2012). *Index of educational disadvantage by school, 2012.* Retrieved 16 July 2016 from https://www.decd.sa.gov.au/sites/g/files/net691/f/index_of_educational_disadvantage_by_school_2011.pdf.

Gutiérrez, K., Morales, P. Z., & Martinez, D. (2009). 'Re-mediating literacy: Culture, difference, and learning for students from nondominant communities'. *Review of Research in Education, 33*, 212–245.

Hattam, R., Kerkham, L., Walsh, J., Barnett, J., Bills, D., Lietz, P., & Tobin, M. (2011). *Final Evaluation Report: Supporting Improved Literacy Achievement (SILA) pilot project.* Retrieved from Adelaide: Centre for Research in Education, University of South Australia.

Hill, S., & Comber, B. (2000). 'Socioeconomic disadvantage, literacy and social justice: Learning from longitudinal case study research'. *Australian Education Researcher, 27*(3), 79–97.

Johnson, K., & Hayes, D. (2007). 'Supporting student success at school through teacher professional learning: The pedagogy of disrupting the default modes of schooling'. *International Journal of Inclusive Education, 11*(3), 371–81.

Kerkham, L., & Hutchison, K. (2005). 'Principles, practices and possibilities'. In B. Comber & B. Kamler (eds.), *Turn-Around Pedagogies: Literacy interventions for at-risk students* (pp. 109–123). Newtown: Primary English Teaching Association.

Lankshear, C., & Knobel, M. (2004). *A Handbook for Teacher Research: From design to implementation.* Maidenhead: Open University Press.

Lewis, O. (1966). 'The culture of poverty'. *Scientific American, 215*(4), 19–25.

Lingard, B. (2011) 'Policy as numbers: Ac/counting for educational research'. *Australian Educational Researcher, 38*(4) 355–82. doi:10.1007/s13384-011-0041-9.

Luke, A. (1992). 'The body literate: Discourse and inscription in early literacy training'. *Linguistics and Education, 4*(1), 107–129.

Mercer, N., & Edwards, D. (1981). 'Ground-rules for mutual understanding: A social psychological approach to classroom knowledge'. In B. Mayor & A. K. Pugh (eds.), *Language, Communication and Education* (pp. 350–363). Kent: Croom Helm Ltd / Open University.

New London Group. (1996). 'A pedagogy of multiliteracies: Designing social futures'. *Harvard Educational Review, 66*(1), 60–92.

OECD. (2012). Program for International Student Assessment (PISA). Retrieved 16 July 2016 from https://www.oecd.org/pisa/home/.

Peterson, C. (2005). 'Teacher-student networks: Using technology-infused curriculum to turn around students at risk'. In B. Comber & B. Kamler (eds.), *Turn-Around Pedagogies: Literacy interventions for students at risk* (pp. 47–62). Newtown: Primary English Teaching Association.

Sellar, S., & Lingard, B. (2015). 'New literacisation, curricular isomorphism and the OECD's PISA'. In M. Hamilton, B. Maddox, & C. Addey (eds.), *Literacy as Numbers: Researching the politics and practices of international literacy assessment* (pp. 17–33). Cambridge: Cambridge University Press.

Smith, D. (ed.) (2006). *Institutional Ethnography as Practice.* Lanham: Rowman & Littlefield.

Smyth, J. (2003). 'A high school teacher's experience of local school management: A case of the "system behaving badly towards teachers"'. *Australian Journal of Education, 47*(3), 265–282.

Snyder, I. (2008). *The Literacy Wars: Why teaching children to read and write is a battleground in Australia.* Nest, NSW: Allen & Unwin.

Tyack, D. & Tobin, W. (1994). 'The "grammar" of schooling: Why has it been so hard to change?' *American Educational Research Journal, 31*(3), 453–479.

# 1

# POVERTY NOW

The educational outcomes and life chances of young people are shaped by the conditions of their upbringing. In this chapter, we provide an overview of the conditions experienced by children in the four schools in which we conducted our research, under the headings Place, Policy and People. We describe the conditions associated with place by tracing the socioeconomic histories of the neighbourhoods served by these schools, and some of the experiences of people who live there. The emergence of inequality as an issue of concern is traced through policy initiatives in both Australia and the United Kingdom. In the second part of the chapter, we locate our study within the tradition of educational research conducted in the northern suburbs of Adelaide, and provide an overview of selected projects that have been influential both in Australia and overseas. This section focuses on the concept of place as a site of research, and adds to the description of relevant prior literature commenced in the Introduction.

Our intention in this chapter is to provide background information about the contexts in which the research was conducted, as well as information about research conducted in these contexts. We acknowledge that there are many ways of representing the conditions described in the sections below. As authors, we settled on the following after much discussion and collective writing: We agreed that in order to read the descriptions of schooling, leadership practices and pedagogical repertoires described in later chapters, it would help to know more about these places, and the people who live and work there. Our interest in the impact of the overwhelming evaluative context of schooling on leadership and pedagogical practices, particularly those practices related to the teaching of literacy, also requires an understanding of policy frameworks; not just those of the present, but also the legacy of past policy, and funding practices.

## Place: tracing the production of poverty

The shifting fortunes of communities in the northwestern fringe of Adelaide, centred around the suburb of Elizabeth, provide the backdrop for three of the schools in our study, while the fourth is located in one of the regional 'port' towns of South Australia. In all four schools, these fortunes have been integrally linked with industry, particularly manufacturing. In this section, we provide a brief historical tracing of the social and economic influences on the communities in which the four schools in our study are located.

Established in the 1950s, as part of a housing development programme intended to alleviate the State's housing shortage, the original housing estate, named Elizabeth, occupied 3,000 acres of land (City of Playford, 2015). It was composed of two large industrial areas, totalling 1,100 acres, situated in the west and south and separated from the residential areas by green corridors. The co-location of these spaces was intended to provide residents with easy access to places of employment, and industry with a large local supply of workers. The largest single industrial site was developed by General Motors Holden Pty. Ltd, which commenced operating in 1958 (Pocius, 2013).

In the 1960s, soon after the creation of these sprawling estates and factories, Australia's manufacturing industry peaked. At that time, it accounted for one in four dollars of national output. However, by the turn of the century, this figure had dropped to only one in eight (Commonwealth of Australia, Productivity Commission, 2004). The death knell for manufacturing in the area sounded during the final year of our study, when General Motors Holden announced that it would cease operating from 2017. These shifts in the local economy of the northern suburbs reflect deep structural changes in the national economy due to technological change and increased international competition. The ascendancy of service industries has reduced the demand for unskilled labourers in manufacturing and agriculture, which has contributed to a relative decline in demand for such occupations. In the early 1980s, three-quarters of unskilled men had full-time jobs, but in recent times the number has dropped to fewer than 60% (McLachlan, Gilfillan & Gordon, 2013).

These changes have significantly impacted upon the now aging housing estates. According to the Australian Bureau of Statistics Index of Relative Socioeconomic Disadvantage (IRSD), these estates are among the most disadvantaged areas in Adelaide. The index has a base score of 1,000 for Australia: scores above 1,000 indicate relative advantage and those below, relative disadvantage. The index score for South Australia is 984, indicating the relative disadvantage of South Australia compared to Australia. The index score for Elizabeth is 788.

This low score represents the accumulation of multiple factors that contribute to the experience of disadvantage for people who reside in the area. For example, compared to other metropolitan areas of Adelaide, Elizabeth ranks among those with the highest percentage of children living in jobless families; the highest percentage of the population aged from birth to 24 years with a profound or severe disability; and the highest hospital admission rates for children and young people aged from birth to 24 years (Glover, Hetzel, Tennant & Leahy, 2010).

Additionally, in terms of educational outcomes, compared to other metropolitan areas of Adelaide, Elizabeth ranks among those with the lowest participation rates in secondary schooling of 13- to 17-year-olds; the highest number of students reading at levels below the national minimum standard in Years 3, 5, 7 and 9; the highest rates of early school leavers; and the lowest rates of young people aged 19 years who had completed Year 12, the final year of secondary schooling (Glover et al., 2010).

By comparison, the area around the 'port' school in our study has an IRSD score of 884. The area was established much earlier than Elizabeth. It had a population of less than 150 people in the mid-1840s, but this figure increased as its port became a regional hub for the transportation to Adelaide first of wool, and then of grain and flour. The school recorded its first enrolments in 1877. Since 1889, the town's economy has been closely tied to heavy industry, which has impacted on the health of the population, especially of young children (Taylor, 2012). The industry responsible for the pollution that affects health is the single biggest employer in the area, accounting for 17% of all workers; and it indirectly supports the employment of more than 2,500 people in the area (Nyrstar, 2012). According to 2011 Census data (Australian Bureau of Statistics, 2014), the most common occupations in the area included Labourers (18.1%), Technicians and Trades Workers (15.6%), Machinery Operators and Drivers (14.1%), and Community and Personal Service Workers (14.0%). The unemployment rate (13.8%) was double that of the State and of Australia as a whole. More than 30% of all children below 16 years of age were in families with very low incomes, indicating particularly high levels of disadvantage. Reading scores for Year 3 children (in Government schools) living in rural South Australia were well below average, and the town was among those with the lowest outcomes.

These kinds of neighbourhoods epitomise the structural changes affecting advanced industrial economies across the globe since the end of the Second World War, and particularly since the 1980s. Urban and peripheral industrial areas like these, built to serve locally concentrated industries, and/or to accommodate expanding urban populations or alleviate inner urban housing pressures, were always relatively poor (Power, 1997; Young & Willmott, 1957). They also historically had low levels of formal educational attainment – since formal qualifications were not a requirement for labour market entry – although often alongside rich local ecologies of learning and teaching through local cultural societies, workers' educational associations and political activism (Rose, 2002). Yet work was relatively plentiful and rates of pay typically sufficient to support family life and participation in local activities. The effects of globalisation and technological change are now well documented. First came rapid job losses. These set in train a series of consequences in response to the economic shock. Although locally variable, these include population decline, low housing demand and physical dereliction; loss of shops and community services; declining mental and physical health; loss of hope, community tensions, vulnerability to crime, antisocial behaviour and drug-dealing (Lupton, 2003; Thomson, 2002; Wilson, 1997). Next came job replacement, usually much more limited in number as the new economy laid down its jobs in different places than the old. Jobs were also of a different kind: the new volume labour of late capitalist economies, such as packing, food processing, warehousing and distribution; or service jobs, such as cleaning, catering and hospitality. These new jobs have typically been less secure and less well paid than manufacturing jobs, and they are often organised around shift work or antisocial hours – creating a new working 'precariat' vulnerable to a low-pay, no-pay cycle, and a set of economically marginalised neighbourhoods where people depend on this kind of work if any at all (Shildrick, MacDonald, Webster & Garthwaite, 2012; Standing, 2011).

But at the same time, other places and people have benefited from economic change. Recent attention has been focused on the top 1% – the elites whose incomes and wealth have expanded exponentially, greatly widening inequality (see for example Dorling, 2014). In the United States, for example, the share of total gross income of the top 1% was nearly 20%, more than double its share in 1979 (Atkinson, 2015). The ratio of the 90th income percentile (the near top) to the 10th (the near bottom) is also often cited. Between 1984 and 2008, across most Organisation for Economic Cooperation and Development (OECD) countries, the household incomes of the richest 10% grew faster than those of the poorest 10%, resulting in widening income inequality (OECD, 2011). Middle incomes have also grown further apart from bottom or near bottom incomes, as the differences between homeowners and renters, and those in secure work and those in insecure work or dependent on state benefits, have become more pronounced. Since the global financial crisis, these widening inequalities, the tough end of which are so visible in Elizabeth and 'the port', have attracted increasing international attention, with academic books such as Thomas Piketty's *Capital in the Twenty-first Century* (2014) and Richard Wilkinson and Kate Pickett's *The Spirit Level* (2010) becoming popular bestsellers. In the words of Barack Obama, it is 'the defining challenge of our time' (The White House, 2013). The relationships in late capitalist economies between affluence and poverty, and between booming downtowns and residualised suburbs, are now so well demonstrated that Stilwell could argue that what needs 'to be explained is why capitalist societies are not even more unequal than they are' (Stilwell & Jordan, 2007, p. 150; see also Massey, 2007).

As these patterns of neighbourhood poverty and intensifying inequality have come to be revealed at national and international scale, we might have expected to see them having a prominent influence on education policy. So many fundamental questions arise for education as a result of economic and social transformations. How do the individual and collective lives of children growing up in neighbourhoods like the ones we describe here come to shape their experiences of, and relationships with, education? How can educators and schools respond? Do schools have to be, or do, something different? What are the implications for school funding, teacher training, curriculum and assessment? From another perspective, one might ask whether, and how, education as currently configured might be contributing to increasing poverty and growing inequality. Can it be expected to change these patterns? Can education transform the individual lives of people living in places like Elizabeth and 'the port', given the economic structures they face? More radically, can education be a tool to transform the economy and society?

However, in practice across the developed world, poverty and inequality have typically remained quite marginal to the work of school systems. To be sure, concerns with inequalities in educational outcomes and concerns about the ways in which poverty affects children and schools have surfaced regularly in policy reviews and have been the subject of numerous policy initiatives. However, as we will expand on in the next section, these efforts have not typically been integrated with or central to mainstream education policy. Instead, they have tended to be short-lived, depending on the support of particular politicians or administrations, and they have not usually been well connected with other social and economic policies to address poverty and inequality themselves.

## Policy: the emergence and development of inequality as an issue of concern in education in Australia and the United Kingdom

More than 40 years prior to the publication of this book, the *Committee of Inquiry into South Australian Education* (Karmel, 1971) provided a comprehensive report of schooling in that state. This report reflected an increasing awareness of the link between social class background and outcomes from schooling that had been previously detailed in large-scale studies in the United States (Coleman *et al.*, 1966) and the United Kingdom (Central Advisory Council for Education, 1967).

The South Australian report was based on evidence that had not previously been collected in Australia on such a large scale, including data about enrolments and teacher qualifications. Jean Blackburn was a consultant to the inquiry. In an interview conducted with her, as part of an *Oral History Project* of the Australian College of Education (Blackburn, 1994), she related some problems she encountered in finding evidence for what required explaining – evidence that could help towards the making of well-founded policy. There was very little available that linked educational outcomes, student achievement if you like, to the social contexts and realities of family lives. The State Department of Education, where it had data that may have been useful, was reluctant to part with it. Chronically underfunded, it had little interest in exposing its own incapacity. One innovative strategy that Blackburn happened upon was the linking of data around the provision of free milk to children in schools and the presence of disadvantaged child populations. It was just enough to contribute to the imagining of a disadvantaged schools programme.

Blackburn's recollections remind us that concerns about inequality are a feature of the last half-century. Blackburn's interest in documenting inequality was not shared by all members of the inquiry. She reasoned that theories of intelligence were so dominant that these members believed that the link between IQ and educational outcomes were self-evident and therefore did not warrant further investigation. Undeterred, Blackburn's research showed that reduced outcomes from schooling occurred in areas where the least resources were available, and that these areas of most need served the children of families who experienced high levels of disadvantage.

The Committee (Karmel, 1971) recommended the establishment of a disadvantaged schools programme. While this recommendation was not implemented in South Australia, Karmel and Blackburn were subsequently appointed joint commissioners of the *Interim Inquiry into Australian Schools* by the newly elected Whitlam Labour government. They replicated and extended on a national level the work they had done in South Australia. One of the key recommendations of the national Karmel report was the establishment of the *Disadvantaged Schools Program* (DSP) (Karmel, 1973). These reports were watershed moments in the history of schooling in Australia. For the first time, inequality in educational provision was mapped, recognised as a problem and made the focus of government policy. The purpose of the DSP was to improve participation and outcomes of students from low socioeconomic backgrounds by providing additional funding to schools serving the poorest 15% of students, calculated using an index of socioeconomic status drawn from data collected by the Australian Bureau of Statistics. DSP funds targeted whole-school change and improving school–community relationships.

> It operated on the basis that socioeconomic disadvantage generally limits the range of educational experiences and opportunities available for students; that the concentration of disadvantage in particular communities presents particular problems for schools serving those communities; and that school structures, curriculum and teaching practices contribute to the reproduction of educational disadvantage.
>
> *(Cobbold, 2007, p. 80)*

Twenty years after the establishment of the DSP, Connell (1994) expressed a sense of 'outrage' and 'urgency' with modern school systems for continuing to fail children living in poverty. There was mounting evidence from analysis of compensatory programmes, including from a study of the DSP that Connell co-authored, that it was possible to 'make a difference' through education for young people living in poverty (Connell, Johnston & White, 1991; Hatton, Munns & Dent, 1996; Randell, 1978). However, progress was hard won and often not sustained:

> Those programs that do produce changes happen to have found one of the variety of ways – which may be situational and temporary – of bolstering teachers' agency, increasing their capacity to manoeuvre around constraints and grapple with the contradictions of the relationship between poor children and schools.
>
> *(Connell, 1994, p. 139)*

Successive governments continued to support the DSP and sustained a belief that differences in educational achievement associated with social inequality were amenable to solutions through policy. The ability of government to influence educational outcomes continues to drive related policy but, during the Keating government (1991–96), the practice of 'broadbanding' was adopted – budget allocations for all equity programmes were combined into one payment. This change in programme delivery was intended to reduce the costs associated with administering a range of equity programmes (Cobbold, 2007). Broadbanding arguably provided states with more flexibility to target funding towards perceived local needs, but it also had the potential to reduce expenditure in some areas in favour of others. It was not entirely surprising then that in the first budget of the Howard Liberal government in 1996–97, funding for social disadvantage was converted to funding for literacy, languages, special learning needs, school to work transition, and quality outcomes.

A consequence of this change in funding was that social justice in schooling was reconceptualised as the achievement of literacy standards (Comber, Green, Lingard & Luke, 1998). While DSP funds had previously supported literacy improvement (Thomson, 2002), they had also been used to support a much broader range of outcomes, 'including improving attendance and participation, increasing retention rates, involving parents in decision-making, broadening teacher repertoires and altering school policies and structures' (Cobbold, 2007, pp. 80–81). The policy move away from broad questions of social justice made it possible for schools to emphasise the needs of individual students or particular groups of students, rather than use funding for specific equity programmes that targeted whole-school change. This meant that funding could be used in ways that contributed to underlying structural inequalities in society that impact on schools, while avoiding scrutiny of this fact (Comber *et al.*, 1998). Significantly, it also points to a shift from a critical focus on the way in which school practices can exacerbate inequalities to a focus on removing the barriers to students accessing standard pedagogies and curricula that are assumed to be widely beneficial.

Despite decades of economic growth, and an economy that did not fare as badly as others during the global financial crisis of 2007–08, Australian education systems continue to fail children living in poverty, and the number of children living in poverty is increasing. In 2014, poverty was about one third higher in Australia than the OECD average level (11%), and poverty is increasing, with one in seven Australians living below the poverty line, and one in six Australian children living in poverty (Australian Council of Social Service, 2014).

In recent years, the *Review of Funding for Schooling: Final Report* (Gonski *et al.*, 2011), chaired by high-profile Australian public figure and businessman David Gonski, renewed calls for equity-based funding. The major recommendation of the report, that schools be funded according to the needs of their students and what is required to educate each one of them to a high standard, is yet to win the support of major political parties in Australia.

Readers of this book from the United Kingdom may be struck by the familiarity of this story. Under the New Labour government, from 1997–2010, educational inequalities were increasingly prominent in political discourse and in policy interventions.

Funding became increasingly redistributed towards schools in areas of greatest disadvantage. However, at the same time, there was an increasing focus on improving the standard of education through centrally prescribed pedagogies and, as data became increasingly sophisticated, an increasing focus on standardised tests as the benchmark of success and the arbiter of school performance (and survival). Enabling students to 'access the curriculum' and be the recipients of high-quality teaching became central, rather than scrutiny of that curriculum and pedagogies *per se* (Lupton & Obolenskaya, 2013). And while additional funding did enable a wide range of additional programmes to develop, particularly the use of learning mentors and the development of 'full-service' or 'extended' schools (Dyson & Kerr, 2014), the central question of what would really need to change in the school system to achieve more equitable outcomes was not fundamentally addressed. The same trend continued, and indeed was intensified, under the Conservative/Liberal Democrat coalition government from 2010–15, which introduced a *Pupil Premium* – additional funding for schools for disadvantaged children, to be spent specifically on increasing their individual attainment (Lupton & Thomson, 2015). Using the funding for whole-school change was initially seen as not an appropriate use of the money, although recent research commissioned by the Department for Education has emphasised the importance of whole-school approaches, emphasising leadership and staff development and prioritising high-quality teaching, rather than alighting on individually focused add-on initiatives in isolation.

Meanwhile, levels of child poverty in the United Kingdom have remained stubbornly high at around 28% (after housing costs). Sixty-two per cent of children in households whose incomes are below the official 'poverty line' of 60% of the median are in households with at least one adult in work, reflecting the failure of the contemporary labour market to deliver sufficiently well-remunerated work (especially for women working part-time) to keep families out of poverty. Yet at the same time as the *Pupil Premium* increased the loading of school funding towards disadvantaged schools, the UK government also introduced a raft of reductions to State support for low-income families, resulting in what are now predicted to be large increases in rates of child poverty (Browne & Hood, 2016). The effects of these welfare reforms on children are already being widely reported in the forms of increased levels of hunger, lack of concentration at school, lack of adequate winter clothing or shoes, and families' reduced capacity to pay for treats and trips, including educational ones (Bragg *et al.*, 2015; Herden, Power & Provan, 2015; Kemp, Cole, Beatty & Foden, 2014). As scholars across the globe have pointed out, attempting to achieve more equitable outcomes for children through educational policies is a project that can only ever be partially successful while deep poverty persists. While schools can make a difference, systematic efforts to achieve educational equality must also involve addressing the 'causes of the causes' (World Health Organisation, 2008) of educational underachievement by poor children, through policies to raise family income, provide adequate housing and health care, skills training, employment and social protection, among other social policies (Anyon, 2005; Berliner, 2013; Lupton & Thomson, 2015).

Moreover, in both countries (and more broadly in other Anglophone countries), efforts to close socioeconomic gaps in the achievement of literacy standards and other results in standardised tests are being pursued in the context of broader policy regimes and discursive climates that are working against the interests of more disadvantaged citizens. Despite rising protest about levels of inequality and the propensity of late capitalist economies to reproduce it, governments of the right and centre-right have sought to mobilise concerns for the worst-off within a discourse of resilience and responsibility, bringing forward policies to support the 'deserving' poor in their efforts to achieve social mobility while castigating (and cutting funding for) the 'undeserving' and 'over-dependent'. In the fourth edition of its *Poverty in Australia* report, the Australian Council of Social Service (2014) concluded that: 'It will take leadership from our elected representatives and governments who must ensure that addressing poverty is central to public policy making. This includes budget processes and decisions, which have in recent times run directly counter to reducing poverty' (p. 6). Di Bartolo (2005) argues that there is increasing public apathy and political indifference to the needs of those living in poverty.

In response to widespread criticism of his Budget for cutting social services and supplementary support, the then Federal Treasurer, Joe Hockey (2014), argued that governments have never been able to achieve equality of outcomes. Key to governing a fair and just society was 'more targeted' spending on welfare, health, education and defence. In his view, it is the responsibility of government 'to provide equality of opportunity with a fair and comprehensive support system for those who are most vulnerable', and 'after that it is up to individuals in the community to accept personal responsibility for their lives and their destiny'. Eschewing the idea that a government should use the taxation and welfare system as a tool to 'level the playing field', Hockey argued: 'We must reward the lifters and discourage the leaners.'

In his comments, the Treasurer invoked the great egalitarian dream of equality of opportunity, or getting to the 'starting line', that obscures the inherent social and economic inequalities of capitalism. This kind of 'race' attributes inequality of outcomes to the efforts and talents of individuals. According to this ideology, poverty is a result of not having tried hard enough, and of having squandered opportunities. The construction of poverty as a problem amenable to solution through individuals working harder, and for their part children performing better, allows governments to constitute social welfare as an unaffordable privilege. Such thinking is fundamental to a neoliberal logic and to a human-capital approach to education. It lets Government 'off the hook' in terms of providing equity-based funding or advancing what Fraser (2005) terms a 'politics of redistribution'.

In the next section, we extend our discussion to consider the impact on schooling of conceptualising poverty as a product of the failings of individuals, and the poor as different in ways that are lacking or deficient. In her analysis of contemporary debates about the place of poverty in current political regimes, Angelique Bletsas (2012) argues that there is an 'affluence governmentality'. She points out that the issue is not simply in how different groups conceptualise poverty (as either a 'problem' of individuals or a 'problem' of structures), but in recognising how rule takes place through one or other of those conceptualisations. Governing takes place through particular problematisations. In the next section, we explore current problematisations of poverty through the experiences of our participants. We consider how they are governed, particularly through educational discourses, and what forms of governing practices, such as surveillance and discipline, are enabled when poverty is attributed to individual rather than structural causes. What are the lived effects of this formation on those who are poor?

## People: living in poverty

> I hate it when people bag the northern suburbs, but I think it has changed, or I'm just getting older … I think people are finding it harder, and the people coming and going all the time, there's a lot of that happening … [nobody has their own home anymore] … Just the hardship of families … And, the amount of children in like foster care …
>
> I don't believe anyone is better than anyone, we just all live different lives anyway … I just try and be myself … and not, you know, judge them or tell them off for not putting lunch in the child's lunchbox. They don't want to be told off, they want people to understand …
>
> I find a lot of families just want to, in their own little way they want to feel a part of it, and they want to know as much as they can about their child's learning. That's what I see from a lot of them. Even when you think they're not interested, they do want to know. Like we do good news calls, and the families you think wouldn't care, they're just so happy that they've had a good phone call rather than: *Come and pick your child up, he's been naughty* … I've always, and to this day I'll still stick up for the northern suburbs, because I've grown up here. Like I was at football with my son, and this gentleman said: *Where do you live?* And I went, *Elizabeth,* and he looked straight at my feet and then back at my face, and I said: *Yes, some of us wear shoes, and some of us are really nice people.* So, you know, you've got your families that are lovely, yeah, you get the same families everywhere.

The statement above was made by a parent of a child attending one of the schools in our study. It describes the demeaning imposition of other people's values and misconceptions on those living in the socially disadvantaged northern suburbs of Adelaide. In an insightful analysis, Peel (2003) describes the ways that so-called 'disadvantaged' communities (people living in poverty) are portrayed. Communities such as these are often labelled 'badlands', 'wastelands' or 'wantlands', in 'a dangerous form of storytelling' (p. 28) that appears in the form of both 'poverty news' by journalists and 'poverty knowledge' by social scientists. At their best, these narratives elaborate what it means to live 'decently' in a context of growing socioeconomic inequality. At their worst, they represent the experience of poverty by focusing on what is wrong with people experiencing a range of social and economic hardships and on their 'bad decisions, rather than on what might be wrong with the context in which those decisions have to be made' (p. 23). Peel argues that poverty news tends 'to portray poor people as "trapped", "excluded" or "powerless", rather than as people who might know something very important about the problems and their solutions' (p. 24). Poverty news often presents 'an ominous unease', where the crucial narrative is what 'they' may do to 'us', or the way poverty undermines 'the perceptions of Australia as an egalitarian or decent society' (p. 24). In both poverty news and poverty knowledge, 'the danger lies in its capacity to do moral or even physical harm to people' (p. 24), instead of highlighting the injustice of poverty in a wealthy society. In Chapter 6, we describe how children living in poverty are governed by schooling practices that attribute disruptive behaviour and low achievement to the material circumstances of their lives, which are lacking, rather than to the discourses of schooling, which are constituted by anxieties about the risk they pose, and expectations that they will fail.

Educational researchers working in high-poverty schools have also observed a 'pedagogy of poverty', which Haberman (1991) described as a 'basic urban style', characterised by giving information, asking questions, giving directions, monitoring seatwork, giving tests, assigning homework, settling disputes, punishing noncompliance, and so on. In Chapter 5, we describe examples of these kinds of practices, which were visible in many of the classrooms in which we conducted research for this book. Core elements of this 'style' have also been observed in other studies comparing pedagogies in middle-class and working-class schools in New Zealand and the United Kingdom (Lupton & Hempel-Jorgensen, 2012; Thrupp, 1999). Hempel-Jorgensen (2009) notes the different effects of this pedagogic style on children's identities as learners. Working-class children experiencing pedagogies of poverty constructed a notion of an 'ideal pupil' as someone who was compliant and pleased the teacher by following instructions and not misbehaving. Middle-class pupils in more advantaged schools, where pedagogic styles focused less on behaviour, control and a focus on mastery of basic skills and knowledge, thought that the ideal pupil preferred by the teacher would be someone who was 'fun' and contributed original ideas. Pedagogies of poverty clearly left striking impressions on children in the primary school, configuring their orientations towards learning and schooling.

Pedagogies of poverty have other underpinnings too, not least the daily realities of teaching in many high-poverty classrooms and schools. These realities, differing from place to place, include inadequate levels of staffing and other resources to meet students' widely differing needs; the requirement to do 'social work' alongside teaching; and the need to constantly respond to the emotional fallout of deep poverty and marginalisation – highly charged emotional climates; regular incidents of conflict; and students who are disengaged from or angry about the demand to comply with an educational project that promises little for them (Thrupp, 1999; Lupton, 2006). As Lupton (2006) shows, these can grind teachers into impoverished pedagogies in order to get through the lesson or survive the day, regardless of whether they subscribe to cultures of poverty. As a result, these very pedagogies exacerbate the effects of these pressures on student engagement and participation. As Haberman (1991) recounts:

> Unfortunately, the pedagogy of poverty does not work. Youngsters achieve neither minimum levels of life skills nor what they are capable of learning. The classroom atmosphere created by constant teacher direction and student compliance seethes with passive resentment that sometimes bubbles up into overt resistance. Teachers burn out because of the emotional and physical energy that they must expend to maintain their authority every hour of every day. The pedagogy of poverty requires that teachers who begin their careers intending to be helpers, models, guides, stimulators, and caring sources of encouragement transform themselves into directive authoritarians in order to function in urban schools.
>
> *(p. 291)*

While Haberman was writing over two decades ago, he recently revisited this work in the US context. He concluded that, in the interim, educational policy settings have not enhanced pedagogy.

> It is a source of consternation that I am able to state without equivocation that the overly directive, mind-numbing, mundane, useless, anti-intellectual acts that constitute teaching not only remain the coin of the realm but have become the gold standard.
>
> *(Haberman, 2010, p. 45)*

Similar observations have been made in the United Kingdom, where decades of competence-based teacher education, standardisation of practice, stringent inspection and increasing performance pressures have reduced teacher professionalism and autonomy across the board in all schools, not just the most disadvantaged. Importantly, these have been particularly restrictive in schools with high levels of disadvantage, where teachers are most under pressure to establish 'the basics' and increase test results using tried-and-tested methods, and where improving 'behaviour' is seen as crucial to increasing schools' reputations within increasingly marketised systems.

It is ironic too that the standardisation of practice and increasing performance pressure in these settings was motivated partly by attempts to remove the effects of 'culture'-of-poverty thinking from the classroom. For equity-minded politicians and officials in many advanced economies, the elimination of 'low expectations' of children in poverty has been a prime motivator for pedagogic standardisation, more frequent and rigorous inspection and stronger accountability for performance, in order that young people are not let down by inadequate teaching.

Yet these are precisely the schools where impoverished, mundane, anti-intellectual pedagogies are likely to do most damage, since many students will not come from families and communities with access to the kinds of educational and cultural resources that supplement and align with what is offered at school.

Scrutinising, standardising, and de-risking pedagogy to avoid failing students in poverty may have precisely the opposite effect. Investigating these kinds of links between policy and practice has been a key contribution of research conducted in education, particularly the ethnographic kind. The intentions of policy makers, and the commitments of school leaders and teachers, often have unintended consequences. In the case of young people who live in poverty, the stakes are higher, because they rely more on education than their affluent peers to improve their life chances. At the same time, a range of concerns about their welfare, the utilisation of their human capital, and the potential problems and dangers they present to society intensify sometimes misguided efforts to produce policy and practice that addresses these concerns. These issues are among those that have been investigated in research conducted in the northern suburbs of Adelaide. Since the previously discussed Karmel Report (1971), a series of major studies has mapped the local conditions of teaching and learning in these changing social and economic conditions. Below we provide a brief account of this body of research.

## Educational research in the north: key contributions to understanding poverty

This book is the latest contribution to a substantial archive of empirical educational research that has been conducted in Adelaide's northern suburbs schools over the past 40 years. While not an exhaustive list, the following selection reflects the extensive and long-term nature of this research:

- Early studies of educational inequality drawing upon extensive interviews, *Making the Difference* (Connell, Ashenden, Kessler & Dowsett, 1982) and *Teachers' Work* (Connell, 1985).
- A review of the Disadvantaged Schools Program, *Running Twice as Hard* (Connell *et al.*, 1991).
- Longitudinal Studies of Schooling, *100 Children go to School* (Hill *et al.*, 1998).
- *A case of intention deficit disorder? ICT policy, disadvantaged schools and leaders* (Thomson, Nixon, & Comber, 2006).
- *Making Hope Practical* (McInerney, 2004).
- *Schooling the Rustbelt Kids* (Thomson, 2002).
- Connecting Lives and Learning: Renewing pedagogy in the middle years. (Prosser, Lucas & Reid, 2010).
- Research into educational aspirations (Bok, 2010; Hattam, Woodley-Baker & Lucas, 2012; L. Smith, 2011).
- Recent doctoral studies by DECD educational leaders from northern region public schools (Rogers, 2013; Semmens, 2014).

In the remainder of this chapter, we describe in more detail four of these studies, chosen because of their relevance to the research reported on in this book. We begin with R. W. Connell's scholarship, based upon research conducted jointly with Dean Ashenden, Susan Kessler and Gary Dowsett. *Making the Difference* (Connell *et al.*, 1982) focuses on interviews with 14-year-old students in independent and State comprehensive schools in Sydney and Adelaide; while *Teachers' Work* (1985) provides detailed descriptions of the life and work of teachers. Our research continues to demonstrate a key finding of this earlier work – that teachers' learning and their repertoires of practice are key to school change. We also refer to Connell's (1991) review of the DSP, conducted with Ken Johnston and Viv White.

We then discuss Pat Thomson's book *Schooling the Rustbelt Kids,* which included primary and secondary schools in the northern suburbs of Adelaide (Thomson, 2002). Thomson provides evidence that policy as usual in the western world, characterised by outcomes-based and standardised approaches, does not work in schools located in disadvantaged communities. Thomson argues that schools have to do more with less, and that they need enabling policy environments, not policies that limit educational outcomes to spelling, reading and writing.

We complete this introduction to prior relevant studies in the north by discussing the project known as *Redesigning Pedagogies in the North (RPiN)*, which was conducted by a large team of researchers based at the University of South Australia working in partnership with an equally large team of partners employed by the Department of Education and Children's Services. Based in secondary schools, the participating teacher–researchers worked with university researchers to reimagine middle schooling so that it integrated the everyday experiences and expertise of young people (Prosser, Lucas & Reid, 2010; Hattam, Zipin, Brennan & Comber, 2009).

## Making the Difference  *(Connell* et al.*, 1982) and* Teachers' Work *(Connell, 1985)*

Both books by Connell and colleagues highlight the ways in which schooling (re)produces social stratification, which in northern suburbs secondary schools in South Australia means 'running twice as hard' and attempting to innovate against a system that normalises the conditions that produce inequality. This research attempted to think past the deficit accounts of these schools and the communities that they serve, and importantly to bring teachers back into the policy debates as the key actors of reform and innovation. These texts are framed by the historical debates that gave rise to what we would today call 'curriculum studies' (Pinar, 2012), especially focusing on what was the dominant form of curriculum ('competitive academic curriculum') and how that was enacted through the local rationality of schools, manifesting in teachers' work. These texts also assert a political project for the profession that argues for teachers as organic intellectuals, who were engaged in curriculum reform in the interests of working-class students, and for a version of the devolution of schools of a social democratic kind, and not the version on offer today. Significantly, these texts report on what was going on in schools during the time of the DSP. In the final chapter of *Running Twice as Hard*, a review of the DSP published in the year that the programme closed down, Connell and colleagues (1991) state:

The program does make a difference to the way innovation occurs and is sustained, in schools ... It has enriched offerings and stimulated imaginative teaching and community projects across a broad front ... The DSP has also had the unplanned effect of stimulating the growth of a network of teachers, consultants and parents ... These networks have built up a body of expertise on issues of poverty and education, and provide an informed context for discussions of policy in the area. This expertise is a major educational asset, and we consider that it should be fostered and applied more systematically.

(p. 264)

## Schooling the Rustbelt Kids *(Thomson, 2002)*

Thomson provides what might be understood to be a regional ethnography, involving data from interviews with 36 principals, photographic material and references to statistical data sets and the international literature. This book is framed by concerns for (re)production of privilege and disadvantage, analysing the processes of educational inequality, innovatively attending to place, providing narratives that account for life in northern suburbs schools, engaging in a critique of policy regimes in place at the time, and outlining a political project for those committed to improving teaching and learning in these schools. *Schooling the Rustbelt Kids* aimed to provide an account of 'the everyday realities of rustbelt schools', 'in the hope that the telling is also a form of "narrative justice", and that stories might contribute to much needed shifts in policy and understanding' (p. xv). When dominant deficit representations of people and the places where they live are carried in narratives told about them by others, the power of the word is only too clear. On this very theme, Thomson writes:

The north is a locality which, on stable and credible measures of hardship, emerges as [one of] the most disadvantaged in the nation, but whose spokespeople wanted to avoid all mention of the word disadvantage and assert instead their assets and advantages. It is hardly surprising that this is the case. ... It was the labelling of a whole city and its people to which northern suburbs residents responded, knowing from experience that words do matter.

(p. 99)

The first half or more of *Schooling the Rustbelt Kids* takes the reader into schools and, through various textual strategies, introduces us to some of the students, the challenges of school principals and the frustrations of teachers. This part of the book is all about contextualising that which is too often missing from knowledge about schools that informs policy-making today. We are introduced to Vicki and Thanh and the sorts of knowledge they bring to school, in what Thomson refers to as their 'virtual school-bag' (pp. 1–2). Thomson then provides an account of the suburban region that she names as either a post-industrial city or a rustbelt, and attempts at least to position her account of schooling in a wider social framing. Too often, educational studies fail to acknowledge the social context, and then push too much of the responsibility for making *the* difference onto schools, when other social policy is also in play, such as housing, labour market and employment, and health.

Her account of 'toil and trouble' is especially revealing, and provides some measure of the challenges for those working in northern suburbs public schools. To summarise her key point: These schools are by and large well managed, but 'because so much … teachers' time is taken up with the unavoidable tasks of keeping order and attending to welfare issues, orderly students … actually have less teacher attention' (p. 49). Importantly also, '[t]he school represents (the) social order [in some communities] and is often called upon to rectify neighbourhood discipline if parents cannot' (p. 54). Importantly, what this results in is 'time taken managing order and welfare, and the resulting lack of time and resources to do as much as might be done to change curriculum, pedagogy and school practices' (p. xiv).

In her chapters on the social context of schools, Thomson outlines a range of factors that affect individual schools, such as changes in the labour market, changes in families and families under pressure, changes in migration and diaspora, and transience. She mentions that schools are also affected by the resources that local communities have (or have not), such as community infrastructure, employment networks and availability of voluntary labour, as well as the age of the locality and school facilities, and neighbourhood narratives. The research for this book was conducted during the early years of the Howard government, which extended from 1996 to 2007. Critically, it was the time when federal government funding formulas were changed, and the rationale for equity funding, that had been argued on the grounds of redistributing resources to the most needy, had lost its power. On this theme, Thomson asserts:

> What exists as state and federal funding practice is not a resources distribution technology for reducing dis/advantage and distinction. It is not more resources for doing more. Rather it … both consolidates and enhances the differing capacities of schools to provide all children with equal life chances.
>
> *(p. 109)*

Thomson ends her analysis with a brief outline of a political project for those committed to a schooling system that can 'provide all children with equal life chances'. This would involve:

- remembering that schools and the 'social' are imbricated. Policy attends to schooling as a key site of social formation that undermines the history of social stratification.
- keeping idealism and realism in productive tension. Our idealism doesn't lead to blaming these schools; nor does our realism mean we lower our expectations.
- acknowledging contingency against assertions of 'fixed and unquestionable outcomes', and exploring and innovating at the local level to develop the kinds of pedagogy and curriculum that might better meet the needs, interests and knowledges of their particular students' (p. 183).

- accepting that 'complexity matters' (p. 183), and that we need policy that enables local-level solutions to unique challenges that are often screened out in one-size-fits-all policy regimes.
- sustaining a 'holistic, integrated regional policy framework' (p. 184).
- providing adequate resources based on the profiles of 'individual schools and their capacity to raise adequate funds, their specific enrolments and neighbourhood assets' (p. 186).
- understanding that 'democratic work builds local assets' (p. 189).
- supporting further research.

The final half of *Schooling the Rustbelt Kids* continues the work of Connell and colleagues, and provides an account of the neoliberalising of policy, and also a critique that calls into question the too-easy claim made by contemporary policy, that the problems are always located in the schools, and with leaders and teachers, and that policy is, by its very nature, the solution. Thomson argues persuasively that, in fact, the solutions are always located in schools, and that policy is often part of the problem.

## Redesigning Pedagogies in the North (RPiN) *project (Hattam et al., 2009)*

The rationale for RPiN mostly accepted the explanation for inequality contained in the cultural reproduction thesis (Hattam *et al.*, 2009), but took up Delpit's (1988) thesis that we need to connect young people's lifeworlds to the academic curriculum. The argument for lifeworld relevance of the curriculum is not a new idea, and it has taken various forms. For RPiN, the following alternatives were worked on: funds of knowledge (Moll, Amanti, Neff & Gonzalez, 1992); place-based education (Gruenewald, 2003; Kerkham, 2011; Kerkham & Comber, 2013; G. Smith, 2002); youth and popular culture (S. Atkinson & Nixon, 2005; Duncan-Anrade, 2004; Nixon, 2003; Sefton-Green, Nixon & Erstad, 2009); and a local literacies approach (McLaughlin, 1996; Street, 1994). As RPiN developed, the project's aims shifted to these questions: How can teachers build pedagogy that engages the lifeworlds of their students and that enables success? How can high expectations be sustained for student learning and positive relationships? One of the key challenges for RPiN was how to describe an emergent alternative to traditional teaching approaches. Of some note here is the shift from *curriculum* studies to new *pedagogy* studies (Hattam & Zipin, 2009, p. 298). During this time, there had been national interest in pedagogy studies, and RPiN provided an alternative approach to the *productive pedagogies* research in Queensland (Hayes, Mills, Christie & Lingard, 2006), and the subsequent New South Wales version of this approach, *Quality Teaching* (Gore, 2007; Ladwig, 2007). RPiN asked participating teachers to reflect on their pedagogy and to describe the challenges they faced. The RPiN teachers argued that traditional chalk-and-talk approaches based on 'imparting knowledge' from teacher to student fail in most cases. Instead, they attempted to articulate an emergent, innovative alternative that was yet to be fully elaborated. The alternative was described by them using terms such as 'student-centred', 'negotiated', 'constructivist' and 'thematic'.

In sustaining positive student–teacher relationships whilst working to provide challenging learning experiences, the teachers described their pedagogies as 'student-centred'. This term invokes such practices as activity-based learning, problem-solving approaches and using lots of opportunities to work in groups. The term also refers to the various ways that teachers are attempting to involve the students in negotiating what goes on in the classroom and in the curriculum. Many teachers referred to 'building on their students' prior experiences' or 'extending areas of interest'. The idea of using a 'thematic approach' – choosing a curriculum theme that has some cross-curricular possibilities – as a basis for such negotiations was reported. Many teachers grappled with designing 'relevant' learning opportunities, a difficult task that required talking/listening to the students. Another often-used term was 'constructivist', a term that we inferred to mean 'starting where the kids are at'. This term also infers greater sensitivity by teachers to the ways that students construct their own meanings. What the teachers described gave a strong sense of the kinds of teaching that was going on: 'explicit teaching', 'scaffolding', modelling analysis, summarising and lots of practical/activity-based tasks. Moreover, 'getting to know the students' went beyond merely building relationships – 'knowing the students' enabled teachers to design relevant and rigorous curriculum that provided intellectual challenge and supported academic success. Rich descriptions of the teachers' alternative pedagogies were documented in an edited collection, *Connecting Lives and Learning* (Prosser *et al.*, 2010). RPiN concluded that curriculum and pedagogical innovation that led to engagement and success in middle years was possible if teachers were supported in ways described above.

Patterns of inequitable outcomes from schooling extend across the sweep of time. Researchers have investigated the continuing and changing ways that these patterns have been produced, and reproduced, through the practices of schooling. Beginning with Connell *et al.*'s (1982) study, conducted in the late 1970s, and concluding with the research reported in this book, conducted in the second decade of the following century, the recurring nature of these outcomes suggests that there are endemic and seemingly intractable features of schooling in the poorest neighbourhoods and regions in the country. The correlation of poverty and inequitable educational outcomes seems inexorable. But the places and people that feature in the research are not, as policy rhetoric and media discourse too often has them, hopeless and helpless, grim, feral and dull-witted. Children, young people, their families, teachers and schools do, in difficult circumstances, find ways to do more than simply get by. The schools that we visited and the people we encountered were doing it tough, but with a determination to do more than just survive. Previous research documents reservoirs of hope, resistant practices and small stories of change in such places, and in the everyday lives of the people who live there. Our research finds these things too. It is important to remember this as the story in this book as it unfolds.

## Conclusion

The schools that feature in this book could in some respects be described as exemplary. By this we do not mean that they consistently set a high standard in their teaching and leadership of literacy, or that they provide examples of good practice to be held up and followed (although some of these can be found within the book). Rather, they are outstanding examples of the realities of developing children's literacies in the time/space moments that represent the intersections of deep postindustrial poverty with neoliberal educational and social policies. These examples, varying in local detail, will be recognisable in affluent nations across the globe.

The areas in which these schools are situated were the engines of economic growth in the industrial era. The legacy of their industrial past is still evident in high rates of ill-health, low skills and low incomes. More acutely, they are presently experiencing the ongoing fallout from de-industrialisation, with entrenched poverty and marginalisation as labour market structures and geographies are reconfigured in increasingly unequal ways. Yet the testimonies of residents bear witness to the ways in which the problem of poverty created by global and local economic restructuring is being redescribed as originating in the poor themselves, highlighting their alleged multiple 'failures' – welfare dependency, low aspiration, criminality and immorality. State support is being withdrawn to 'incentivise' aspiration and social and spatial mobility, while no longer supporting those not deemed 'deserving' or sufficiently independent.

Educational inequalities are centrally important for the many young people in these areas whom the school system fails to engage and support, and for policy makers who realise that both economic growth and greater equity depend on more widespread educational success. In the following chapters, we critically examine at the local level of schooling if the remedies prescribed are adequate for the task, and if governments pay sufficient attention to the redistribution of resources. More importantly perhaps, we question the increasing focus on individual students rather than on whole-school change, and on the structures and processes of schooling that produce disadvantage. We describe in detail a range of pedagogical practices which are, on the one hand, developed in a discursive climate that blames and seeks to discipline the poor and, on the other, are standardised and regulated by education policies that seek to 'drive up' the performance of poor children in narrowly defined tests, and to hold teachers to account on these results.

## References

Anyon, J. (2005). 'What "counts" as educational policy? Notes toward a new paradigm'. *Harvard Educational Review, 75*(1), 65–88.

Atkinson, A. (2015). *Inequality: What can be done?* Cambridge: Mass. & London: Harvard University Press.

Atkinson, S., & Nixon, H. (2005). 'Locating the subject: Teens online @ ninemsn'. *Discourse, 26*(3), 387–409.

Australian Bureau of Statistics (2014). *Australian Bureau of Statistics: Census for a Brighter Future.* Retrieved 10 May 2016 from http://www.abs.gov.au/websitedbs/censushome. nsf/home/Census?opendocument.

Australian Council of Social Service (2014). *Poverty in Australia 2014.* Retrieved 9 June 2016, from http://www.acoss.org.au/poverty-2/.

Berliner, D. (2013). 'Effects of inequality and poverty vs. teachers and schooling on America's youth'. *Teachers College Record, 115*(12).

Blackburn, J. (1994). *Oral history project.* Interviewer: T. Ryan. 5UV Radio Adelaide, at the University of Adelaide. Retrieved 10 March 2016 from http://nla.gov.au/nla.obj-217264631.

Bletsas, A. (2012). 'Spaces between: Elaborating the theoretical underpinnings of the "WPR" approach and its significance for contemporary scholarship'. In A. Bletsas & C. Beasley (eds.), *Engaging with Carol Bacchi: Strategic interventions and exchanges* (pp. 37–51). Adelaide: University of Adelaide Press.

Bok, J. (2010). 'The capacity to aspire to higher education: "It's like making them do a play without a script"'. *Critical Studies in Education, 51*(2), 163–178.

Bragg, J., Burman, E., Greenstein, A., Hanley, T., Kalambouka, A., Lupton, R., McCoy, L., Sapin, K. & Winter, L. (2015). *The impact of the 'bedroom tax' on children and their education: A study in the city of Manchester.* Manchester Institute of Education. Retrieved 30 March 2016 from http://www.seed.manchester.ac.uk/medialibrary/research/Bedroom-Tax-Final-Report.pdf.

Browne, J., & Hood, A. (2016). *Living standards, poverty and inequality in the UK: 2015/16 to 2020/21.* Institute for Fiscal Studies. Retrieved 17 July 2016 from http://www.ifs.org. uk/uploads/publications/comms/R114.pdf.

Central Advisory Council For Education (England) (1967). *The Plowden Report: Children and their primary schools.* Retrieved 17 July 2016 from http://www.educationengland.org.uk/ documents/plowden/plowden1967-1.html.

City of Playford (2015). *History of Playford.* Retrieved 12 May 2016 from http://www.play-ford.sa.gov.au/page.aspx?u=1339.

Cobbold, T. (2007). *The great school fraud: Howard government school education policy 1996–2006.* Paper prepared for the Australian Education Union. Australian Education Union. Southbank, Victoria.

Coleman, J. S., Campbell, E. Q., Hobson, C. J., McPartland, J., Mood, A. M., Weinfeld, F. D., & York, R. (1966). *Equality of Educational Opportunity.* Washington, D.C.: U.S. Dept. of Health, Education, and Welfare.

Comber, B., Green, B., Lingard, B., & Luke, A. (eds.) (1998). *Literacy Debates and Public Education: A question of 'crisis'.* Canberra: Australian Curriculum Studies Association.

Commonwealth of Australia, Productivity Commission (2004). *Trends in Australian Manufacturing.* Retrieved 17 July 2016 from http://www.pc.gov.au/research/support-ing/manufacturing.

Connell, R. (1985). *Teachers' Work.* Sydney: Allen & Unwin.

Connell, R. (1994). 'Poverty and education'. *Harvard Educational Review, 64*(2), 125–149.

Connell, R., Ashenden, D., Kessler, S., & Dowsett, G. (1982). *Making the Difference: Schools, families and social divisions.* Sydney: George Allen & Unwin.

Connell, R., Johnston, K. M., & White, V. (eds.). (1991). *Running Twice as Hard: The Disadvantaged Schools Program in Australia.* Geelong, Victoria: Deakin University Press.

Delpit, L. (1988). 'The silenced dialogue: Power and pedagogy in educating other people's children'. *Harvard Educational Review, 58*(3), 280–298.

Di Bartolo, L. (2005). 'Educational polarisation in Brisbane: Rawls's least advantaged and the myth of choice'. *Australian Educational Researcher, 32*(3), 63–82.

Dorling, D. (2014). *Inequality and the 1%*. London: Verso Books.

Duncan-Anrade, J. (2004). 'Your best friend or your worst enemy: Youth popular culture, pedagogy and curriculum at the dawn of the 21st century'. *Review of Education, Pedagogy and Cultural Studies, 26*(4), 313–337.

Dyson, A., & Kerr, K. (2014). 'Out of school time activities and extended services in England: A remarkable experiment?' *Journal for Educational Research Online, 6*(3), 76–94.

Fraser, N. (2005). 'Reframing justice in a globalising world'. *New Left Review, 36*(November/December), 1–19.

Glover, J., Hetzel, D., Tennant, S., & Leahy, K. (2010). *Understanding Educational Opportunities and Outcomes: A South Australian atlas* (9780646529882). Retrieved 12 May 2016 from http://www.publichealth.gov.au/pdf/atlases/sa_education_2009/Education.pdfhttp://nla.gov.au/nla.arc-121032-20100630-1607-www.publichealth.gov.au/pdf/atlases/sa_education_2009/Education.pdf.

Gonski, D., Boston, K., Greiner, K., Lawrence, C., Scales, B., & Tannock, P. (2011). *Review of Funding for Schooling: Final report*. Commonwealth of Australia: Department of Education, Employment and Workplace Relations. Retrieved 10 May 2016 from http://www.schoolfunding.gov.au.

Gore, J. (2007). 'Improving pedagogy: Challenges of moving teachers toward high levels of quality teaching'. In J. Butcher & L. McDonald (eds.), *Making a Difference: Challenges for teachers, teaching, and teacher education*. Rotterdam: Sense.

Gruenewald, D. (2003). 'The best of both worlds: A critical pedagogy of place'. *Educational Researcher, 32*(4), 3–12.

Haberman, M. (1991). 'The pedagogy of poverty versus good teaching'. *Phi Delta Kappan, 73*(4), 290–294. doi:10.2307/20404620.

Haberman, M. (2010). '11 consequences of failing to address the "pedagogy of poverty"'. *Phi Delta Kappan, 92*(2), 45.

Hattam, R., Woodley-Baker, R., & Lucas, B. (2012). *Rethinking equality/aspirations-achievement/pedagogy/university-school relations*. Paper presented at the Australian Association for Research in Education Conference, Sydney, 4 December 2012.

Hattam, R., & Zipin, L. (2009). 'Towards pedagogical justice'. *Discourse: Studies in the Cultural Politics of Education, 30*(3), 297–301.

Hattam, R., Zipin, L., Brennan, M., & Comber, B. (2009). 'Researching for social justice: Contextual, conceptual and methodological challenges'. *Discourse: Studies in the Cultural Politics of Education, 30*(3), 303–316.

Hatton, E., Munns, G., & Dent, J. N. (1996). 'Teaching children in poverty: Three Australian primary school responses'. *British Journal of Sociology of Education, 17*(1), 39–52.

Hayes, D., Mills, M., Christie, P., & Lingard, B. (2006). *Schools and teachers making a difference: Productive pedagogies and assessment*. Sydney: Allen & Unwin.

Hempel-Jorgensen, A. (2009). 'The construction of the "ideal pupil" and pupils' perceptions of "misbehaviour" and discipline: Contrasting experiences from a low-socioeconomic and a high-socioeconomic primary school'. *British Journal of Sociology of Education, 30*(4), 435–448.

Herden, E., Power, A., & Provan, B. (2015). *Is welfare reform working?: Impacts on working age tenants: A Study of SW HAILO*. Case report 90. Retrieved 17 July 2016 from http://sticerd.lse.ac.uk/dps/case/cr/casereport90.pdf.

Hill, S., Comber, B., Louden, B., Reid, J.-A., & Rivalland, J. (1998). *100 Children go to school: Connections and disconnections in the literacy experience prior to school and in the first year of school. Vols 1–3*. Canberra: Department of Education, Employment Training and Youth Affairs.

Hockey, J. (2014). *A budget for opportunity*. An address to The Sydney Institute by the Federal Treasurer, Retrieved 12 June 2016 from http://jbh.ministers.treasury.gov.au/speech/009-2014/.

Karmel, P. (1971). *Education in South Australia. Report of the committee of enquiry into education in South Australia 1969–1970.* Retrieved 17 July 2016 from http://web.education.unimelb.edu.au/curriculumpoliciesproject/Reports/download/SA-1975-Karmel1971.pdf.

Karmel, P. (1973). *Schools in Australia: Report of the interim committee of the Australian Schools Commission.* Retrieved 10 March 2016 from http://apo.org.au/source/interim-committee-australian-schools-commission.

Kemp, P., Cole, I., Beatty, C. & Foden, M. (2014). *The impact of changes to the local housing allowance in the private rented sector: The response of tenants.* Department for Work and Pensions, UK. Retrieved 17 July 2016 from http://www4.shu.ac.uk/research/cresr/sites/shu.ac.uk/files/impact-lha-prs-tenants.pdf.

Kerkham, L. (2011). 'Embodied literacies and a poetics of place'. *English Teaching: Practice and Critique, 10*(3), 9–25.

Kerkham, L. & Comber, B. (2013). 'Literacy, place-based pedagogies and social justice'. In B. Green & M. Corbett (eds.), *Rethinking rural literacies: Transnational perspectives* (pp. 197–217). New York: Palgrave Macmillan.

Ladwig, J. (2007). 'Modelling pedagogy in Australian school reform'. *Pedagogies: An International Journal, 2*(2), 57–76.

Lupton, R. (2003). *Poverty street: The dynamics of neighbourhood decline and renewal.* Bristol: The Policy Press.

Lupton R. (2006). 'Schools in disadvantaged areas: Low attainment and a contextualised policy response'. In H. Lauder, P. Brown, J. Dillabough and A. H. Halsey (eds.) *Education, Globalization and Social change.* Oxford: Oxford University Press, pp. 654–672.

Lupton, R., & Hempel-Jorgensen, A. (2012). 'The importance of teaching: Pedagogical constraints and possibilities in working-class schools'. *Journal of Education Policy, 27*(5), 601–620.

Lupton, R., & Obolenskaya, P. (2013). *Labour's record on education: Policy, spending and outcomes 1997–2010.* Social policy in a cold climate working paper 3 WP03. Retrieved 17 July 2016 from http://sticerd.lse.ac.uk/dps/case/spcc/wp03.pdf.

Lupton, R., & Thomson, S. (2015). *The Coalition's record on schools: Policy, spending and outcomes 2010–2015.* Social policy in a cold climate working paper 13 WP13. Retrieved 17 July 2016 from http://sticerd.lse.ac.uk/dps/case/spcc/WP13.pdf.

Massey, D. (2007). *World city.* Cambridge: Polity Press.

McInerney, P. (2004). *Making Hope Practical: School reform for social justice.* Flaxton, Qld.: Post Pressed.

McLachlan, R., Gilfillan, G., & Gordon, J. (2013). *Deep and persistent disadvantage in Australia.* Australian Government Productivity Commission. Retrieved 17 July 2016 from http://www.pc.gov.au/research/supporting/deep-persistent-disadvantage.

McLaughlin, T. (1996). *Street Smarts and Critical Theory: Listening to the vernacular.* Madison, WI: University of Wisconsin Press.

Moll, L. C., Amanti, C., Neff, D., & Gonzalez, N. (1992). 'Funds of knowledge for teaching: Using a qualitative approach to connect homes and classrooms'. *Theory into Practice, 31*(2), 132–141.

Nixon, H. (2003). 'New research literacies for contemporary research into literacy and new media?' *Reading Research Quarterly, 38*(4), 407–413.

Nyrstar (2012). *A new Port Pirie: Transforming the future.* Retrieved 17 July 2016 from http://www.portpirietransformation.com/index.php/the-redevelopment.

OECD (2011). *Divided we stand: Why inequality keeps rising.* Retrieved 5 June 2016 from http://dx.doi.org/10.1787/9789264119536-en.

Peel, M. (2003). *The Lowest Rung: Voices of Australian poverty.* Cambridge, UK: Cambridge University Press.

Piketty, T. (2014). *Capital in the Twenty-first Century.* Cambridge, Mass. & London: Harvard University Press.

Pinar, W. (2012). *What is Curriculum Theory?* New York: Routledge.

Pocius, D. (2013, December 19). Elizabeth Industrial area. (Weblog post). Retrieved 6 June 2016 from http://playfordspast.blogspot.com.au/search/label/Elizabeth.

Power, A. (1997). *Estates on the Edge: The social consequences of mass housing in northern Europe.* London: Palgrave Macmillan.

Prosser, B., Lucas, B., & Reid, A. (eds.) (2010). *Connecting Lives and Learning: Renewing pedagogy in the middle years.* Kent Town, South Australia: Wakefield Press.

Randell, S. K. (1978). *The Disadvantaged School Program: A program to improve the quality of education for the disadvantaged.* Paper presented at the Quality in Australian Education Conference.

Rogers, B. (2013). *Educational Leadership: Cultivating plurality in a dialogic teacher 'public space'.* Unpublished thesis (EdD). School of Education. University of South Australia.

Rose, J. (2002). *The Intellectual Life of the British Working Classes.* New Haven and London: Yale University Press.

Sefton-Green, J., Nixon, H., & Erstad, O. (2009). 'Reviewing approaches and perspectives on "digital literacy"'. *Pedagogies: An International Journal,* 4(2), 105–127.

Semmens, B. (2014). *The public secondary school principal in contemporary times: Subjectivity, resistance and the limit to neoliberal sensibilities.* Unpublished thesis (PhD). School of Education. University of South Australia. Retrieved 5 June 2016 from http://search.library.unisa.edu.au/record/UNISA_ALMA21105849310001831.

Shildrick, T., MacDonald, R., Webster, C., & Garthwaite, K. (2012). *Poverty and Insecurity: Life in low-pay, no-pay Britain.* Studies in poverty, inequality and social exclusion. Bristol: Policy Press.

Smith, G. (2002). 'Place-based education: Learning to be where we are'. *Phi Delta Kappan,* 83(8), 584–594.

Smith, L. (2011). 'Experiential "hot" knowledge and its influence on low-SES students' capacities to aspire to higher education'. *Critical Studies in Education,* 52(2), 16–177.

Standing, G. (2011). *The Precariat: The new dangerous class.* London: Bloomsbury.

Stilwell, F. J. B., & Jordan, K. (2007). *Who Gets What?: Analysing economic inequality in Australia.* New York: Cambridge University Press.

Street, B. (1994). 'What is meant by local literacies?' *Language and Education,* 8(1/2), 9–17.

Taylor, M. (2012, July 19). 'Lead poisoning of Port Pirie children: A long history of looking the other way'. *The Conversation.* Retrieved 17 July 2016 from http://the-conversation.com/lead-poisoning-of-port-pirie-children-a-long-history-of-looking-the-other-way-8296.

The White House. (2013, December 4). Remarks by the President on economic mobility. Office of the Press Secretary, The White House. Retrieved 16 July 2016 from https://www.whitehouse.gov/the-press-office/2013/12/04/remarks-president-economic-mobility.

Thomson, P. (2002). *Schooling the Rustbelt Kids: Making the difference in changing times.* Crows Nest, NSW: Allen & Unwin.

Thomson, P., Nixon, H., & Comber, B. (2006). 'A case of intention deficit disorder? ICT policy, disadvantaged schools and leaders'. *School Effectiveness and School Improvement,* 17(4), 465–482.

Thrupp, M. (1999). *Schools Making a Difference: Let's be realistic!* (1st ed.). Buckingham, England & Philadelphia: Open University Press.

Wilkinson, R., & Pickett, K. (2010). *The Spirit Level: Why equality is better for everyone.* London & New York: Penguin Books.

Wilson, W. (1997). *When Work Disappears: The world of the new urban poor.* New York: Vintage Books.

World Health Organisation (2008). Closing the gap in a generation: Health equity through action on the social determinants of health. Retrieved 30 June 2016 from http://www.who.int/social_determinants/thecommission/finalreport/en/.

Young, M., & Willmott, P. (1957). *Family and Kinship in East London*. London: Routledge and Kegan Paul.

# 2

# STUDYING SCHOOLS

In this chapter, we introduce the four schools at the heart of our research: Sandford, Easton and Highfield, located in Adelaide's northern suburbs, and Riverview, located in a regional country town and 'port' community. We explain how we approached studying them. We set out our understandings of the schools as places that are constituted by local conditions, situated within much broader contexts; as sites of learning for children from diverse backgrounds, whose life experiences cannot always be easily understood or reduced to numbers; as institutions with long histories of school reform; and as places of work for teachers whose practices are highly diverse and associated with a range of effects. We explain how these understandings helped us to make sense of what we observed during the three years in which we visited each school. During these visits, we spent time with the principals and we maintained contact with small groups of teachers, students and parents. We conducted the study in order to understand literacy leadership and pedagogies, as well as the constraints and possibilities afforded by the location of the schools within contexts spanning the local to the global.

All the schools are located in communities with relatively high levels of social and economic disadvantage, ranking either in the most disadvantaged Category 1 (Sandford and Highfield), or Category 2 (Easton and Riverview), on South Australia's Index of Educational Disadvantage (IED), which is used to allocate resources to schools based on need.[1] As such they have, as will be seen, some 'family resemblances' resulting from their status as 'disadvantaged' schools. Their present and future realities seem equally tied to structural inequality, changes in the labour market and changes in policy that portend reductions in health care, public transport and other services on which families living in poverty depend. All these communities confront bleak employment prospects, and the certainty of continued entrenched and intergenerational disadvantage that has limited the future prospects of many of the students and their families. These socioeconomic contexts are a central feature in the ecologies of these schools, an issue that is often either conveniently glossed over or deliberately ignored in current education policy in Australia.

Yet the schools are also richly varied, both in terms of their distinctive material locations and the wider social events and processes taking place in their neighbourhoods. Recent studies of schools in disadvantaged communities (Lupton, 2005; Thomson, 2000, 2002; Thrupp & Lupton, 2006) have made compelling arguments for understanding the 'nuances of context' (Thrupp & Lupton, 2006) in order to recognise that 'disadvantaged schools' are not all the same, and do not face the same challenges as each other. We therefore start by further exploring the local contexts of the schools in ways that suggest the kinds of demands made on resources, as well as the pedagogical and curriculum decisions made in the schools.

However, we do not mean to suggest either that the descriptions of local conditions are all that there is to know and understand about the schools, nor that practices and relationships in the schools can simply be read off from these descriptions. On the contrary, the sense of growing familiarity with our research sites that might develop over the course of the first half of the chapter is intended to be disrupted and called into question by our reading of context, our approach to understanding the complex lives of young people, the nature of change in schools, and our understanding of the challenges faced by teachers and school leaders in these schools. These are unpacked in the second half. We conclude the chapter with a brief overview of how we conducted the research.

## The schools and their communities

### Riverview Primary School

Riverview Primary is the oldest of the four schools, having opened in 1877. Many of the buildings are old, but have attractively presented exteriors, including the original 1876 stone building where the current administration offices are located. There is a Children's Centre on the same campus, for children from birth to eight years of age. A new four-class unit for the Year 6/7 classes was built during 2010, funded by the federal government's Building Education Revolution grants to schools. Each classroom has an interactive whiteboard. The school has access to an oval and soccer field situated across the main road from the school, a shared resource with the local council. The oval is a popular place for the community on weekends and for school sports.

Two hundred and twenty-four students are currently enrolled at Riverview. There are 11 classes supported by 15 teachers, three non-instructional time (NIT) teachers, one Resource Centre manager, and eight part-time school support officers (SSOs). The SSOs are actively involved with the teachers in their learning teams, and provide in-class intervention support for students with specific learning needs. In addition, there is one Aboriginal community education officer (ACEO), as well as three front-office SSOs. Two SSOs are assigned to each year level learning team to support student learning. Special programmes are in place to provide intensive support for students in the areas of English, mathematics, coordination and social skills. Additional targeted funding enabled a Learning Centre to be established at the commencement of the 2015 school year.

The leadership team consists of the principal, deputy principal, student support focus teacher and two coordinators. One of the coordinators has responsibility for the Learning Centre and is supported by 1.1 full-time equivalent staff and two SSOs. The aim of the Learning Centre is to provide timely short-term intervention to targetted students to extend their learning potential, and to recognise students for their creativity and sporting abilities through providing alternative enrichment programmes.

Riverview's principal, Angela, described the school as serving an area that has undergone many changes. Some old homes have been demolished, many others have been renovated to reduce possible lead pollution and many homes are for rent. According to two staff members who have worked for several decades in the school, Riverview used to be considered 'the affluent school' in the town. The processes that have led to residualisation of Riverview were set in train with changes in the dynamics of the town, sharpened by the economic downturn of the 1970s and increasing public awareness of the 'lead issue'. People moved out of the larger, older homes around Riverview, and out of the 'lead vein' produced by the smelting of lead, silver and zinc. However, in the mid-1950s and then the mid-1960s, new primary schools were built to ease the enrolment pressure at Riverview and a Catholic school was established nearby in 1967. People employed in better-paid jobs chose to send their children to the other schools, and built homes away from Riverview. People moving into the area tended to be transient families, many of whom had moved in to the Riverview area for its cheaper housing.

Of Riverview's current student population, 11% have been identified as students with disabilities, 38% have difficulties with speech and language and 37% of students are supported through the Resource Entitlement Scheme (RES).[2] Aboriginal students make up 40% of the student population, the highest proportion of any of the four schools. 75% of students are eligible for School Card support.[3]

## Sandford Primary School

Sandford is a larger school than Riverview, with 424 students enrolled in 2015 and a staff of 39, including 11 classroom teachers in their first five years of teaching. Established in 1960 as separate junior primary and primary schools, Sandford has since undergone many changes. It was renamed in 1994, and underwent significant refurbishment. In 2011, the junior primary and primary schools were amalgamated, and it is currently a combined Preschool–Year 7 school under one administration.

When we completed the study, Sandford had five leadership positions: principal, deputy principal, senior leader (Intervention/Resilience for Learning portfolio), senior leader (Curriculum, Literacy and Numeracy portfolio) and a coordinator for the early years (Preschool–Year 2). It was not unusual for these roles to change, especially with a change in school leadership. For example, the position of assistant principal with responsibility for literacy improvement that existed at the start of the study disappeared in the second year of the project. The teaching staff includes 28 full-time and seven part-time classroom teachers and two special education teachers; part-time staff includes an Aboriginal education teacher, an English as an additional language or dialect (EALD) teacher, and a librarian. In addition, Sandford has employed a positive psychology coach and a speech pathologist coach (to assist with oral language and phonological awareness). Both of these positions reflect the school's site improvement priorities that were developed to address concerns around the increasing complexities of students and their families, especially in the early years.

The school provides a first language-maintenance programme in Swahili and Kaurna (a local Indigenous language). Specialist teaching focuses on physical education, science and an R–4 Indonesian programme. Every class R–7 has access to one-on-one information and communications texchnology (ICT) devices:

- R–2: tablet computers for young children
- Years 3–5: tablet computers
- Years 6–7: tablet computers
- Preschool and Special Classes have access to iPads
- Every classroom has an interactive whiteboard.

The school has demountable classrooms for four early years classes; a four-classroom junior primary years block with an enclosed substantial 'wet area' for art and other extra-curricular activities; a four-classroom primary years block; an indoor gymnasium and a large outdoor covered learning area used for assemblies and lunch time activities, as well as special occasions such as Book Week parades.

Although mainly a white working-class neighbourhood, there is a relatively large Aboriginal population, and there have been recent significant demographic changes. Growing cultural diversity is reflected in the increasing number of speakers of Dinka, Vietnamese and Kirundi. While the majority of families (85%) in the neighbourhood still reflect the English origins of the first immigrants to settle in the area, almost 10% of families speak two or more languages, and refugees from South Sudan and Burundi make up 2% of the neighbourhood (compared to 0.1% for South Australia overall) (Australian Bureau of Statistics, 2014). Sandford's community is also changing because a new super school[4] and new housing development are attracting more young working families into the suburb, bringing a 'new feel' to the school, as the principal, Gavin, described it.

In 2015, the enrolment of 424 included 63 Aboriginal students, 43 EALD students and 58 students verified with a disability.[5] Eighteen of these verified students attend two special classes supported by the northern region and located on the campus. Fourteen preschool students who were identified as needing transitional speech and language support commenced Reception in 2015. Seventy per cent of students are approved for a School Card.

## Easton Primary School

Easton was one of the first R–7 schools in the Elizabeth area, opening in 1958. By the time of our study, it was the largest of our four schools, with 512 students enrolled at the beginning of the 2015 school year, and another 60 students expected by the start of 2016. In 2015, there were 13 classes in Junior Primary (R–2), and 12 classes in Primary (Years 3–7). Thirty-seven teachers are employed at the school, including a librarian, two special education teachers, a part-time EALD teacher and a part-time Aboriginal Education teacher. Classroom teachers are supported by 11 SSOs, who either work in the administration office or provide support in classrooms or the Learning Centre.

During 2013–15, a new gymnasium and a new early years Learning Centre were constructed, and several classrooms and learning areas were refurbished. A new extension to the Learning Centre provides new facilities for the school's intervention programmes. All classrooms have access to an interactive white-board. Easton provides specialist teaching in the areas of science, music and physical education.

The housing around Easton is mixed in quality, but many are run-down, semi-detached houses that have not been maintained either by their renters or by Housing SA.[6] Few houses are owner occupied. Not far from the school are the remains of a small shopping centre, where only one shop shows any sign of activity. People go to the town centre, about two kilometres away, for day-to-day shopping. The neighbourhood around Easton is affected by the same economic and demographic changes that are remaking Sandford – the closure of the car industry, new housing development and the new super schools. Increasing numbers of young families, more working families and aspiring middle-class people are moving to the area, according to the school principal.

The two new 'super schools' nearby were fully enrolled soon after they opened. Although a number of students who lived in the vicinity relocated to the new super schools in 2011, overall enrolments at Easton did not fall significantly. For some parents who might prefer to have their children enrolled at a super school, the only option was to enrol at other, less well-appointed local schools. Enrolments in Easton's preschool have continued to grow since 2013. In fact, a big increase in the number of preschool children in the area came to the attention of the previous Regional Director, who argued for reopening a preschool that was closed two or three years previously.

Enrolments in 2015 included 31 EALD students (9%) and 53 Aboriginal students (10%). Fourteen per cent of students are verified with disabilities. Fifty-one per cent of students are approved for a School Card. Easton has a highly transient student population (about 30%). During 2014, 85 students transferred to other schools, and 120 students came to Easton from elsewhere. (At classroom level, this equates to an average of four students per class leaving and six students arriving during the year.)

## *Highfield Primary School*

Like Easton, Highfield Primary opened in 1958. The school was rebuilt and upgraded in 1981, and in 2010–12, federal funding was used to significantly refurbish more than one-third of the school. In addition to the 11 classrooms and science and non-instruction time (NIT) class spaces, the main building has a large drama room, activity hall, staff room, art/technology room, two courtyards and a centrally located resource centre that accommodates a bank of computers. The school has two large ovals, primary and junior primary playgrounds, and shared play areas. There are shaded areas with seating for students. The courtyard, drama room and hall are available for lunchtime activities.

The smallest of the four schools, Highfield had 234 students enrolled in 2015. There were 10 mainstream class teachers, two teachers attached to the regional special classes, a school counsellor and a part-time teacher librarian. Support staff included an ACEO, who liaised with Aboriginal families (17.5 hours per week), and there were 50 available hours per week for SSOs, who support intervention programmes.

Highfield is located in an area where the South Australian Housing Trust constructed many of the homes for low rental. These have seen relatively recent refurbishment or redevelopment. However, much of the community is experiencing the effects of long-term and compounded disadvantage and unemployment. The school serves a highly transient population and a high proportion of the students are from single-parent or blended families. In 2015, 58% were students identified with disabilities, including the students in the two special classes; 29% were Aboriginal; and 24% of students did not speak English as a first language – by far the largest proportion in any of the four schools. Eighty per cent of students were eligible for School Card support, making this school the most socioeconomically disadvantaged school in the study.

Table 2.1 summarises some of the key characteristics of the four schools.

## Leadership and literacy in the four schools: an introduction

Details about both the leadership and practice of literacy pedagogies in Riverview, Easton, Sandford and Highfield schools form the substance of the chapters that follow in this book. Below, we provide some initial illustrations of how the schools were responding to the contexts in which they were located and to the need to address the seemingly intractable problem of low performance of their students in literacy.

As indicated in the Introduction, for the most part, the students in all four schools scored low on literacy achievement according to the National Assessment Program – Literacy and Numeracy (NAPLAN). Negligible numbers of students achieved scores in the top quartile, and a small number in the second quartile. The majority of the students were placed in the bottom two quarters for literacy testing, with some movement between these bottom quarters in some years (more details

**TABLE 2.1** School enrolments in 2015

| School | Total enrolment | IED category | School Card | EALD | Aboriginal | Special needs / NCP* ** RES support | Verified disability |
|---|---|---|---|---|---|---|---|
| Riverview | 244 | 2 | 75% | 3 (1.2%) | 100 (40%) | 92 (38%) speech/ language | 11% |
| Sandford | 424 | 1 | 70% | 43 (10%) | 63 (14.8%) | 14 (3%) (mainly preschoolers with speech & language issues) | 58 (13%) (18 attend Special Class) |
| Easton | 512 | 2 | 51% | 48 (9%) | 53 (10%) | 16% | 14% |
| Highfield | 234 | 1 | 81% | 58 (24%) | 68 (29%) | 58 (24%) | 135 (58%) (includes two Special Classes) |

* NCP = negotiated curriculum plan, a plan designed for students with additional learning needs, but who are not verified as students with a disability
** RES = Resource Entitlement Scheme for South Australian public schools indicates the resources schools will receive for: Industrial Entitlements (Authority of Certified Agreement) – the resources that are mandated from the enterprise bargaining process); Commonwealth and State Government initiatives – the resources required to support students with special needs and resources – specific projects from both State and Commonwealth governments; and Discretionary Allocations – discretionary allocations made to schools as part of the staffing process or in recognition of special circumstances.

about these results are provided in the Appendix). Three of the schools had been identified as so-called failing schools and were compulsorily selected to be part of the Supporting Improved Literacy Achievement (SILA) project in South Australia that was discussed in the Introduction.

A key point is that change over time of the performance of students in literacy is very difficult to interpret and explain. In the three city schools, the student population was highly transient and only about half of the students at any given year level sat consecutive tests. This situation makes the determination of 'student gain' at cohort level a fraught concept. At Riverview, the results varied greatly from year to year and it is very difficult to provide suitable explanations for the changes. In 2013, Riverview was ranked in the top 25 schools across Australia for improvement in NAPLAN scores and the following year dropped back to scores of previous years. Our analysis indicates that in this case, the very good result could be explained in part by a number of years of very focused and school-driven professional learning and the relative stability of staffing. These conditions were undone in 2014 and the failure to consolidate the good result was not surprising. But such straightforward explanations in these volatile contexts are not easy to come by.

The fact that relatively so few children across these four schools performed well in literacy tests was of course great cause for concern and was taken very seriously by each of the principals. NAPLAN data were analysed carefully in all the schools, and this analysis informed the development of *School Improvement Plans*[7] and the focus for professional learning. Schools also used a range of other assessment data, such as Running Records[8] and tests of comprehension, vocabulary and spelling. These were of more immediate use to teachers for planning their literacy programmes and for informing changes to classroom practice. They also provided evidence of the small gains that students had achieved and that NAPLAN could not capture.

In different ways, all of the schools made literacy improvement a major goal and invested considerable time and resources, giving it priority in terms of professional development for teachers and support staff. Each school was required to allocate time each day to literacy activities, and they were also required to articulate their approaches to literacy learning in the form of an 'agreement' that was designed to align teachers' practices around a set of agreed approaches. In subsequent chapters, we provide examples of the so-called 'literacy block' and 'literacy agreement'. Below, we briefly describe some of the ways in which educational leaders took context into account when supporting and maintaining literacy learning and some of the ways the contexts in which the schools were located impacted on their efforts. We illustrate a range of ways in which the schools were actively mobilising their available resources in the cause of literacy improvement. We follow these descriptions with an explanation of how we attempted to make sense of the efforts of educational leaders and teachers in these contexts and how we reconciled their efforts with the knowledge that the problem of underachievement in literacy was seemingly intractable.

While school leaders contended with complex contexts, leadership itself was never far from precarious. Over the course of our research, educational leadership in the schools we studied changed when leaders took up jobs elsewhere, retired, or their role descriptions were varied. This kind of movement in key positions in a school sometimes has a knock-on effect. For example, Principal Gavin – who had worked very effectively on changing the culture at Sandford and challenging teachers to keep the focus on learning – accepted a secondment to central office to manage a State-wide literacy and numeracy project. At almost the same time, the school counsellor accepted a position elsewhere. The repercussions of the departure of two significant leaders in the school was to be felt for the next 12 months, as their positions were temporarily backfilled: the deputy principal became acting principal; the senior leader (curriculum, literacy and numeracy) became deputy principal (as a consequence of which she was not able to maintain her role in providing professional learning in one-on-one literacy chats with classroom teachers (see Chapter 3); and an outstanding early-career teacher agreed to act as school counsellor.

The principal of Easton Primary, John, had been in a leadership position at an inner-city 'leafy green' school for five years before taking up his position at Easton, where he was in his seventh year as principal. He reflected that although 'people who may be ignorant about the school' might turn away from coming to a school in the area, he felt that the school 'has a really positive reputation, particularly around literacy, and many families come here because of that reputation'. Its history had been strongly shaped by a charismatic and innovative leader, whose interest in focusing intensely on literacy teaching and developing leadership amongst the teachers had, at least for the period of his tenure, created fertile ground for new ideas and practices.

## Hogwarts: a short-term, targeted intervention

Easton school devised an innovative approach to providing an intervention programme for students who were struggling with literacy, a programme that they called Hogwarts. Middle- and upper-primary students went to Hogwarts for extra writing, reading and comprehension to boost their confidence and specific skills. For early-years students, Hogwarts was focused on giving additional time and attention to the 'Big 6'[9] to complement what was happening in classrooms and so that teachers could organise their programming around the 30-minute absence of the students. Typically, the students going to Hogwarts worked in small groups, and at any given time there would be students from multiple year levels in the Learning Centre. Each group of learners was supported by a highly skilled SSO or an intervention teacher. On one visit, we noticed that a group of four Year 6/7 students had organised themselves, and had already started on the learning task for the session, before the intervention teacher had arrived. The principal commented that calling the school's intervention Hogwarts had made a much stronger impact than he had ever imagined. As he described it:

> Those kids will be there lined up after recess, you know, ready to go in. They don't need to be reminded. The kids who come at 9.30 or 10 o'clock or 10.30 will know: 'I've got to go soon; I've got to go soon.' A relief teacher going into a room will be quickly told: 'I'm going to intervention now', so if the teacher has forgotten to write that on the program, they'll quickly know about it.

There had also been positive responses from parents, who could 'explicitly see that extra help and intervention is happening'. From our perspective, it isn't just the name that has created such enthusiasm for the programme. It is the way in which the students are respected and supported to be successful in their learning, and that they are not retained in the programme once they have reached their learning goals – there is no stigma attached to going to Hogwarts, because it is a short-term programme. In addition, the student data it uses and generates is available to the classroom teachers, who participate in making decisions about students' learning needs and how Hogwarts can address them. In schools in general, such decisions are more often left to the professional judgement of a special education teacher, who may or may not have direct contact with the classroom teachers.

## Enrichment programme to support growth

At Riverview, teachers developed support and intervention programmes for students who were unlikely to achieve literacy benchmarks and targets. Students who achieved 'high results but not growth' were also on Principal Angela's radar. Her enrichment programme challenged them to go beyond 'cruising'. She actively involved herself in 'performance for learning' observations of 'students in the middle'. She gave them feedback and spoke with them about goal-setting and targets. From her perspective, students who might otherwise 'fall really quickly' responded positively to her acknowledgement of their progress and ongoing interest in their achievements. Angela's level of active face-to-face engagement with learners stood out and demonstrated to her colleagues how highly she valued key practices, such as thoughtful feedback. Creating and sustaining conditions for learning – for teachers and for students – was foremost in her day-to-day practice as an educational leader.

## Supporting a range of needs

Across all these schools, EALD students were not large in number, but they did require additional learning support. Sometimes this was in the form of in-class SSO support; sometimes the students were included in a small group that was withdrawn for more focused teaching. Students with special learning needs were typically assessed by outside consultants (e.g. speech pathologists), who would support classroom teachers to develop Negotiated Curriculum Plans (NCPs). Each of these students was allocated additional one-on-one or small-group support that was targeted to their specific learning needs. Verified students with disabilities could be placed either in mainstream classrooms or in a Special Class, depending on their capacity for independent learning and functioning in a classroom.

These examples are intended to illustrate that our research schools were actively involved in supporting literacy achievement. The fact that they were having limited or fleeting success was something we wanted to understand. We included them in our research because our sources and our analysis of changes in literacy achievement suggested that there was something interesting going on in each site. We did not want to describe what they were doing wrong in order to diagnose the problem and suggest how they might fix it. Neither did we want to describe what they were doing right so that it might be 'upscaled' and used as a model for good practice. Instead, we wanted to describe and gain insight into the impact of standardised testing and reporting, residualisation, and shifting social and economic conditions, as described in Chapter 1. In the next section, we describe how we approached this research project, including the assumptions that underpinned it and how our prior experiences shaped it.

## Studying the four schools

We approached our study of these schools not as blank slates, but with specific histories of engagement with them and with schools like them. We also brought our familiarity with extensive relevant educational research literatures. We thus brought some important prior understandings, what might also be called assumptions, to our research that shaped our choice of research design, the data generation tools that we used, and our analysis, which are detailed later in this chapter. Below we describe how some of these prior understandings shaped our research dispositions and made us 'tune in' to the schools in particular ways. The four Australian-based researchers also endeavoured to shake up our assumptions and understandings by working together on analysis of the data from the case study schools. Regular critical debriefs of our school visits, shared reading of transcripts of interviews, co-constructing profiles of school leaders and co-authoring of critical incidents produced complications and complexity in our interpretations of what was going on. This continued throughout the project and into the writing of this book. The involvement of the two England-based researchers in writing took this problematisation a step further. Our aim is to produce an account that honours the complexity of the work and raises questions for policy and practice.

## Students do not appear in schools with a 'background' in tow

It is common to hear school students described as being from a particular kind of 'background'. And indeed, Table 2.1, and our descriptions of the intakes of the schools, suggests that certain background characteristics are important to know. When this is said or written, the word background is usually accompanied by a descriptor that denotes cultural or linguistic heritage, or perhaps socioeconomic status. More often than not, this terminology signals some kind of 'problem' that the student possesses and that the school must take account of. Reference to an individual student's language background, for example, often indicates lack of dexterity in spoken or written English; it flags to the school that it may need to make extra effort, and also that there is a potential claim for additional funding for language support for these students. Similarly, having an Aboriginal or Torres Strait Islander background signals heritage, but also flags a set of potential issues that schools may need to recognise – cultural practices such as funerals, for example – and signals that there may be particular systemic interventions available, such as Aboriginal Education Worker support or Homework Centre funding. Background is also used more generically, as in 'troubled' or 'difficult' background, and here again it is a signal that there is something about the student as a person, and perhaps as a member of a social group, that warrants particular attention by the school and may require and deserve systemic resources.

The notion of background thus carries with it an ambiguous set of notions: of the kinds of exclusions that schools produce, and their obligation to not do so; the entitlement of particular groups of students to additional resources; and of the individual deficiencies of students related to their social positioning. Mostly, however, the actual result is that the tag background is interpreted negatively (Comber, 1998). The backgrounds of students who are not from minority or disadvantaged groups are taken for granted and are rarely thought worthy of comment, while what is 'wrong' or missing from the backgrounds of others becomes the focus of attention.

Educational researchers (Comber & Kamler, 2004; Hattam & Prosser, 2008; Smyth, Down & McInerney, 2010; Valencia, 1997, 2010) have documented the prevalence of 'deficit discourse' in schools where large numbers of students have the kinds of backgrounds that are correlated with less apparent school success. In such situations, lack of educational success is attributed to backgrounds where:

- the individual student is deficient – they are 'slow', or have some kind of dis-ordered condition; they don't know enough English; they are poorly behaved; they have no ambition;
- the family is deficient – children haven't been read to every night; their parents don't know how to parent, or just don't care in the right way; they watch too much television; they don't want their children to do well;
- the neighbourhood is deficient – there are whole streets of people who don't work; there is nothing organised to do; there are no role models.

Missing from these accounts is recognition that the ways in which troubled, troublesome and troubling children get to be this way is complex and socially produced by multiple relations, policies and agencies. Missing from these accounts is, for instance, any notion that there is not one best way to parent, that some social groups have been systematically oppressed for generations and that what we count as aberrant is culturally specific and produced. And, most importantly, missing from these amalgams of accounts of families, homes and lives is any account of the kinds of cultural, linguistic or cognitive resources that the students may possess (González, Moll & Amanti, 2005). These lacunae work against teachers looking for the ways in which students' home/neighbourhood/online/community/subcultural knowledges, experiences, practices, narratives and tel-eologies might not only be a bridge to the knowledge that currently counts in school, but also might ultimately point to the ways in which schooling might become more inclusive and socially just.

The reductive simplification implied by the notion of background works against more nuanced and cultural–sociological understandings of the production and reproduction of unequal schooling, and society more generally. While it can act as a kind of self-fulfilling prediction of failure, trouble and lack of academic attain-ment, mostly background works to obscure rather than illuminate our understand-ings of why things are as they are, and what might be done about them.

Thus, in this research, we looked to see how teachers and schools categorised and explained their students. We chose research data generation and analytic meth-ods that would be sensitive to the language of research and policy texts and their associated actions and resourcing. In other words, the discourses, categories and descriptors we employ can rapidly become part of the problem we seek to inves-tigate and ameliorate. We attempted to make our standpoint clear at the outset in working with educators from the central department, regional office and, of course, the school leaders and teachers. For example, we made explicit reference to, and provided resources from, our earlier work where we coined the term 'turn-around pedagogies'. We combined classroom observation with 'purposeful conversations' (Burgess, 1988) and the collection of school artefacts, as we describe in more detail in the last section of this chapter. The results of this approach can be particularly seen in Chapter 5, where we consider 'fickle literacies'.

### Complex, not simple, understandings are needed of the relationships between neighbourhoods and schools

In the first part of this chapter, and in previous ones, we have tried to introduce the areas and the schools to readers who are unfamiliar with them in ways that quickly paint a picture. We have drawn out some of the similarities between the contexts of the schools and highlighted statistics that can be compared and which convey particular understandings of the kinds of places they are. We have described the schools as sitting in these neighbourhoods as though in a container. However, this is not how we understand the schools.

The four schools were known to us before we started this research. As explained in the previous chapter, most of the research team had been involved in the northern suburbs for a long period of time, and had a connection with the area in which the regional or port school was located. We therefore had a strong sense of the histories of the broader political, economic, cultural and social shifts that had affected the children, their families and the neighbourhoods they lived in. Our understandings went beyond thinking of schools and their 'contexts'.

We approached the schools thinking of them as embedded in wider relations, networks and flows within their geographical area. We understood them not only as distinctive material locations, but also as having family resemblances resulting from their status as 'disadvantaged' schools (see Chapter 1). We also understood that what happened inside the school was produced by wider social events and processes. Thus, when we were told about student transience, we knew this to be a social phenomenon of family mobility, a serious problem in the two regions where we had long been working. We understood – as did many of the school staff – that families had to move house frequently because of the workings of public–private housing, the local labour market and more punitive national approaches to welfare benefits. These conditions in turn were produced by decades of decline of the regional manufacturing industries, as well as shifts in public housing and welfare policies, themselves part of the overall move away from a welfare state.

But, despite commonalities amongst them, the four schools were also unique. They had particular histories, but also their own distinctive set of staff and students. The schools were particular and unique, not as a result of a rational managed process, but rather through people and material objects being 'thrown together', as Doreen Massey (2005) puts it, over time, and somewhat serendipitously. Despite the apparently fixed descriptions we have given at the start of this chapter, we saw each school as constantly changing. We have written snapshots frozen in time.

In reality, each school was a temporary community in which there were some shared understandings as well as competing stories. There was ongoing negotiation of the nature and composition of the institution, what it might and should do, who the school 'catchment' included and what it needed, and what the possibilities for action were and how these were constrained.

We were concerned to try to understand the changing nature of the school, the ways in which people made sense of it and their jobs, and the basis on which their decisions were made. Our commitment was thus to a longitudinal study, limited in scope but able to do 'deep' data generation. This meant that we had to establish relationships with the schools, teachers and children, and to take on board the kinds of living ethical practices that come from sustained research engagement in one place. We also had to become familiar with each of the school cultures and their implicit and explicit rules and conventions, as well as experience the rhythm of school days, terms and years. We thus adopted an ethnographic methodology.

## Finding out about schools and classrooms

While there is a long tradition of school and classroom ethnography (e.g. Armstrong, 1980; Ball, 1981; Jackson, 1960), it is still a minority pursuit in educational research. This may be because ethnography requires both time and an intellectual and emotional commitment and engagement on the part of the researcher and the school staff. It may also be because it is a methodology which foregrounds the interpretation of the researcher. While a range of methods are used, including relevant statistical data and sometimes surveys, it is an approach which relies fundamentally on the researcher being *in situ*, keeping comprehensive notes, listening carefully, and then providing their interpretation of what they have seen and experienced (Van Maanen, 1988; Walford, 2008).

Ethnographic methodology has the advantage, however, of focusing on the everyday, on change over time, and on micro transactions and interactions. These are then placed in wider social and cultural contexts in order to answer general ethnographic questions such as: What's going on here? How do the participants experience life in this school? How do they understand their work? How does it come to be like this? What matters? What goes unnoticed?

Our interpretations of what was going on in classrooms and staffrooms were also informed by an institutional ethnography, following the approach of Dorothy Smith (2005). Smith is interested in discovering the ways in which people's work is organised and hooked up beyond what might be visible at the local level. Taking the perspective that people are experts in what they do, she investigates how they activate texts as part of their everyday work. In terms of the present study, we wanted to understand how teachers made sense of the so-called literacy agreements,[10] given the wider imperatives of NAPLAN and the emphasis on teacher quality. It is important to remember too that teachers' work to improve student literacy performance competes with other immediate priorities of managing a class. These schools also had behaviour agreements in place. Teachers juggled these priorities amongst others, with many of them also under the pressure of being employed on short-term contracts. In the past decade, a range of policies and practices – emerging from national and state governments, multinational publishers, private consultancies – have placed an unprecedented emphasis on literacy, to the point where there has been a proliferation of tests, kits, and 'specialists' that may well be overwhelming, even for experienced teachers.

In this context, it is not surprising that principals emphasised student targets and differentiated, explicit teaching. It is also important to note, however, that principals also sought to find balance and consistency, in an attempt to mediate competing demands and contradictions.

Place-based research methods are those which focus on the ways in which schools are both patterned and specific, located in space/time and engaged in various stretched-out relations and meaning-making practices (Thomson & Hall, 2016). Researchers using place-based methods reject the notion, as do we, that either schools or students are somehow removed from the rest of their lives when they are inside the school, and/or the only ways in which neighbourhoods and families matter is when they are seen as problematic and in need of 'fixing'. Understanding the school as a place which has an ongoing trajectory, and is always in the middle of 'travel', also means that researchers coming into the school must get to grips with the history and implied future of the school, as well as its present. Place-based methods draw on cultural geographies and urban planning approaches, often using case study or ethnographic methodologies.

We draw particularly on place-based methods in order to understand the patterned but specific nature of each of the four schools we studied and the ways in which this is imbricated in an education system and the public sector, and in wider social, cultural, political and economic relations.

### The challenge to improve classroom practice is greatest in high-poverty communities

We assumed from the outset that the challenge to improve classroom practice is greatest in high-poverty communities, because the standard classroom – or 'normal' – practice is less likely to work here. Not because young people in these settings are less capable of success at school, but because these settings often carry the burden of residualisation; they must rely upon the resources of first-time teachers (and sometimes leaders), and they must cope with high turnover of both students and staff. While individual teachers in these settings are able to make a difference by improving the outcomes of students, the recent evaluation of the SILA project (see Chapter 1) affirmed the importance of considering the school (not the teacher) as *the* site of reform. In which case, decades of research in disadvantaged schools suggests the following key features for productive models of whole-school change:

- having coherence between school aims, curriculum, pedagogy and professional development;

- having a focused school improvement plan that is owned by staff and designed to enact reform;
- improving literacy outcomes be using unsettling deficit views of young people and their communities;
- getting teachers from out behind the classroom door and normalising a culture of peer accountability; and
- nurturing a school-wide professional learning community that promotes critical reflection by teachers (Hardy, 2010).

If the focus for whole-school reform is curriculum and pedagogy, then what do we know about 'actually existing pedagogies' (Lingard, 2007) that dominate in schools serving high-poverty communities? Without being extensive, recent Australian studies such as the *Queensland School Reform Longitudinal Study*, the *Changing Schools, Changing Times* project, and *Redesigning Pedagogies in the North* (RPiN) provide useful findings. For example, Lingard (2007) refers to the dominant pedagogies as pedagogies of indifference or pedagogies of the same, summarised as being strong in care for students, but as pedagogies that mostly 'fail to work with and across differences', and also 'fail to make a difference in their lack of both intellectual demand and connectedness to the world' (p. 246) (see also Lingard & Ladwig, 2001; Hayes, Mills, Christie & Lingard, 2006). This view was confirmed by Hayes and colleagues (Hayes, Johnston & King, 2009): 'classrooms practices are very traditional, following predictable routines, and are largely unsuccessful as far as formal learning is concerned' (pp. 251–2) (See also Connell, Johnston & White, 1991; Knapp & Shields, 1995). Hayes *et al.* (2009) argue that 'these conditions may be widespread and not limited to high-poverty contexts. However, in challenging circumstances, more is riding on the efficacy of classroom practice because poor families are highly dependent on schooling for their educational resources' (p. 252).

But then, as Hayes *et al.* (2009) argue, '[t]he key issue is not what kinds of pedagogies improve educational outcomes but how to support the development of the kinds of pedagogies that we have good reason to believe will work. As in the past, the sticking point remains practice' (p. 253). They point out that the present model for improving pedagogy involves adopting the relevant institutionally supported framework. In Australia, these models have varied slightly from state to state, but they generally include a set of descriptions of the kinds of pedagogies, and in some cases assessment processes, that have been shown to work somewhere at some time. The nuances and particularities of successful adoption and implementation are omitted, and all that's assumed to be required is faithful adoption of the framework. This approach shows no sign of continued success in disadvantaged schools, as it is local knowledge about practice that largely determines what kinds of pedagogies get adopted and enacted. As a consequence, 'improvement relies upon being able to develop new knowledge about what is possible in these contexts, and this is primarily a pedagogical challenge associated with supporting the professional learning of teachers and leaders' (Hayes *et al.*, 2009, p. 263).

If we are to take 'context' seriously, then we need to be examining and analysing the 'ecology of school' (Eisner, 1988, p. 24). Whilst it is possible to argue that individual teachers are able to make a difference by improving literacy outcomes for students, all teachers work in schools that serve specific communities, and hence pedagogy is developed and enacted in response to specific existential conditions. Each school has unique buildings and other material resources, and their own cultural practices, and hence their own 'regimes of truth' (Foucault, 1980, p. 131) about their students and 'what works'. Whilst it is possible for individual teachers to develop innovative practices, their sustainability is very much related to the enabling conditions, or not, of their school. The design of our research assumed that 'educational' leadership is enacted in unique schools defined by their singularity and required research approaches that are capable of making sense of that uniqueness. As such, we are interested in how principals and teachers and others working in primary schools develop and sustain their own rationality, or logics, and how this informs practice – in particular, the 'actually existing pedagogies' (Lingard, 2007, p. 246). We want to argue that actually existing pedagogies are constituted in schools where teachers interpret policy rationales through local 'regimes of truth' that operate in each school. We can think about the 'regime of truth' for any school in terms of: how 'good' leadership is understood; the dominant rationalities of practice – that is, what works here, and what is understood as 'good' pedagogy; and, what are the 'truths' about the students and their families that circulate in talk amongst the teachers?

School-level regimes of truth offer a certain level of self-evidence, or 'a scheme of interpretation' (Garfinkel, 1967), through which classroom life can be, and is, made recognisable and intelligible. Actually existing pedagogies arise in response to locally diagnosed problems, and are sustained as an 'ongoing practical accomplishment' (Freebody & Freiberg, 2011, p. 80), constituted out of 'practical reasoning' or 'practical theorising' (p. 80) at the local school level. Those working in schools use the conceptual resources available within their school to co-construct meaningful narratives of practice that solve existential and local problems and, in general, 'work to ensure the smooth running of situated everyday activities [i.e. pedagogy]' (p. 83). Pedagogy, then, develops in response to the question: what does [my] pedagogy have to do? Such a question focuses our attention on what pedagogy has to do in specific 'local' contexts, and in response to particular groups of students. In disadvantaged schools, this means responding practically to existential problems and the needs of complex school communities.

## Policy is not simply implemented in schools

Despite the wishes of policy-makers, and to their great frustration, policies do not have uniform take-up in schools. Policies are refracted and diffracted at every level – from their translation into administrative guidelines, funding schemes and curriculum materials, through their emphases and support offered by regional and district staff, to the relative importance placed on any particular policy in a given school.

Schools are always dealing with multiple policy agendas simultaneously, from literacy performance to regional restructures. They also have their ongoing issues to deal with. As we have seen in the snapshots of our four schools, this can range from ongoing issues between families that come to school, to high rates of family illness. School principals thus always weigh up any new initiative and consider how it might assist, alter or hinder the direction of change they have been nurturing. They also consider the regulatory regime that surrounds the policy in question. Principals are known to put some policies on the shelf and wait to see if anything happens as a result of their benign neglect. And when they do bring a policy into the ongoing life of the school, they make decisions about how it will be handled.

Principals are responsible for planning, resourcing and staffing the activities that bring policy into the school culture, systems and practices. However, what they can do varies enormously. Schools are variously able to support policies, and are always in the game of making choices about what is most important at any time, given where the school is 'at'. They also have different kinds of resources to put behind policies, including expertise and time for professional development.

Middle managers and teachers also interpret policies and what they are meant to do. They have different levels of experience and commitment to any policy, as well as possessing pedagogical repertoires that may be more or less conducive to change. Staff get various kinds of support and scrutiny and choose – more or less enthusiastically – to participate in developing the overall school response to a new policy initiative.

It is hardly surprising, given the various points of interpretation, ownership and action, that the ways in which policies appear between and within schools vary enormously. The question in which we are interested then is not simply how NAPLAN has been interpreted and hooked into the actions of educators, but also why, given the level of variation and commitment possible even across four schools, this particular policy has been so influential and powerful. How has this policy, as opposed to the many others that come into and at schools on a regular basis, managed to get right inside classrooms, and change teacher and leader practices? Our research has had to follow the trajectory of the NAPLAN policy into schools. It may even be the case that it is not NAPLAN per se, but the unrelenting emphasis on standards of performance and public accountability in the form of *My School*, that is the bigger player here. The employment contracts of senior leaders at district and state levels, and indeed in some schools, include improved NAPLAN performance targets. To investigate these related phenomena, we set out to interview principals and teachers about their understandings of the policy and local variants concerning what it means for their everyday practice. We closely watched and recorded what and where changes were occurring. We followed texts, meetings and newsletters, and attempted to understand how leadership in these schools translated into classroom practice and also then to student learning.

## Teachers are not identikit teaching machines

Many policy-makers offer generic views of 'good teachers' and their 'best practice'. Performance management regimes are often designed around rubrics, which suggest that there is a preferred way to teach all young people, regardless of who they are and where they are – despite talk of differentiation and personalisation. For instance, in parts of the United States and in some areas in England, there is an accepted formula for 'the lesson' – an introductory plenary in which a specific learning outcome is explicated; direct instruction is followed by individual or small-group practice, and then a concluding summary is made, at which time homework is also given out (Thomson, Hall & Jones, 2010). We take a very different approach to teachers' work than this.

We understand that all teachers have pedagogical repertoires, which they call on variously and adapt for different curriculums, classes and children. A pedagogical repertoire involves more than simply being able to teach a four-part lesson, or to keep a running record of progress, or to adhere to the national curriculum. A teacher's repertoire is a tangle of, for instance: finding, recognising and using prior knowledges, experiences and interests of children; strategies to maintain order; the capacity to improvise in response to minute-by-minute changes in the classroom; careful and responsive listening; experiences and understanding of scoping and sequencing a curriculum module; subject knowledges and the connections between foundational concepts and supporting meso-concepts; diagnostic strategies and interventions – why is this child behaving like this and what can I do? – and much more. Educational researchers have carefully observed and theorised the practices of teachers, and we know them to be highly diverse and variously 'effective'.

Teachers build their repertoires in part through teacher education. They also draw on their own experiences of being taught, as well as on various professional learning opportunities available to them inside and outside school. Some beginning teachers may arrive in their first schools with repertoires that are well suited to their new posts. Others may need considerable time and support to build the kinds of know-how that they need in order to support the learning of all of the children in their classes. Most teachers add to their repertoires over time.

Thus, and importantly for our research, we had no expectation that all teachers would deal with literacy policy and testing regimes in the same way. They would bring the various repertoires at their disposal to this task. Our interest was not only in seeing how the teachers responded, but also in understanding which parts of their teaching repertoires were now in play, and what new strategies they might have to learn. Our observations and interviews were deliberately designed to elicit data about teacher repertoires and how they were framed and delimited in current circumstances. A range of such repertories is described in Chapters 4, 5 and 6.

## How we conducted the research

In the first year, we surveyed primary school leaders from 16 of the 32 SILA schools (see Introduction).[11] We investigated their perspectives on school practices and on regional and departmental supports that have made a positive difference to student literacy learning in their school. The survey investigated trends and questions about educational leadership, which emerged from the SILA evaluation, including the nature of professional learning, the forms of literacy learning, the cultures of learning and aspiration reflected in school structures and processes, and the distribution of leadership. The survey also examined commonalities and differences in the leadership models employed in primary schools with respect to leading literacy curriculum and pedagogy. The four schools in this study were selected from the 16 in consultation with the Department for Education and Child Development.

We engaged in 'purposeful conversations' (Burgess, 1988) with educational leaders, including but not limited to principals, and work-shadowed them for over a week, at times nominated by them, in order to get a sense of the ways in which they operated as leaders and their rationales for their approaches. We invited them to identify key events and practices that they believed made a positive difference to teachers' knowledge and practice. We collected NAPLAN data for the period we were studying schools.

We followed up the leads identified by the survey and by educational leaders to investigate how these practices were experienced by teachers. Key events and practices were observed and recorded, including school closure days, staff meetings, data analysis meetings, year-level planning and review meetings. Relevant artefacts were collected. We invited teachers to participate in interviews and focus groups about their understandings of leadership and literacy pedagogy.

We undertook selected observations during literacy lessons, nominated by teachers, where they were employing practices that they believed had a positive impact on their students. These lessons were photographed and video- or audio-recorded, subject to consent from teachers, students and their caregivers. The researchers reviewed selected segments of lessons with classroom teachers, who were invited to interpret aspects of the pedagogy from their perspectives.

We worked closely with volunteer teachers in each school to investigate and document the ways in which pedagogies were employed to make a difference for students with difficulties. Each volunteer teacher selected a small number of students who were having ongoing difficulties with literacy. In this phase, we developed case studies of pedagogies the teachers designed and negotiated in the interests of particular students. Together with the teachers, we documented their effects using a range of data sources, including student artefacts and performances and the results of in-school and standardised assessments as appropriate.

In conclusion, we have developed a research approach for doing theoretically informed empirical work in and with schools – a multisite school ethnography that is sensitive to temporality, place and space, and aims to discern the complexity facing principals and teachers. In the next chapter, we 'enter' the schools through our encounters with educational leaders. We begin to make the data we collected available and to offer an interpretation of these local conditions that critically engages with the material we have presented in the first three chapters, including relevant prior research, histories of place, policy legacies and current contexts, and our own experiences. While our ethnographies offer powerful snapshots, they are of course partial and do not lend themselves to generating easy sets of implications for policy and practice. Rather, these accounts from schools raise questions about how next to support educators and communities in terms of the increasing gaps between the wealthy and the poor.

## Notes

1 The Index is calculated using the following measures: parental economic resources (ECO), parental education and occupation (EDU), aboriginality (AB) and student mobility (MOB). Schools are ranked according to an overall score, then separated into seven categories.
2 Resource Entitlement Scheme (RES) for South Australian public schools indicates the resources schools will receive for: Industrial Entitlements (Authority of Certified Agreement) – the resources that are mandated from the enterprise bargaining process); Commonwealth and State Government Initiatives – the resources required to support students with special needs, and resources-specific projects from both State and Commonwealth Governments; and Discretionary Allocations – discretionary allocations made to schools as part of the staffing process or in recognition of special circumstances.
3 The School Card scheme offers financial assistance for students attending government schools and whose families are on low incomes. It contributes to covering education expenses.
4 The public school system opened three 'super schools' in the early 2010s in or near the northern suburbs. The term 'super schools' was designated as a way of talking up the new investment in school infrastructure.
5 Students with disabilities are those students who are verified by a Department for Education and Child Development (DECD) psychologist or speech pathologist as eligible for the DECD Disability Support Program. Verification requires evidence of both an impairment and of the ways in which a student's impairment does, or will, impact significantly on progress in the curriculum and on his/her ability to participate in learning activities and the school community.
6 Housing SA is the name of the local State government department responsible for public housing stock.
7 Each government school is required to document priorities, targets, strategies and evaluation measures in a three-year School Improvement Plan that is reviewed in an annual cycle of planning and of reporting to DECD and to the local community.
8 Running records are used to document students' reading behaviours as they read aloud from a book that approximates their reading level; quantitative scores are calculated on the basis of errors and self-corrections. Level 26 indicates independent reading.
9 The 'Big 6' – oral language, phonemic awareness, phonics, fluency, vocabulary development and comprehension strategies – was strongly promoted by the DECD and the Northern Regional Office. It has become commonplace in the literacy block in most early-years classrooms in South Australia.
10 Each school developed literacy agreements following recommendation from the SILA reviews. They were intended to promote shared understandings of literacy and 'good literacy practice' across year levels. See Chapter 3 for a full discussion.
11 Some of the SILA principals had moved on or retired, and not all of the principals in the remaining schools wanted to participate in a follow-up study.

## References

Armstrong, M. (1980). *Closely Observed Children: The diary of a primary classroom*. London: Writers and Readers Ltd.
Australian Bureau of Statistics (2014). *Australian Bureau of Statistics: Census for a brighter future*. Retrieved 24 April 2014 from http://www.abs.gov.au/websitedbs/censushome.nsf/home/Census?opendocument.

Ball, S. (1981). *Beachside Comprehensive: A case study of secondary schooling*. Cambridge: Cambridge University Press.

Burgess, R. (1988). 'Conversations with a purpose: The ethnographic interview in educational research'. In R. Burgess (ed.), *Studies in Qualitative Methodology: Conducting qualitative research* (pp. 137–155). Greenwich, CT: JAI Press.

Comber, B. (1998). 'The problem of "background" in researching the student subject'. *The Australian Educational Researcher, 25*(3), 1–21.

Comber, B., & Kamler, B. (2004). 'Getting out of deficit: Pedagogies of reconnection'. *Teaching Education, 15*(3), 293–310.

Connell, R., Johnston, K. M., & White, V. (eds.). (1991). *Running Twice as Hard: The Disadvantaged Schools Program in Australia*. Geelong, Vic.: Deakin University Press.

Eisner, E. (1988). 'The ecology of school improvement'. *Educational Leadership, 45*(5), 24–29.

Foucault, M. (1980). *Power and Knowledge: Selected interviews and other writings*. New York: Pantheon.

Freebody, P., & Freiberg, J. (2011). 'Ethnomethodological research in education and the social sciences: Studying "the business, identities and cultures" of classrooms'. In L. Markauskaite, P. Freebody & J. Irwin (eds.), *Methodological Choice and Design: Scholarship, policy and practice in social and educational research* (pp. 79–98). Dordrecht; London: Springer.

Garfinkel, H. (1967). *Studies in Ethnomethodology*. Cambridge: Polity Press.

González, N., Moll, L., & Amanti, C. (2005). *Funds of Knowledge*. Mahwah, NJ: Lawrence Erlbaum.

Hardy, I. (2010). 'Critiquing teacher professional development: Teacher learning within the field of teachers' work'. *Critical Studies in Education, 51*(1), 71–84.

Hattam, R., & Prosser, B. (2008). 'Unsettling deficit views of students and their communities'. *Australian Educational Researcher, 35*(2), 89–106.

Hayes, D., Mills, M., Christie, P., & Lingard, B. (2006). *Teachers and Schooling Making a Difference: Productive pedagogies, assessment and performance*. Sydney: Allen & Unwin.

Hayes, D., Johnston, K., & King, A. (2009). 'Creating enabling classroom practices in high poverty contexts: The disruptive possibilities of looking in classrooms'. *Pedagogy, Culture & Society, 17*(3), 251–264.

Jackson, B. (1960). *Life in Classrooms*. New York: Holt, Rhinehart &Winston.

Knapp, M., & Shields, P. (1995). 'Academic challenge in high poverty classrooms'. *Phi Delta Kappan, 76*(10), 770–776.

Lingard, B., & Ladwig, J. (2001). *The Queensland School Reform Longitudinal Study: Final Report*. Brisbane: The State of Queensland (Department of Education).

Lingard, B. (2007). 'Pedagogies of indifference'. *International Journal of Inclusive Education, 11*(3), 245–266.

Lupton, R. (2005). 'Social justice and school improvement: Improving the quality of schooling in the poorest neighbourhoods'. *British Educational Research Journal, 31*(5), 589–604.

Massey, D. (2005). *For Space*. London: Sage.

Smith, D. E. (2005). *Institutional Ethnography: A sociology for people*. Lanham, MD: AltaMira Press.

Smyth, J., Down, B., & McInerney, P. (2010). *Hanging in with Kids in Tough Times: Engagement in contexts of educational disadvantage in the relational school*. New York: Peter Lang.

Thomson, P. (2000). '"Like schools", educational "disadvantage" and "thisness"'. *Australian Educational Researcher, 27*(3), 157–172.

Thomson, P. (2002). *Schooling the Rustbelt Kids: Making the difference in changing times*. Crows Nest, NSW: Allen & Unwin.

Thomson, P., & Hall, C. (2016). *Place Based Method for Researching Schools*. London: Bloomsbury.

Thomson, P., Hall, C., & Jones, K. (2010). 'Maggie's day: A small scale analysis of English education policy'. *Journal of Education Policy*, *25*(5), 639–656.

Thrupp, M., & Lupton, R. (2006). 'Taking school contexts more seriously: The social justice challenge'. *British Journal of Educational Studies*, *54*(3), 308–328.

Valencia, R. (2010). *Dismantling Contemporary Deficit Thinking: Educational thought and practice*. London: Routledge.

Valencia, R. (Ed.) (1997). *The Evolution of Deficit Thinking: Educational thought and practice*. London: Routledge Falmer.

Van Maanen, J. (1988). *Tales of the Field: On writing ethnography*. Chicago: The University of Chicago Press.

Walford, G. (ed.) (2008). *How to Do Educational Ethnography*. London: Tufnell Press.

# 3

# EDUCATIONAL LEADERSHIP PRACTICES

## Making and remaking the school

Understanding school leadership cannot be separated from understanding the workings of current policy regimes and the legacies of past policies. Nor can it be divorced from leaders' places of work – schools and their locations within local, national and global contexts. Thus the previous chapters provide the necessary multilayered contextual information that is integral to the central concern of this chapter – how school leaders work with their colleagues to develop schooling practices that reflect their collective understanding of the purpose of education and the needs of their students. As noted in Chapter 2, we have found it useful to think of schooling, as described by Freebody and Freiberg (2011), as an 'ongoing practical accomplishment' (p. 80) that is constituted out of the 'practical reasoning' or 'practical theorising' (p. 80) of people working together in particular situations. In our research we have been keen to understand the part leaders play in making sense of, and then making and remaking, their schools. When we use the term 'educational' or 'school leader', we are not limiting our comments to the principal, head or head teacher, terms that are used interchangeably throughout the book to signal the similar but differently named leadership positions in schools in Australia and elsewhere. Our conceptualisation of the concept of leader extends beyond this role to include those with other designated leadership roles, as well as teachers and others who exercise educational leadership in schools.

In the current policy regime, leadership practices are unavoidably orientated by market mechanisms based on consumer 'choice'; new steering-at-a-distance forms of public management; and performativity, as Ball (2008) suggests. Policies that operate through devolution, choice and accountability generally assume that school leaders will cooperate, or at the very least comply, with their enactment. Devolution, the delegation of authority to the school for decisions about resource allocation – or school-based management as it is known in the United States and United Kingdom – comes with 'new audit and risk management procedures and new lines of accountability that delimit' (Thomson, 2010, p. 9) what can be done locally. The tension between what is right locally and what is mandated is especially felt in public schools serving high-poverty communities. By way of an example, as we discussed in Chapter 1, Australian schools are not currently funded according to the socio-economic needs of their students. Hence, the inequitable allocation and distribution of resources at the local level gets managed by school-based educational leaders.

Our work in teasing out how new policy technologies get taken up in actually existing schools, and how school principals work against delimiting framings as they respond to the unique challenges of their school, has led us to conceptualise educational leadership in a larger sociopolitical and cultural context. But we also take account of the material places where the schools are located and their unique geographies and histories, as detailed in Chapter 2.

One way to take local context seriously is to foreground the ways in which school leaders problematise their work. Not only is leadership 'a more complex, comprehensive and extensive concept than that of management' (Grace, 2000, p. 236), but researching school leadership requires the dispersed view of leadership that we have adopted, which includes not only the principal, but also teacher–leaders, and sometimes students and parents. Investigating educational leadership, as defined in this study, is not limited to a particular role or to a particular conceptualisation of the purpose of this role, but we have focused our investigation on leadership in relation to teaching and learning practices specifically related to literacy.

We begin our analysis in this chapter with a close reading of the work of Gavin, the principal of Sandford. In so doing, we draw inspiration from an early, book-length school ethnography, conducted by Berlak and Berlak (1981), who set out 'to provide a language for examining the larger issues that are embedded in the particulars of the everyday schooling experience' (pp. 3–4). The notion of 'dilemmas' emerged for these authors as they grappled with the accounts of life in schools from teachers and school leaders. They found it difficult to render their data using a positivist view of causality that attempts to generate a hierarchy of factors. 'We could not easily formulate answers that represent our observations' (Berlak & Berlak, 1981, p. 22):

> Our effort to describe and understand our recorded experiences led us by increments to develop a language, a set of concepts that would more adequately represent the complexity we had experienced. … we developed … a set of what we came to call 'dilemmas' that appeared to have great promise for representing complexity of the phenomena without overlaying our own educational or political preferences on our descriptions.
>
> *(Berlak & Berlak, 1981, p. 22)*

In the period since Berlak and Berlak wrote about dilemmas, critical scholarship has challenged educational researchers to make explicit their own educational or political preferences, and to make these part of what needs to be accounted for and analysed. One of the means by which we attempt to do this is by making visible our research processes, and detailing how we noticed the particulars of everyday activities in the schools in our study. Our purpose is not just to lay bare our approach, but also to provide knowledge that might facilitate a critical engagement with our research. We acknowledge that our efforts to describe and understand these activities represent one possible reading among many. Hence, the dilemmas that we describe in this chapter 'cast two concerns as one' – our observational efforts to describe the work of educational leadership in schools, where there are high levels of poverty, and our analytical efforts, informed by the research literature, to make sense of this work. This movement, between analysed data and thinking about how they might be explained, is integral to ethnographic research (Coles & Thomson, 2016).

## Poverty and its effects come to school

Early in the school year, each researcher work shadowed a school principal for approximately a week, leaving when it was considered inappropriate to remain – for example, when the principal had a meeting with students, parents or staff who had not agreed to be part of the research project. During this intense period of observation, the researcher and principal debriefed when an opportunity arose. In addition, the principals were interviewed a number of times during the course of the project and notes were made of informal chats that occurred randomly in the playgrounds, staff rooms and corridors.

The section that follows employs short vignettes to give a sense of the work of the principal at Sandford, who we call Gavin, during the work-shadowing week, and on a range of specific occasions when the researcher was invited to participate and/or observe.

### Pupil-free day, January 24, 8.45am: a new school year

It's the first of two days of meetings for the educators at Sandford. The children return the following week. The staff will prepare and participate in professional development together. They are meeting in the staff room, and every chair is taken. There is an enthusiastic buzz of post-holiday conversation. The space is organised in a circle (as far as is possible). Gavin, the principal, welcomes everyone back to school. He's casually dressed and wearing the school T-shirt. It's a hot summer's day. He observes that they will be revisiting their 'common agreements' (literacy, behaviour routines and structures), and reminds them they will have 'preschoolers on the school grounds'.

In a low-key manner, Gavin then explains that he has been a principal for 14 years in three different schools, and that the best advice he had received was to 'get the staffing right'. He continues:

'Well, we've got the staffing right. We've got people that want to be here, to have relationships with kids and families, each other, and develop a positive culture, to support our kids and families. We've got no new people. Everyone wants to be here.'

With that, Gavin then hands over to two colleagues, the school counsellor and the assistant principal: literacy improvement, to run the first session of the day.

This initial observation was telling. It showed the approach to leadership that Gavin sought to negotiate with the staff, and the key messages he sought to convey in his very short welcome. Without any detailed analysis of what was said and how, we can see that Gavin employs a dispersed leadership approach, at least in this instance. We can see him reiterating his theme. First, he briefly establishes his credibility in terms of his experience. He then uses his brief welcome to recognise the staff (they are addressed as 'the right people' because they 'want to be here'), whilst at the same time reminding them of his expectations ('a positive culture'; 'have relationships with our kids and families').

In this short welcome, one of the major challenges of working in schools located in high-poverty environments is implied – the difficulty of attracting and retaining a stable, experienced teacher workforce. Gavin had also worked at continuity; there were 'no new people', which would allow the school simply to 'revisit our agreements'. Later, we learn that Gavin had actively sought to appoint a talented teacher from his previous school and to have his most promising early-career teachers win further contracts and be made permanent at the school. In his three years at the school, 'getting the right staff' had been a key mission (c.f. Thomson, 2002). When he arrived, 75 per cent of the staff had been on short-term contracts. In the three years of his tenure thus far, he had managed to make eight permanent positions. However, 40 per cent of staff remained on short-term contracts.

### 24 January, 1.30–3.00pm

That same day, staff had time to prepare their rooms. Every teacher had moved classrooms at the end of the previous year (partly to accommodate early childhood teachers and children together) and all were busily organising their spaces. Gavin visited every teacher individually and introduced the researcher to each staff member during this walk around the school. Late in the day all teachers visited every other teacher's room and each host teacher briefly introduced their plans for the start of the year.

### Work-shadowing 18–22 January: doing leading, moment-by-moment, day-by-day

Before school on 18 January, Gavin gives the researcher the plan of the week.

### First lesson

Then it's off to the preschool, where Gavin releases one of the staff to catch up on planning. On the way to the preschool, Gavin explains that he sees this as part of his teaching. He has chosen the preschool with the hope of meeting parents and carers as they drop off the young children. He also likes to meet all the children and know them by name. He communicates meaningfully with the children, asking questions and giving feedback about their activities, for example noticing a missing jigsaw puzzle piece, offering to read a story that children are leafing through, sitting on the floor with children and so on.

## Back in office

After the preschool lesson that same day, Gavin and I have agreed to discuss the research. Soon after I sit down, a parent rings and is put through to his office. 'Yep. Have you gone to the police? I think you need to go to the police.' The call continues, with Gavin trying to make it clear to the parent what he is responsible for and what he isn't. The student referred to is not at school that day. The parent is making accusations against another person. The call ends with Gavin promising to have a conversation the next day, but he concludes by saying: 'My job is to support the whole school and maintain the wellbeing of everyone here'. He has spent about seven minutes on the phone, and has to follow up on the matter briefly with others out of his office. When he returns, he begins to talk about the desperate need to upgrade the facilities at Sandford, and the delays in central office following up the procurement process so that the builder can commence working. He lists what will be done: new carpet where it has been destroyed, removal of bench, fixing air-conditioners, blinds in rooms, tinting on windows, soft-fall surface in playground – this is not large-scale work, but these items have been held up for some time. He then explains the budget situation, programmes, teachers' union difficulties and the problem with lack of social capital on Governing Council.

## After morning tea

Gavin needs to telephone the parent who had called earlier. He makes several other follow-up phone calls and then introduces a new topic, namely two teachers who are on leave for stress and legal matters, meaning that they cannot be replaced substantively. As Gavin explains the problem, it becomes clear that as a principal he has inherited a number of local, unfolding problems – disputes between families and also absent teachers with ongoing, significant issues. Quite apart from how school leaders intend to work on the culture with parent and teacher communities, on taking up their appointments, they do not enter a vacuum. Relationships are already in place. A new principal must wrestle with such legacies.

The opening narrative provides a brief insight into the range of everyday practices of one 'educational leader' – a mix of ongoing encounters that make up the typical principal's day, each requiring decision and action (cf. Wolcott, 1973). The daily work of school leaders can be read as pedagogical interactions for the purpose of influencing teaching and learning (Lingard, Hayes, Mills & Christie, 2003). While pedagogy is a core concern of educational leadership, and pedagogical leadership is not limited to classroom pedagogies but also includes other pedagogical activities, such as teacher professional learning, community counselling (Hayes, Christie, Mills & Lingard, 2004), the above description of Gavin's leadership practice shows that his daily work extended beyond pedagogical concerns, and included:

- talking to staff at the beginning of the year in ways that acknowledge specific ways of thinking about the work;
- working at sustaining continuity of 'the right' staff, so that the teachers can develop sustainable and collaborative whole-school approaches to teaching and learning;
- visiting classrooms regularly to model ways of talking to students and to provide 'productive' feedback to teachers;
- reculturing the school through every encounter, specifically through managing relationships between the school and parents, especially when things go wrong; and
- sustaining a dispersal of leadership practices, especially for developing school plans, professional development activity and evaluating 'good' pedagogy.

Attending to the everyday matters arising from the effects of poverty on local neighbourhoods constitutes a disproportionate amount of leaders' work; this is time that they are therefore unable to devote to more obviously educationally focused work, and it demonstrates that the absence of equity-based funding comes at a cost at the local level. Such matters can have a domino effect. For example, when Gavin is unavoidably called away, the assistant principal: literacy improvement becomes acting deputy (because the deputy becomes acting principal), and has to spend her day dealing with children who have been sent to the office for behavioural transgressions. This means she is unable to conduct her regular 'literacy chats' with early-career teachers. Dealing with these kinds of problems is unavoidable and requires expertise and time. The knock-on effect is clear – other people in the school need to step in and step up. The expertise that has been built up in the school over time – expertise about literacy, for example  – can no longer be put into action in the innovative ways that the leadership team had originally devised.

There are a number of ways to understand such scenarios. If we consider how leadership practices can be designed and sustained in high-poverty schools in order to enhance literacy teaching and learning, then these actual work demands need to be named and considered for what they take from the resources available and what is at stake. The school is never a sealed institution, but a porous, dynamic meeting place that must be negotiated daily by all participants (Comber, 2016). While the school leader may have a vision of ways of developing the knowledge and practices of the teachers, and work towards consistency and common goals, the immediate demands of parents, children and teachers, both in and outside of the school, impact on what can be accomplished, quite apart from the demands of the education department or sector. This line of argument complicates the opening portrayal in this chapter. What is going on is not self-evident. The very idea of 'leadership' becomes more difficult to pin down. In what follows, we attempt to make visible (following Smith, 2006) at least some aspects of the complex work that leaders attempt and accomplish.

## Making sense of what is made visible in the work of leaders

The dilemmas that Berlak and Berlak named in the 1980s are echoed in more recent scholarship with respect to the difficult choices and multiple agendas that educational leaders grapple with day-to-day. Critical Leadership Studies (CLS) aims to provide powerful explanatory accounts of what is happening to principals' work and their subjectivities, and of how educational leadership itself is being constituted by policy. CLS also aims to provide hopeful accounts of how educational leadership might contribute to advancing more socially just outcomes in educational institutions, including, in this case, schools. Thomson, Hall and Jones (2013) argue for a (post)critical tradition of leadership studies that 'mobilizes social theory in order to reproblematise dominant ways of thinking about leadership and change' (p. 156). Gunter (2001) explains that CLS challenges notions of visionary leaders and seeks to understand their experiences in contested policy spaces by 'engaging with real life real time practice, so that the experiences of practice are both captured and theorised' (p. 104).

For instance, writing about the 'supply problem' facing the schooling sector internationally, Thomson (2009) highlights the demand to focus on 'contemporary pressures, dilemmas and tensions' (p. 2) that surround leaders' work. In her conclusion, she summarises a contemporary dilemma for school leaders in terms of a struggle to manage the existential demands of the work, whilst being loaded with more and more tasks from the system's policy. The 'head's daily regime of "encounters" with all and sundry is necessary and time-consuming. Heads have no choice but to meet crises and unpredictable events head on' (Thomson, 2009, p. 150). Meantime, 'policy-makers ... keep pushing more and more tasks onto schools' (Thomson, 2009, p. 150).

Gunter (2012) provides another version of this same dilemma and pushes the analysis further by defining her inquiry in terms of understanding 'the relationship between the state, public policy and knowledge', and specifically how school leadership is made knowable, especially for policy-making. Gunter outlines persuasively how 'the leadership of schools' is problematised by policy in the United Kingdom, and we would agree that there are similarities in Australia. This problematisation assumes that leaders can be recruited to the cause of 'delivering national reforms locally' (Gunter, 2012, p. 2). Under the logic of neoliberalising governmentality, educational systems require 'a centrally designed and regulated form of leadership ... with head teachers left with [only] tactical options about efficient and effective implementation' (Gunter, 2012, p. 2). While the first part of Gunter's diagnosis is applicable to the Australian context, it cannot account for the scope for tactical autonomy that school principals have in Australia, even though the school year and their school profiles are increasingly organised and hooked up nationally by the National Assessment Program – Literacy and Numeracy (NAPLAN) and *My School*. Beyond these federal requirements and demonstrating compliance to demands for effectiveness and efficiency, principals in Australia still have some say over a wider terrain, including school structures, school culture, pedagogical practices and the extent to which accountability technologies, such as national testing, distort life in schools. This kind of autonomy is available to some, but not all, head teachers in England – namely, those that are 'successful' in text, exam and inspection regimes. Different kinds of head-teacher autonomy are distributed according to audit measures (Thomson, 2014).

Gunter goes on to argue, and again we think accurately, that school leaders are now constituted in policy texts as 'transformational leaders' who are responsible for distributed decision making, which enables 'a totalising reform strategy where all could be responsible and accountable for standards' (Gunter, 2012, p. 2) and learning outcomes. Reading Thomson and Gunter together, we could assert that those who take up school leadership positions now work in policy regimes that intensify their work, diminish and particularise their autonomy, and render them responsible for achieving systems imperatives (e.g. Niesche & Thomson, 2016).

For all of the principals in our study, the most significant dilemma was a variation on the one defined above by Thomson and Gunter: how to work with/against the logic of contemporary policy. This concept of with/against we borrow from Lather (1991) as shorthand for the ethical work of all educators working in disadvantaged schools. On the one hand, educators have no choice but to work with the policy logics of the times, such as high-stakes testing, short-term contracts for school leaders and national curriculum. All leaders struggle with how to interpret and enact policy logics in their own schools, and work the tension between being seen as a 'good' corporate citizen (i.e. implementing policy logics in the 'right way') vis-à-vis the existential demand to interpret policy in ways that are responsive to the specificity of their own contexts. In addition, working with/against involves engaging with contemporary schooling policy that asserts a logic of devolution that permits, and even expects, local 'interpretation' of policy (Thomson, 2008). However, our research draws attention to the diminishing space for such local interpretation and, in some cases, to where policy undermines the key project of the local primary school to serve the educational needs of the local community. The repercussions of this undermining are especially evident for schools serving high-poverty communities.

As a conceptual framework for examining leadership in schools, we have attempted to show that CLS provides analytical tools that we believe strongly resonate with the schools we have been studying. These tools include explanatory accounts of principals' work, particularly how it is being constituted by policy, and hopeful accounts of how educational leadership might contribute to advancing more socially just outcomes in educational institutions. In the next section, we illustrate the form that these kinds of explanatory hopeful accounts might take, by further detailing some of the difficult choices and multiple agendas that the educational leaders we observed grappled with on a daily basis.

## The dilemmas of leaders' work

We encountered each school at a specific point in time. The narratives that educational leaders related at each site reflected this temporality by identifying similar plot points – moments in time – connected by different story lines. The plot points included the state of the school when they arrived; the local conditions that impacted on their work; the changing diagnosis of problems and the assembling of responses from available resources; their hopes for the future, and their understanding of what they needed to do to get there.

In this section, we attempt to represent the complexity of these narratives through a series of dilemmas that enable us to frame and analyse the work of educational leaders. As a heuristic, dilemmas provide us with a means by which to represent our observations of the work of educational leaders. These dilemmas manifested in various ways and illustrate different sets of complexity. We have chosen four illustrative examples under the following headings:

- serving the local community;
- 'democratically' changing school culture;
- changing pedagogy through whole-school agreements;
- practising 'educational' leadership whilst responding to demands for performativity.

We begin with Riverview, focusing on Angela, the principal, and the dilemmas she encountered relating to serving the local community and 'democratically' changing the school culture. We then give examples from each of the schools in the northern suburbs to illustrate other dilemmas associated with changing pedagogical practice through whole-school agreements. Kathryn, the principal of Highfield, reflects on the use of teacher professional learning to support the implementation of the literacy agreements. Lena, the senior leader: literacy improvement at Sandford, describes the use of literacy chats to support teachers' use of literacy-achievement measures. Robyn, the part-time reading support mentor at Easton, describes her work as a mentor to increase teachers' familiarity with the comprehension strategies in use in the school.

### Serving the local community

Angela was the principal at Riverview Primary. Below, in direct quotes from her interviews, we hear her narrative told with sensitivity to the ways in which poverty shapes students' experiences of, and aspirations for, schooling, and her insistence on high expectations for successful student learning in her analysis of the community in which the school is located:

> Well, it's always been a low socioeconomic area, and we have some families that have experienced about three, and going into the fourth, generation of

unemployment. About 70 per cent of our student population is eligible for the School Card support. We're also getting more and more students that are coming to our school with a lot of difficulties in regards to learning and their social skill development. Our Aboriginal attendance, as well, has actually gone up now to over 30, and that's a significant marked increase for us. Twenty-one per cent of our student population has been identified as students with disabilities. We've got about 40 per cent with speech/language difficulties, and 37 per cent of students are supported through the Resource Entitlement Statement,[1] due to learning problems. So there's a significant number that we're working with.

The challenge for us is how to break that cycle, and we can't do anything with the community in regards to unemployment, but hopefully what we do with the students will actually start breaking down that cycle of unemployment, so there's hope. When I started as principal here four years ago, I'd ask students: 'What are your ambitions? What would you like to achieve?' And a lot of it was: 'Oh, it doesn't matter because I'll do what dad does, just go through Centrelink.'[2] And it's like: 'No, that's not what I want to hear.' So the emphasis now is on sustaining more hope. I think they can see that it doesn't matter what they end up being in their career, whatever it is, as long as they're successful in what it is, and that ambition – to actually improve themselves – is actually starting to change. To get our kids to finish secondary, and to want to actually think about going to university. They have the potential, and that's what we try to share with them: 'You can do it.' What seems most important is that we show that we believe in the kids.

Most of the teachers are up for that challenge and they've got used to me saying: 'You've got to raise the bar.' Even things like when we first started our reform project, we set minimum targets, but that's a disadvantage for our students. That's saying we believe that all they're capable of is the minimum, and I now refuse to have that. My target is that all students will be ready for secondary school by the time they leave this school. There are definite expectations that we have here, not just in terms of the quality of teaching, but it's the whole attitude, and the holistic approach to the profession, that we actually address. We have been doing a lot of work on school values, and attempting to generate a narrative about a shared purpose for our school, and that purpose is concentrating on teaching and learning. I have argued against thinking that: 'These kids come to school with nothing.' No. They come to school with what they have, and it's up to us to move them forward from there, and we need to be contributing to and measuring students' growth.

Angela's account asserts her diagnosis of the purpose of her school: in her words, it is about breaking the cycle of intergenerational unemployment. This translates not only into providing hopeful narratives for the futures of her students, but also into successful achievements at primary school that set them up for success in secondary school. The challenge of imagining and supporting success beyond school for her students meant insisting on the transmission of the message: 'Yes, you can!' in contrast to the message that is likely to prevail in more affluent settings: 'Yes, you will!' Rather than framing her narrative as a demand, Angela affirms that her students can be successful. Importantly, Angela reiterates her affirmation often: in classrooms with students, during staff meetings with teachers and when she meets with parents.

Angela's problematising leads her to refuse to accept what has been the case historically for her school community, and to imagine hopeful innovation – that she might lead her school to realise an alternative future for her students, not the (re)production of social stratification. Importantly, her project as a school leader largely ignores the policy logic of school choice and she takes up instead the challenge of Riverview being a 'good' school for every child who enrols.

Angela demonstrates a matter-of-fact awareness of the socioeconomic conditions faced by families. These need to be recognised and acknowledged, because of the impact they have on the children being taught at her school and because they are the conditions that she and her teachers work within. But Angela insists that these conditions are challenges and should not limit their expectations of children or their determination to 'move them forward'. Angela knows that what she says matters. She has to keep on believing and generating a narrative about a shared purpose.

## 'Democratically' changing school culture

Realising the hopeful imagining for Riverview Primary School, as outlined above, demands leading for change by transforming a culture of complaint, and redesigning pedagogies of lack, over and over. Educational leadership involves ongoing diagnosis of the problems. How the problems are understood shapes the responses that are assembled and put into practice. For Angela, this process required a shift from isolated individual practice, and a concentration on control, to collective practices that emphasise 'kids' learning'.

> I am always reflecting on how far we've come, because when we first started reforming the school we had teachers who were doing their own thing, and it was closed doors and no one was allowed to enter, and no one knew what anyone else was doing. So culturally, you've got sort of deficit views of the kids and their community, which then feeds into sort of low expectations for learning. You have a fetish for student behaviour management done really badly, and no concentrating on teaching and learning. Also, I won't have anything that takes the emphasis away from kids' learning, and specifically from the program we have devised over the past few years.
>
> We actually did focus on reculturing to start off with. We had to change that perception, the kids needed to feel safe here, and teachers had to feel safe, and it was all about their perceptions that they belong here. We worked on changing the expectation for parents, the school values, really. We started to do a lot about the school values, about what is respect, what does it look like, what is trust, what does it look like, all of those things.

And we talk about individual and collective responsibility, so it's not just the classroom teacher's responsibility, it's a collective, so everyone helps that child out. We changed the way we did school planning. Developing the Site Improvement Plan is now a whole-school practice. This is everyone's collective responsibility – and that includes teachers and students. We have a data analysis day every year, where all staff get together to analyse site-based tests, achievement and behaviour data, the NAPLAN, and then we decide what our future directions are going to be.

So what we've been working on for the past few years with staff is developing a common conversation or common language that we use in classrooms. It's so important for kids that they're not having to change every year to a different way of teaching and learning, so that it's very consistent, so that's really made a huge difference. An important aspect of that is we've made up whole-school agreements – for instance, on using word knowledge, and teaching phonological awareness. Another aspect of our shared understanding focuses on our expectations for teachers, and for their professional learning. I assume that teachers are in a profession and that means there are expectations, not just in terms of the quality of teaching, but it's the whole attitude and the holistic approach to the profession, and again it comes back to the trust. We did a lot of work on vales and expectations, and that was both with students and building that relationship with staff.

It's been really interesting to actually see the change, as in the perception of the community. We used to be seen as a school where the focus was on behaviour, you know, it would always be alternative programs for behaviour, and the perception was that the school was rewarding those sort of programs and rewarding students for inappropriate behaviours. That was the perception of them, that the kids that were doing the right thing were actually being penalised because they didn't get to paint the murals or do the garden, or whatever, so that whole perception has now changed. I can walk around now, and visit classrooms, and when I walk in I can't get the teachers' attention because they're so used to me visiting, and the students pay no attention to me either and just keep focusing on their work. The pride in the school has been massive with the students wearing the dress code. The students are very tolerant of difference; they're very accepting of many students. I don't know why, but there's just not 'doing the deficit'; there seems to be a sort of a flourishing of difference, then people have to feel like they're not being put down because they are different.

Angela's narrative gives us insight into the logics of her practice. The reform process that she instigated was being realised through her persistent hopeful and clear-sighted leadership that involved ongoing reflection and analysis – data analysis every day, every year. Angela's story of change – getting a grip on social order in the school, and moving to establish a common ethos centred on learning in general, and literacy in particular – is not uncommon in disadvantaged schools (cf.

Hampton & Jones, 2000; Peacock, 2008; Stubbs, 2003; Winkley, 2002). Here, however, the narrative is specifically situated in the current policy context.

The movement from individual to collective practice was encapsulated in whole-school agreements that contain the common language and understandings of the collective. In the following section, the intended purpose for these agreements is explained. These forms of 'governing texts' (Smith, 2006) are not new, but their realisation through the so-called Literacy Agreements was a feature of the schools in our study that can be traced to the SILA project, as described in the Introduction.

## Changing pedagogy through whole-school agreements

As previously discussed, one of the key strategies of SILA, which investigated 32 schools with the lowest achievement levels and trends in NAPLAN literacy assessments in South Australia, was a school review process that culminated in a public report. The reviews said 'hard things' that required (urgent) attention at the SILA schools, and were often seen as 'creating a catalyst' for reform. SILA school principals reported that these reviews mostly provided an accurate diagnosis of some key challenges with regard to teaching literacy. From our perspective, the analysis provided in the reviews identified significant challenges facing policy and practice in disadvantaged SILA primary schools that also mapped onto existing (inter)national research, including:

- an over-reliance on whole-class, low-level, routine tasks, and hence a lack of challenge and rigour in the learning tasks offered to students (Hayes, Johnston & King, 2009; Lingard, 2007);
- a focus on the 'code-breaking' function of language, at the expense of richer conceptualisations of literacy that might guide teachers' understanding of challenging pedagogies (Gutiérrez, Hunter & Arzubagia, 2009; Luke, 2003);
- the need for substantial shifts in the culture of schools, especially unsettling deficit views of students and their communities (Comber & Kamler, 2004; Hattam & Prosser, 2008);
- a need to provide a more 'consistent' approach to teaching literacy across the school;
- a need for School Improvement Plans in order to implement a clear focus on literacy learning;
- a need to sustain professional learning to produce new knowledge and practice (Hayes *et al.*, 2009).

The project for school change that was outlined by SILA was taken up in different ways by the four schools involved in our research. Each school was clearly focused on improving their students' NAPLAN scores (the measure that was valued by the state education department and broader education community as an indicator of a well-functioning school). They adopted and adapted a range of strategies and programmes in order to achieve better student outcomes, but they also attempted to change pedagogical practices through the development of whole-school literacy agreements.

In each of the schools, locally developed agreements about how to improve literacy were in operation. Their specific intentions for improving literacy were outlined in a document known as a Literacy Agreement. These documents contained site-specific whole-school approaches to literacy teaching. They were intended to address issues identified in the SILA school reviews (as listed above) and guide, improve and focus teachers' pedagogical practices.

The Literacy Agreements typically included a description of the scope and sequence for teaching literacy from Reception to Year 7; the form and timing of assessment tasks; year-level targets for reading, spelling and writing; and guidance on the content and structure of the time allocated each day to literacy activities (known as the Literacy Block in several of the schools). To successfully implement the Literacy Agreements, schools needed to consider teachers' professional learning needs as well as the purchase of resources for classroom programmes. Equally importantly, the agreements were a reference point for professional conversations about students' learning and about the data that provided evidence of students' progress in performance development meetings between teachers and line managers in the leadership team.

The Literacy Agreements were arrived at in a variety of ways, including reinstituting familiar approaches to literacy, and attempting new strategies developed after in-depth discussions about the literacy needs of students and the requirements of the recently introduced national curriculum. For our purposes, it will suffice to comment briefly on what the agreements encompass, so that the examples of individual teachers' practices that we describe in later chapters can be read in relation to the collectively authorised practices that operated in the schools. We then highlight some of the different ways the Literacy Agreements were developed and implemented in each of the schools.

The schools produced literacy folders, assessment folders and induction folders that documented the agreements and made them 'active texts' (Kerkham & Nixon, 2014; Smith, 2006) that guided and regulated teachers' and leaders' understandings of literacy practice. At Easton, for example, each teacher was given a Literacy Folder and an Assessment Folder, essential guides to what was to be taught and assessed at each year level. The Literacy Folder contained:

- Whole-school spelling programme. This included: a scope and sequence, stages of spelling development, guidelines for teaching a balanced spelling programme, examples of focused teaching activities related to the four spelling knowledges (phonological, visual, morphemic, etymological), and a list of websites and print resources for teachers.
- Scope and sequence for teaching comprehension strategies in year levels from Reception to Year 7 (and linked to NAPLAN reading skills). The comprehension skills to be taught included: making connections; inferencing; visualising and visual literacy; summarising, synthesising and determining importance; and

comprehension strategies for nonfiction texts. Examples of teaching activities and readings for teachers were included in a companion Comprehension Folder.

- A copy of teaching resources relevant to the year level, such as handbooks for teaching phonics and grammar.

The Assessment Folder contained:

- Calendar of assessments to be given for each year level each term: Screen of Phonological Awareness (SPA), Running records, Progressive Achievement Test in Reading (PAT-R) (ACER, 2016), spelling tests, Jolly Phonics, sight vocabulary, decoding checklist, NAPLAN, Lexile levels.
- Examples of assessment record sheets such as Screen of Phonological Awareness (SPA); teacher-rating oral language and literacy (TROLL) (Dickinson, McCabe & Sprague, 2003).
- Bedrock word list; Oxford word list; MultiLit vocabulary list (Wheldall, 2006); Running records (Clay, 2000).
- Diagnostic spelling tests (Waddington, 2000; Westwood, 2005).
- Sight vocabulary list.
- Decoding checklist.
- ESL scope and scale data collection.
- Marking rubric for assessing students' writing.

This list of the assessments indicates the priority given to testing and measurement of skills and capabilities, perhaps suggesting that having this data will in its own right lead to improvement. However, this remains contingent on teachers having the ability to interpret and understand the implications of each child's performance in terms of their further teaching and provision of resources and tasks. Many teachers needed time and assistance to learn about how to administer the different tests and make meaning from the results. In some instances, the relentlessness of the testing calendar left little time for reflection and response. In addition, the test results did not always lead to any further resourcing when difficulties were identified, leading some teachers to feel overwhelmed by what students could not do.

In summary, the Literacy Agreements were intended to support a whole-school approach to the teaching of literacy that would result in improvements in student performance. The importance of whole-school approaches emerged in the school reform literature in the form of school-wide professional learning communities (Louis, Marks & Kruse, 1996; McLaughlin & Talbert, 2001). The basis for the claim, which was reflected earlier in Angela's narrative, is that change needs to be understood and supported by teachers who share a vision for their collective action, namely, a sense of shared responsibility for all students' learning. However, Lipman (1998) warns that the conditions that produce these communities – shared decision-making, collaboration, professional development and so on – can be substituted for the goals. In other words, 'they may become ends in themselves divorced from the goals of transforming students' educational experiences' (Lipman, 1998,

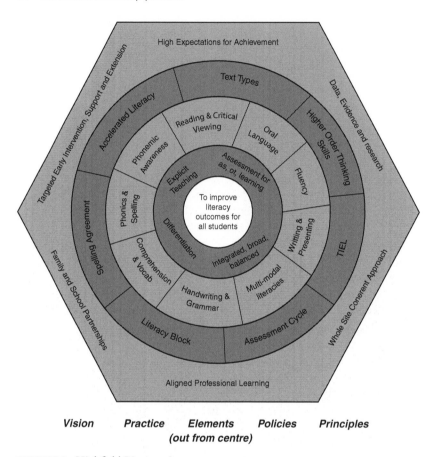

Vision  Practice  Elements  Policies  Principles
(out from centre)

**FIGURE 3.1** Highfield Literacy Agreement.

p. 296). Whether intended or otherwise, the shared and binding nature of the agreements often meant that teachers were required to adopt specified approaches to the teaching of literacy.

At Highfield, the Literacy Agreement was summarised as in Figure 3.1. Many of the programmes and approaches included in this diagram were also being implemented in other schools in our study. This diagram illustrates the wide range of approaches to teaching literacy that were in common use.

The 'literacy pie' illustrated in Figure 3.1 was a lot to digest. Teachers needed a deep understanding of literacy and language and a range of practices to support literacy learning. As in the other schools, support to develop these practices at Highfield came from a range of sources, including locally developed resources, specialist trainers and coaches, targeted professional development and the professional learning teams. One problem that emerged was due to high levels of teacher turnover. Since teachers joining the school came with different knowledge about literacy pedagogy, there was an ongoing need to commit resources to developing the pedagogical approaches required to implement the Literacy Agreements, and to developing recently arrived teachers' understandings of the literacy needs of young people that underpinned these agreements. The educational capital in professional learning teams remains contingent on the membership and their opportunities to engage deeply with complex ideas.

Highfield principal Kathryn recognised the importance of professional learning for 'unpacking and deconstructing' the literacy pie, which she acknowledged was 'a big mind map in my head, I can see it, and it all fits together in my head'. After an unsuccessful attempt at placing all the teachers into professional learning teams, she asked them to select a small group of colleagues they wanted to work with in this way. The following observations are from fieldnotes recorded, and subsequently transcribed, after the weekly meeting of one of these teams.

> The four teachers discussed a teacher observation rubric that one of them had discovered on the web. It's called SOLOM, or the Student Oral Language Observation Matrix, but before they got into the long discussion of that matrix they began with sharing some incidents that had happened related to individual students, involvement of parents and so on. So there was a lot of general chatter to begin with, also some discussion about responses to news about one of them being pregnant, but most of the professional learning community time was taken up with a discussion of SOLOM.
>
> It's not clear to me why they want to use this. The main reason they gave was that the oral language assessment task that they've been using is something they're not happy with. It's not that they find it difficult to use, it's just that they don't find the information it provides terribly useful, so on their own initiative they went looking for something else, and they've come up with this SOLOM matrix. It seems to provide more detailed information about oral language development, but it also includes, on the rubric, descriptions of reading comprehension and spelling and, I think, what they like is the kind of alignment in the levels between those things.
>
> This is a very supportive little group, they're fun to be around and to be with. They clearly like each other very much, respect each other, help each other, share resources, and are really sparky – bouncing ideas off each other all the time. They seem to be able to be very honest; they've been very welcoming of me. They're not afraid to talk about difficulties or to share successes. I think this is a very nice example of a professional learning community, the kind of thing we'd really hope all teachers to be part of. The only thing that I think is perhaps missing is a more experienced teacher, or leader, who could perhaps guide them to maybe think a little bit more deeply about some of the things they're doing, but look, they're actually great and I think as a self-selecting professional learning community it's probably doing everything, and perhaps more, that Kathryn was hoping to do.

Professional learning took on many different forms at Highfield Primary, and Kathryn assembled these learning opportunities for teachers, perhaps using a similar process to how she imagined the components of the Literacy Agreement: 'I've tried to get better at explaining and putting things in writing like this, so people understand what my thinking behind it is.' It was clear that the thinking behind it was complex on a number of levels, including: whose learning was being met, for what purpose, and by which means? In Kathryn's view, a focus on student achievement needed to be accompanied by a focus on the learning of teachers, and on improving what they are doing.

At Sandford Primary, principal Gavin created a leadership position entitled senior leader: literacy improvement. An experienced early years teacher, Lena, was appointed. Her role was to provide in-class support for early-career teachers, including modelling strategies for literacy teaching as requested. However, the most innovative practice we observed was the one-on-one meetings she held with teachers each term. These were known as 'literacy chats'. To these meetings, teachers were expected to bring current data for three students about whom they had some concern; to discuss their progress, and identify goals for the following term. Incidental professional learning was integral to these meetings, where, in response to the teachers' analysis of the data, Lena could insert examples of learning tasks that might extend the students' literacy learning; suggest a focus on a particular aspect of literacy (such as oral language development); propose ideas for teaching 'sight words' or grammar in the context of reading a shared big book with the class; and suggest options for grouping students. She would also critique the practice of rigidly following the programmes promoted in the Literacy Agreement by sharing how she modified her classroom practice to take account of the learning needs of her students.

During the literacy chats, teachers explored the practical and the possible in terms of engaging students in learning in multiple ways. For example, in the following exchange with Carrie, a Reception/Year 1 class teacher, senior leader Lena acknowledges the productive work Carrie is doing with Jolly Phonics and provides examples of how she might enhance the students' learning by varying the learning context and purpose:

*Carrie*:  We do the Jolly Phonics digraph, which we'll do as a class, and on Monday it looks like introducing … Tuesday we're blending, and then there's usually games or something to do with it … Wednesday I'll do it super quick, and that could be another blending one or, you know, more words with it, and every now and then we come up with the alternative vowel, and Friday, there'll be another page of games to use with it, or we'll talk about other digraphs. It's a Jolly Phonics game on the board.

*Lena*:  You could also look at finding a big book or a story that has whatever digraph you're doing as a main focus, and that way you're introducing some big book group reading, and bringing that out in context.

*Carrie*:  I was on a website that, yeah. When would I use that book?

*Lena*:  I would maybe do it on a Friday, as like a consolidating activity, like: 'We've been looking at this digraph all week, let's go through this book and …'

*Carrie*:    'Put our hand up or do the action as soon as we hear it.'

*Lena*:    Yeah, or get a big piece of Perspex, and put it over your big book, and: 'Come and circle the word that has our digraph in it, so come and find it.' Because that way they're also getting in that shared reading, that whole-group comprehension as well, seeing the word, the blend in context, not just as isolated words here, there and everywhere. It's like: 'Well look, here's our word, it's the same word, here it is.' It's that thing you were saying before: 'Here's our word all over here by itself, but look, they're also here, and we know those words because we can read here, and now we can read them here.' And you can read the book, and get them to clap every time that they hear or come to that word, so: 'Clap when you hear the word that's got this digraph in it.'

Lena's suggestions disrupt the tendency to teach strictly according to the methods and sequence of the programme, whilst maintaining a focus on teaching the necessary decoding skills in the context of a shared reading for meaning.

At Easton Primary, a part-time reading support teacher position was created to support the Literacy Agreement. Robyn, a mid-career teacher, was appointed to this position and released from classroom teaching for two days a week. Her main role was to mentor teachers who were unfamiliar with the comprehension strategies included in the school's Scope and Sequence document. The school's analysis of their NAPLAN results indicated that comprehension, specifically inferencing, was a key area for development. We observed Robyn model strategies as teachers requested, such as visualisation, making connections (text-to-self, text-to-text, text-to-world), summarising, and distinguishing between 'interesting' and 'important' information in both fiction and nonfiction texts. After a lesson where a strategy was modelled, she would suggest ideas for further activities that were included in a comprehension folder given to teachers at the beginning of the year, offer advice on how to bring the strategy into the literacy programme and provide time for debriefing. This classroom-focused mentoring was strongly based on a teacher's self-identified professional learning needs and was followed up with questionnaire responses from the teachers, as Robyn explained:

> So, probably again next week, I'll be doing another questionnaire or another bit of thinking around: 'Well, OK, I've worked for two terms now with these people, now who feels they need some more support in those areas? And who is using comprehension strategies, and who isn't? If you're not using them in your classroom, what do you need to keep moving forward?'

As reading support teacher, Robyn was also involved in providing whole-school professional learning at staff meetings. For example, from the Screen of Phonological Awareness (SPA) data, she had identified 'some gaps in students' phonological awareness, their rhyme, all of those Big 6 areas', and it was apparent from questionnaire responses that a number of the teachers 'didn't have that knowledge of the

Big 6,[3] because they weren't here when we taught that'. The Literacy Agreement identified the 'Big 6' as essential components of a balanced literacy programme.

Professional learning needs at Easton were also addressed through year-level professional learning communities (PLCs), where teachers would collaborate on planning units of work, discuss student data and share strategies for supporting student learning, and share professional reading resources. The PLCs were also the taking off point for tentative steps towards collaborative inquiry into aspects of literacy teaching. The principal was keen to have the teachers engage in action research and required them to undertake a one-term project. For example, two of the teachers in our research were exploring aspects of their literacy teaching. Their questions were:

- Does the explicit teaching of comprehension strategies in literacy support students' ability to independently use these strategies in other learning areas?
- How can I successfully incorporate tablet computers into my literacy block?

At Easton, the Literacy Agreements were sustained in different ways through different forms of professional learning, including input from outside consultants, which we do not discuss here. While the agreements prescribed what teachers should teach and assess, the practices that supported the teachers to enact them could open up possibilities for teachers to rethink and reimagine their literacy pedagogy.

We have come to understand that the Literacy Agreements are themselves entangled in a dilemma; they tend to make available a narrow view of literacy that teachers become very skilled at teaching and assessing, at the expense of providing students with challenging literacy tasks. The teachers' goals are strongly aligned to achieving improved NAPLAN scores, the measure by which schools and teaching are judged. Yet, as the principal at Easton acknowledged, there was a cost – teachers were inclined to 'teach safe', to adhere to the letter of the agreements. In the classroom, the predictable and practical tended to be emphasised rather than the creative preparation for the unforeseen and unknown, and this resulted in a narrowing of what was considered to be 'the normal'.

## Practising 'educational' leadership whilst responding to demands for performativity

All of the principals in this study asserted that their schools were committed to enrolling every child who wished to attend. This commitment was seen as fundamental to the purposes of public schools, but they all had stories of how some neighbouring schools worked around this commitment. Marketisation, which is now so central to global schooling policy, asserts a logic of parental choice that presents a key ethical dilemma for leaders in our study (Angus, 2015; Campbell, Proctor & Sherrington, 2009; Morgan & Blackmore, 2013). When pushed, this policy logic now 'forces' schools and school leaders to attract the most academically capable students, or those students who can provide the school with student outcome data, such as NAPLAN results, that will present the school in the best available light. This logic is blind to the realities facing 'actually existing' schools serving high-poverty communities (Lingard, Sellar & Savage, 2014; Thomson, 2010), because providing an opportunity for a good education for every child in the community means taking on not only students who are academically capable, but also students who bring their troubles to school. The principals in our schools reorganised and restructured people and resources in order to provide for such students.

Angela's commitment to a socially just education put her at odds with the notions of school choice and its entanglement in the marketisation of schooling. Her story about the arrival of one particular family is particularly telling in this regard:

> We've had quite a few new students enrolled this term, and a few have significant family issues. Of some note, we recently re-enrolled a family which is returning to our school. This family is being shunted from town to town, and that involves a Year 7 child, one in Year 5 and one in Reception, and the two younger ones are also excluded (taken out of the classroom and either sent to another classroom, or sent home under parent supervision, for a specific time). They just trash classrooms, and we had the police involved for the Year 5 child. The children's mother has argued that we are the only school that can cater for the needs of her children. Taking these children, though, means a change to the complete dynamics of every class that those kids are in. We are used to taking on students who change the dynamics of the classes, but this is extreme. The teachers have all accepted their new enrolments, some a little bit more reluctantly than others, but it means that we have to pull, or redeploy, SSOs, to one-to-one or small-group work. Meantime, funding is getting cut left, right and centre, but we're getting higher and higher needs. Some of our SSOs are working voluntary hours here, just so the students still get the support, because we can't afford the funding.
>
> But it can change classroom dynamics when you get a student that is having a lot of issues, and all of a sudden you put them into a very calm, settled class. It can change everything overnight, which is really challenging for our teachers. With really challenging students, we need to withdraw them from the mainstream classroom, and this is quite counter to our philosophy and values. Some of the recent enrolments have forced us to rethink what we are doing in terms of programs outside of classrooms. Most recently we had to rethink the rationale for our Learning Centre. Initially the vision was to provide for the students who just needed a little bit of timely intervention to give them the confidence to go up. And also the students that needed to be stretched. And in terms of that, it's not just trying to get them even better, you know, but actually to challenge, to go deeper with their thinking, their questioning, actually developing their ... more or less their life skills rather than their school smarts, but also to provide for students that aren't necessarily strong in academics, but have skills in other areas, like in athletics or in art, which we've done this year.

More recently, though, it needs to cater for really troubling school behaviour, which is a bit disappointing, but some students really require one-to-one. But in so doing, they're feeling safe, they're feeling a lot more confident, they are wanting to come to school, whereas before there was no way they were going to school. So things like suspensions for those students have decreased, and we're looking at other avenues to support them than focusing on the Australian Curriculum. Basically we are attempting to address their specific needs, rather than what we can do in a mainstream classroom. The hope is we are going to get them into a mainstream class where they can actually manage their resilience and coping. With these students we actually have a debrief every term: 'Okay, what are our opportunities to improve? What do we need to address? What can we do that's different? What can we do to help?' We've started things like managing the resilience programs, the social skills programs, the tuning-in programs ... For example, one of these children in the Learning Centre is now involving himself more in learning, but in a very hands-on approach. His reading was really low, but we've got him reading recipes so he can cook, following instructions. He's able to do that now with confidence, and then talk about it, and he hasn't had a suspension since. The youngest one, there was a glimmer of hope that we can keep him in a mainstream classroom, but it's a very fine line. At this stage all it takes is: 'I'm going to ring home,' and then he responds. While he's in a mainstream class, he's on a modified learning program, and we do have a lot of support in there with him.

I am very concerned about their family life, and I also know that school is probably their only one safe place that they have. We have to be the champion for each of those children. We needed to reorganise some basic things in the school that could incorporate this difficulty that couldn't be incorporated in the way the school was organised before, so it's not just about them actually, it's the frame they're in.

In this addition to Angela's narrative, which has been threaded through this chapter, we gain an insight into the depth of her concern for every student and the risks that such concern presents to all students. Angela's commitment and values are borne by every teacher and student, who must adjust and accommodate. Her willingness to reframe and 'reorganise some basic things in the school' illustrates another kind of dilemma faced by educational leaders in these kinds of settings on a regular basis – how to meet the learning needs of young people with complex needs.

When the mainstream class doesn't work for every student, the potential for disrupted schooling may be realised in internal suspensions, short-term exclusions from the school, or longer-term placement at another school. Just as a family may be shunted from town to town, so a student may be moved from one disadvantaged school to another where resources may be equally stretched. One young student, Gus, had exhausted his options for remaining at Sandford, because of his increasingly violent behaviour. The school did not have the resources to deal with his daily frustrations in the classroom. The principal had made a request for him to be placed at Easton, two-and-a-half kilometres away, for a ten-week term, in part so that his mother could readily take him to the school.

In this kind of temporary transfer process, leaders need to take into account how to best use the resources in their own school, considering which students are accepted where, and under what circumstances. In the current policy environment, where NAPLAN results can significantly impact on the standing of the school, the dilemma for leaders lies in their commitment to equitable access to education for all students, even if some are not likely to enhance the reputation of the school. We present a fuller account of student Gus in Chapter 6.

## Conclusion

In this chapter, we have attempted to provide contextualised accounts of the work of educational leaders that demonstrates its complexity, messiness, contingency and ethical uncertainty (Kerkham & Comber, 2016). The dilemmas detailed above provide a language for making visible and examining the larger issues that are embedded in the particulars of the everyday schooling experience, in particular the practice of educational leaders.

Our research makes clear that the educational leaders who support literacy learning:

- diagnose or problematise what is most existential in their unique school contexts, whilst simultaneously enacting policy;
- assemble and sustain the conditions for productive learning by all staff and students;
- transform school culture through each encounter with staff, students and parents;
- co-construct a persuasive narrative for the school community that demands high expectations and works towards redesigning pedagogies for engagement; and
- sustain a dispersal of leadership practices, especially for developing school plans, professional development activity and evaluating 'good' pedagogy.

It is likely that policy-makers assume that educational leaders foreground the demands of policy over the existential demands of their unique school contexts, but our research suggests the opposite. School leaders mostly generate their theories for leading their schools through reading their contexts and then working out how policy might be enacted. The dilemmas above illustrate that school leaders are continually involved in a process of 'practical reasoning' and 'practical theory', aimed at breaking the cycle of poverty, optimising available resources, complying with accountability measures, making accommodations that meet the needs of all students and so on.

The resolution of these problems constitutes the accomplishment of schooling. To borrow from Ball (1997, p. 317), such resolutions 'are assembled over time to form a bricolage of memories, commitments, routines, bright ideas and policy effects. They are changed, influenced and interfered with regularly, and increasingly.' While educational policies now leave little room for educational leaders to exercise discernment, those in the schools we studied spoke a form of policy vernacular that was inflected through the specifics of people, histories, narratives, resources and networks located in each local place. They worked within the diminishing space made available to them for local variation and adaptation, and managed to find ways to serve the educational needs of children and their families.

The following chapters continue our examination into educational leadership with a focus on what teachers were doing in classrooms. Observing the pedagogical work of teachers over time afforded us opportunities to examine the impact of a range of conditions on classroom practice, and on what teachers say about how these conditions enable or constrain their work. We found some answers to questions such us: How do teachers interpret the impact of policy on their pedagogical practice? What kinds of leadership do teachers find supportive, and in what ways? How do teachers diagnose and respond to the needs of the children they teach?

Focusing on what teachers were doing in classrooms also provided us with opportunities to compare the impact of their practices on literacy learning. In the next chapter, we describe the uncommon pedagogies of six teachers from across the schools. What went on in their classrooms was unusual, because it was noticeably different to their peers – not because of what they were doing, but because of how they went about their work in supporting their students' literacy learning. In this way, we describe how they too were leaders of literacy learning in their schools.

## Notes

1   Resource Entitlement Scheme (RES) for South Australian public schools indicates the resources schools will receive for: Industrial Entitlements (Authority of Certified Agreement) – the resources that are mandated from the enterprise bargaining process); Commonwealth and State Government Initiatives – the resources required to support students with special needs and resources – specific projects from both State and Commonwealth Governments; and Discretionary Allocations – discretionary allocations made to schools as part of the staffing process or in recognition of special circumstances.
2   Centrelink provides a range of government payments and services for retirees, families, people with disabilities, Indigenous Australians and people from diverse cultural and linguistic backgrounds. The majority of Centrelink's services concern social security payments for pensioners and unemployed people.
3   Explicit teaching of the 'Big 6' – oral language, phonemic awareness, phonics, fluency, vocabulary development and comprehension strategies – was strongly promoted by the Department for Education and Child Development (DECD) and the Northern Regional Office. It has become commonplace in the literacy block in most early years classrooms in South Australia.

## References

Australian Council for Educational Research (ACER) (2016). 'Progressive achievement tests in reading (PAT-R)'. Retrieved 18 July 2016 from https://www.acer.edu.au/pat-reading.
Angus, L. (2015). 'School choice: Neoliberal education policy and imagined futures'. *British Journal of Sociology of Education, 36*(3), 395–413.

Ball, S. (1997). 'Good school/bad school: Paradox and fabrication'. *British Educational Research Journal, 18*(3), 317–336.

Ball, S. (2008). *The Education Debate: Policy and politics in the 21st century*. Bristol, UK: Policy Press.

Berlak, A., & Berlak, H. (1981). *The Dilemmas of Schooling: Teaching and social change*. London: Methuen & Co., Ltd.

Campbell, C., Proctor, H., & Sherrington, G. (2009). *School Choice: How parents negotiate the new school market*. Crows Nest, NSW: Allen & Unwin.

Clay, M. (2000). *Running Records for Classroom Teachers*. Auckland: Heinemann.

Coles, R., & Thomson, P. (2016). 'Between records and representations: Inbetween writing in educational ethnography'. *Ethnography and Education, 11*(3), 253–266.

Comber, B. (2016). 'Poverty, place and pedagogy in education: Research stories from front-line workers'. Radford Lecture. *Australian Educational Researcher, 43*(4), 393–417.

Comber, B., & Kamler, B. (2004). 'Getting out of deficit: Pedagogies of reconnection'. *Teaching Education, 15*(3), 293–310.

Dickinson, D., McCabe, A., & Sprague, K. (2003). 'Teacher rating of oral language and literacy (TROLL): Individualising early literacy instruction with a standards-based rating tool'. *The Reading Teacher, 56*(6), 554–564.

Freebody, P., & Freiberg, J. (2011). 'Ethnomethodological research in education and the social sciences: Studying "the business, identities and cultures" of classrooms'. In L. Markauskaite, P. Freebody, & J. Irwin (eds.), *Methodological Choice and Design: Scholarship, policy and practice in social and educational research* (pp. 79–98). Dordrecht and London: Springer.

Gunter, H. (2001). 'Critical approaches to leadership in education'. *Journal of Educational Inquiry, 2*(2), 94–108.

Grace, G. (2000). 'Research and the challenges of contemporary school leadership: The contribution of critical scholarship'. *British Journal of Educational Studies, 48*(3), 231–247.

Gunter, H. (2012). *Leadership and the Reform of Education*. Bristol, UK: Policy Press.

Gutiérrez, K., Hunter, J., & Arzubagia, A. (2009). 'Re-mediating the university: Learning through socio-critical literacies'. *Pedagogies, 4*(1), 1–23.

Hampton, G., & Jones, J. (2000). *Transforming Northicote School: The reality of school improvement*. London: RoutledgeFalmer.

Hattam, R., & Prosser, B. (2008). 'Unsettling deficit views of students and their communities'. *Australian Educational Researcher, 35*(2), 89–106.

Hayes, D., Christie, P., Mills, M., & Lingard, B. (2004). 'Productive leaders and productive leadership: Schools as learning organisations'. *Journal of Educational Administration, 42*(4/5), 520–538.

Hayes, D., Johnston, K., & King, A. (2009). 'Creating enabling classroom practices in high poverty contexts: The disruptive possibilities of looking in classrooms'. *Pedagogy, Culture & Society, 17*(3), 251–264.

Kerkham, L., & Comber, B. (2016). 'Literacy leadership and accountability: Holding onto ethics in ways that count'. In B. Lingard, G. Thompson, & S. Sellar (eds.), *Testing in Schools: An Australian assessment* (pp. 86–97). London and New York: Routledge.

Kerkham, L., & Nixon, H. (2014). 'Literacy assessment that counts: Mediating, interpreting and contesting translocal policy in a primary school'. *Ethnography and Education, 9*(3), 343–358. Berkeley, California: University of California Press.

Lather, P. (1991). *Feminist Research in Education: Within/against*. Deakin, Geelong, Victoria: Deakin University Press.

Lingard, B. (2007). 'Pedagogies of indifference'. *International Journal of Inclusive Education, 11*(3), 245–266.

Lingard, B., Hayes, D., Mills, M., & Christie, P. (2003). *Leading Learning: Making hope practical in schools*. Maidenhead: Open University Press.

Lingard, B., Sellar, S., & Savage, G. (2014). 'Re-articulating social justice as equity in schooling policy: The effects of testing and data infrastructures'. *British Journal of Sociology of Education*, *35*(5), 710–730.

Lipman, P. (1998). *Race, Class and Power in School Restructuring*. New York: SUNY Press.

Louis, K., Marks, H., & Kruse, S. (1996). 'Teachers' professional community in restructuring schools'. *American Educational Research Journal*, *33*(4), 757–798.

Luke, A. (2003). 'Making literacy policy and practice with a difference'. *Australian Journal of Language and Literacy*, *26*(3), 58–82.

McLaughlin, M., & Talbert, J. (2001). *Professional Communities and the Work of High School Teaching*. Chicago, IL: University of Chicago Press.

Morgan, R., & Blackmore, J. (2013). 'How parental and school responses to choice policies reconfigure a rural education market in Victoria, Australia'. *Journal of Educational Administration and History*, *45*(1), 84–109.

Niesche, R., & Thomson, P. (2016). 'Freedom to what ends? School autonomy in neoliberal times'. In I. Bogotch & D. Waite (eds.), *The International Handbook of Educational Leadership*. New York: Wiley Blackwell.

Peacock, A. (2008). 'If you go down to the woods today … developing a whole school culture where it is safe to take risks'. *Forum*, *50*(2), 214–219.

Smith, D. (2006). 'Incorporating texts into ethnographic practice'. *Institutional Ethnography as Practice* (pp. 65–88). Lanham, Maryland: Rowman & Littlefield Publishers.

Stubbs, M. (2003). *Ahead of the Class: How an inspiring headmistress gave children back their future*. London: John Murray.

Thomson, P. (2002). *Schooling the Rustbelt Kids: Making the difference in changing times*. Crows Nest, NSW: Allen & Unwin.

Thomson, P. (2008). 'Headteacher critique and resistance: A challenge for policy, and for leadership/management scholars'. *Journal of Educational Administration and History*, *40*(2), 85–100.

Thomson, P. (2009). *School Leadership: Heads on the block?* London: Routledge.

Thomson, P. (2010). 'Headteacher autonomy: A sketch of a Bourdieuian field analysis of position and practice'. *Critical Studies in Education*, *51*(1), 5–20.

Thomson, P. (2014). '"Scaling up" educational change: Some musings on misrecognition and doxic challenges'. *Critical Studies in Education*, *55*(2), 87–103.

Thomson, P., Hall, C., & Jones, K. (2013). 'Towards educational change leadership as a discursive practice – or should all school leaders read Foucault?' *International Journal of Leadership in Education: Theory and Practice*, *16*(2), 155–172.

Waddington, Neil (2000). Diagnostic standard and advanced reading and spelling Tests 1 & 2. 2nd edition Adelaide: Waddington Educational Resources Pty Ltd.

Westwood, P. (2005). *Spelling: Approaches to teaching and assessment*, Second edition. Camberwell, Victoria: ACER Press.

Wheldall, K. (2006). *MultiLit (Making up lost time in literacy)*. Retrieved 18 June 2015 from http://www.multilit.com/.

Winkley, D. (2002). *Handsworth Revolution: The odyssey of a school*. London: Giles De La Mare.

Wolcott, H. (1973). *The Man in the Principal's Office: An ethnography*. Prospect Heights, IL: Waveland Press.

# 4

# UNCOMMON PEDAGOGIES

The long-term nature of our research enabled us to pay close attention to teachers' work over an extended period of time. We spent time in classrooms and staffrooms. We walked the hallways and playgrounds. We talked with school leaders, teachers, students and parents. In the process, we became familiar with the routines and practices of each school, many of which were recognisable across the sites in our study. We were not surprised to observe common pedagogical practices, since each school was operating according to literacy agreements, as discussed in Chapter 3 and these detailed what would be taught and assessed in order to 'raise literacy standards'. Although these documents were locally negotiated, they included a number of agreements that were common to all the schools about what counted as 'good' literacy pedagogy. Hence, common features of the agreements included structural arrangements, such as the Literacy Block; approaches to literacy, such as *Accelerated Literacy* (Acevedo & Rose, 2007; Rose, 2010); the teaching of genres; and the adoption of commercially available resources, such as Jolly Phonics (Lloyd & Wernham, 1992) and Lexile reading levels (Metametrics, 2004).

With time, we also came to notice a small number of teachers in each school whose pedagogies stood out. These practices were unusual, not because of what these teachers were doing, but because of how they went about their work. In technical terms, they were adopting similar approaches to other teachers – assessing literacy with running records, providing opportunities for students to work in flexible groupings for guided reading and differentiating learning activities to meet the needs of a range of students. Even so, these teachers' classrooms, and their interactions with students and their families, were substantially different. In this chapter, we describe their pedagogical practices and how they designed and created enriched learning opportunities for their students.

Over 25 years ago, Marilyn Cochran-Smith (1991, p. 280) drew on Gramsci and other critical scholars to insist that 'teaching is fundamentally a political activity in which every teacher plays a part by default or by design' and that as individual educators we cannot excuse ourselves from our responsibilities. She argued that early-career teachers needed to learn how to teach against the grain *in situ* in the company of experienced teachers.

> [T]eaching against the grain is also deeply embedded in the culture and history of teaching at individual schools and in the biographies of particular teachers and their individual or collaborative efforts to alter curricula, raise questions about common practices, and resist inappropriate decisions.
>
> (*Cochran-Smith, 1991, p. 280*)

The challenge of teaching against the grain now takes place in settings subjected to the demands of markets and their associated mechanisms, including increased competition between schools (largely driven by externally developed performance measures), diversification of choice for families and accreditation of teachers against professional standards. In this context, teachers' work is frequently reduced to technical concerns about how to improve students' performance outcomes on standardised tests. The imperative to implement 'what works' trumps the value of teachers' professional judgement about what is needed and appropriate. Hence, teachers are expected to adopt evidence-based practices. The problematic assumption here is that a very limited range of evidence counts, namely, that produced by correlational statistics, such as randomised control trials. Hence, teacher professionalism does not count as being able to produce evidence-based practice. Rather, what counts as evidence is produced somewhere else, supposedly through 'gold standard' research, completely ignoring the specificity of context. Hence the nuances of what works in different places, at different times, with different children and families, are missing.

Researchers have attempted to describe what good teachers do. Drawing upon their past efforts, we can say that the teachers we describe in this chapter viewed children's cultural and linguistic backgrounds, or their 'virtual schoolbags' (Thomson, 2002), as important resources. They assumed that their students had the capacity to engage with high-expectations curricula (Dudley-Marling & Michaels, 2012) and frequently involved students and teachers in extended conversations around texts, problems and the focus content. Importantly from our perspective, critical educational researchers need to document this work. In literacy studies, we see this as part of a move towards positive discourse analysis, where we seek to understand at a deeper level the kinds of classroom discourse that work to open up possibilities for students (Comber, 2006b, 2016b; Rogers & Mosley Wetzel, 2013). In such cases, teachers position children as people who already have knowledge that they can articulate and, moreover, they highlight the potential of what can be learned in the classroom collective.

Despite the constraints and demands of their everyday working contexts, along with the heightened insistence on performance targets, uncommon pedagogies were visible when the teachers described in this chapter opened their classrooms to families and connected with their communities. They recognised and valued their students' interests and range of background knowledge. These teachers created opportunities for students to engage both academically and socially in the culture of learning they created in their classrooms. They designed learning tasks that demanded complex thinking and language. Their practices, while ambitious and 'against the grain' of the more typical school literacy routines that are discussed in Chapter 5, suggest possibilities for complex and rich pedagogies in schools where they are hardest to accomplish.

In addition, teachers' own histories impact on their interpretive resources for reading, understanding and enacting school policy, whether that might be behaviour, literacy or dress codes. As discussed in the Introduction to this book, our standpoint as educational researchers working in high-poverty contexts is to work against the pervasive deficit discourses that prevail in discussions of 'the poor' and at the same time to contest the blame apportioned to teachers for unequal educational outcomes. For these reasons, we have chosen to begin our discussions of teachers at work by portraying instances of inclusive, creative and critical literacy pedagogies. It is important to learn from these accomplishments and to document how they were achieved, in order to move beyond reproducing narratives of school failure. This is not to romanticise heroic teachers; rather it is to understand what matters, where and how, and with whom, and to begin to understand how this is negotiated in practice. Students' learner identities are deeply impacted by teachers' everyday discursive practices, which position them in particular ways – both opening up and shutting down conversations.

We will argue that the uncommon pedagogical practices we observed were a combination of professional knowledge about literacy and pedagogy and a set of dispositions towards students and their communities. This combination enabled teachers to invent ways of being and relating in the classroom that distinguished their practice from that of their peers. In other words, simply knowing a pedagogical approach does not automatically translate into 'better literacy teaching'. And equally important, 'liking the children' is not enough to make one a better teacher. It is how teachers put together a range of discursive and material practices, underpinned by principles of respect and recognition, that enables the design and enactment of situated, enabling pedagogies (Comber, 2016a). Such practices are contingent upon recognition and respect for the children and their families.

In this chapter, we look closely at a number of examples of uncommon pedagogies demonstrated through what teachers say and do and the messages they convey to their students about learning. In the next section, we elaborate briefly on the notion of 'turn-around literacy pedagogies' because that was a key starting point for our study. Next, we present case studies of two teachers, working at Highfield Primary School, who were able to sustain such practices over time: Suzy, a very experienced teacher working in an early-childhood classroom, and Alicia, an early-career teacher working with a Year 6/7 class. Highfield's principal had invested considerable resources in systematically building teachers' knowledge of reading pedagogy. In addition, we will show how Suzy and Alicia turned to their students with respect visible in their everyday classroom discourse and infusing their literacy lessons and interactions.

Following our close-up look at the Highfield classrooms, we survey a range of promising, but more ephemeral, practices, where there were signs of teachers deliberately expanding their repertoires to connect with their students in productive ways: at Riverview, teacher Jason first worked with a Year 6/7 class and then in a Learning Centre environment; at Sandford, teacher Carrie worked with a Year 1/2 maths class, and her colleague Lara with a Year 3/4 class; and finally at Easton, Andrea taught a history unit with her Year 2/3 class. These cases are important because they show glimmers of promising pedagogies; however, for different reasons in each case, these proved difficult to sustain. These cases also indicate the ways in which several teachers were able to work creatively across the curriculum, beyond the literacy lesson, to begin to induct children into the discourses of different subject areas. Finally, we draw out some implications for supporting this complex and sometimes fragile work. As we discuss in Chapter 5, default models of practice and deficit views of young people never disappear.

## Teachers who stood out from their peers

In the Introduction, we discussed research conducted by Comber and Kamler (2005), which showed that when teachers worked as researchers to understand their local communities and families, to explore an expanded view of literacy and to learn from research, they were able to make changes to their classroom practices and positively shift students' identities towards being capable and successful literacy learners (Comber & Kamler, 2005). As a consequence, teachers revised their understanding of their students' capabilities, and increased their expectations for academic achievement, because they questioned previously held deficit assumptions about their students and their families. They recognised that different children bring valued – albeit different – knowledges and experiences to school. The problem of poor performance was recast as a pedagogical challenge, rather than an inevitable consequence of growing up in poverty. An important element of redesigning their pedagogy was a 'permeable curriculum' (Dyson, 1993), whereby children could make use of their home and peer language, culture and knowledge as they assembled academic knowledge and school literacies.

As the study on which we report in this book evolved, it began to emerge that only a small number of teachers demonstrated classroom practices that incorporated these understandings in a way that improved the learning opportunities of their students. Teachers' logics of practice (Bourdieu, 1990) were more commonly underpinned by deficit assumptions about children and families living in poverty, which generally limited or provided weak opportunities for learning. In addition, as we have previously argued, an increasingly performative, audit-based culture in schooling, that is operationalised through high-stakes, standardised measures of achievement, has become the authorised keystone to improving literacy outcomes. There is evidence to suggest that the annual National Assessment Program – Literacy and Numeracy

(NAPLAN) has solidified literacy as a set of measurable, discrete skills and led to a narrowing of the curriculum and of literacy learning (Comber, 2012; Klenowski, 2014) and/or to teachers appropriating some of the political rhetoric around national testing (Hardy, 2014).

Notwithstanding this, a small number of teachers stood out in each school because their practice was substantially informed by elements of turn-around pedagogy (Table 4.1). In particular, they turned to their students and their families and created classrooms of trust where all children eagerly participated. They drew on a range of educational discourses and practices that went beyond the dominant accountability rhetoric and behaviour regulation that so dominates policy and school talk at this time. This afforded them opportunities to build productive pedagogical relationships with young people and, for some, with their families.

In the remainder of this chapter, we draw upon observations recorded in our field notes and interviews to describe these uncommon pedagogical practices. These descriptions are intended to contain sufficient detail about what it was about each teacher's practice that stood out, while also showing that many of their approaches were familiar and recognisable among their peers. We aim to show that teachers engaged their students in successful literacy learning by turning around to young

**TABLE 4.1** Teacher pseudonyms, experience and feature of 'turn-around pedagogy'

| Teacher's pseudonym | School/class | Teaching experience | Feature of turn-around pedagogy |
|---|---|---|---|
| Suzy | Highfield Reception/Year 1 | More than 15 years | Family and student experience incorporated in classroom practices; complex understanding of learning ecologies. |
| Alicia | Highfield Year 6 | Less than five years | Student interests and perspectives made central; deep knowledge of reading pedagogy; positioning students as active collaborators. |
| Jason | Riverview Year 6/7 | Less than five years | Designing academically demanding open-ended tasks that engage students 'at risk' of not succeeding. |
| Carrie | Sandford Year 1/2 | Less than five years | Connecting everyday life to curriculum tasks that engage students in creative responses and academic knowledge. |
| Lara | Sandford Year 2/3 | More than 15 years | Strong knowledge of literature and science pedagogy; incorporation of popular culture into expanded literacy practices. |
| Andrea | Easton Year 3 | Less than five years | Connects important place learning with students' interest in researching their place history, using primary sources. |

people and their families, by turning their pedagogy to popular culture and new literacies, by turning to knowledge produced by educational research and through their ongoing reflection on their own practice.

## Suzy: connecting learning at home and school

Suzy was an experienced teacher at Highfield, where she taught students in the first two years of school. She had come to teaching after initially studying and working in early childhood education. Suzy first came to our attention because her classroom was always open before school, with parents and carers dropping off children and staying to chat with Suzy, or each other. Some joined in small reading groups with their child, or other people's children; others quietly watched the literacy learning activities on display in the room, which included children from Reception to Year 7 working together and with adults. The following description of Suzy's classroom was constructed from our field notes.

> In Suzy's Reception/Year 1 class, the walls were covered with posters of letters, words, images, numbers and colours that she regularly pointed to in order to help the children associate sounds and ideas with letters and words. The classroom doors were opened ten minutes before class began. Older and younger children, some with their parents, were warmly welcomed and offered lots of suggestions for things to do as they trickled into the room. There were puzzles, games, toys and readers to share.
>
> Suzy was in full flight, noticing people and emotions, and directing activities by pairing adults and older children with Reception children. She was demonstrating how to turn each interaction with a child (and adult) into an opportunity to learn about literacy or, in her words, a *teachable moment*.
>
> Some 'return' parents and older children were adopting the same kinds of practices as Suzy. They were sitting with children, helping them to read, using their fingers to point, sounding out letters and making associations with the resources in the room.
>
> The classroom was a hive of activity. Suzy was quickly discerning whether a child needed some additional support. She was generous with her hugs and supportive comments. She was extremely reassuring with both the children and adults. The phrase she used most with the parents was: 'Don't stress about that.' She often reassured parents that their children were doing REALLY well and illustrated it with an example. She would also say to the parents that the children loved it when they joined in, but that it was: 'OK if they weren't able to stay'.

Suzy's practice stood out because she consistently invited parents, carers and siblings to be actively involved in the classroom. The success of her efforts was demonstrated by their willingness to return frequently and to participate in early-morning literacy and learning activities. For Suzy, reaching out to parents provided her with insights into family practices and the lives of the students. It enabled her to sustain strong pedagogic relationships beyond the classroom. Her insights, and her recognition of families as 'resource-full' (McNaughton, 2002), shaped Suzy's responses to students' learning in the classroom, as we describe later.

Conversations with Suzy were replete with references to 'making connections'. She liked to explain how she would 'build on the familiar', which involved acknowledging the language and literacy resources of the families of the students she teaches. She described her pedagogical relationships with parents as 'travel[ling] through this journey like a school community family' and cited Bronfenbrenner's (1979) concept of ecology and community as her inspiration. She was also familiar with the concept of a 'strengths-based approach' (Clifton & Harter, 2003) to working with children and families living in poverty. Suzy's description of her students and their families was not steeped in deficit language. She invested in accessing and utilising their resources to make a positive difference for young people. Suzy's observations of children interacting with each other and at work in the classroom provided her with insights into their interests and their learning. She noted that: 'the families provide that additional information that helps me create a picture, more so of the whole child'. She explained that input from families is 'massively important' because:

> It's not until I've got the families that I get a context of the outside community and the other things that come into play to help form who that child is, and why they think in a certain way, or do things in a certain way, or possibly why they're struggling in certain ways. So the families are very important in that whole context for me.

She made deliberate use of the time at the beginning and end of the school day to include parents in the learning journeys of the students and, indeed, to acknowledge and support the parents as teachers themselves:

> If they say they are reading at home, I can have the opportunity to say: 'Wow!' I can affirm them as a teacher: 'Well, you should take some credit for this because, basically, there are two teachers at play here. You're listening and I'm listening.' And it gives me an opportunity to direct them in the next step: 'Would you like some more sight words to practice with them?' ... Or if they're not, I will use it as an opportunity to say: 'Well, wow, look how far they've travelled. Imagine if we are both teaching.' And I'll use it in that sense, and I'll say: 'Come back and tell me when you've had the chance to hear them. I bet you won't be disappointed.' I like to share with them, in an everyday way, some strategies that they may be able to use to support them with teaching their child.

In Suzy's classroom, teaching moments were made possible in the smallest interactions, yet their effects rippled beyond a one-to-one conversation. Suzy's strategies for including parents and carers were guided by her recognition of family strengths, difference and diversity and were visible in her conversations with them when they visited the classroom. At the end of the day, children would often read aloud to the whole class, including parents and carers in the room. Suzy used that time to 'notice and name' (which she identifies as a 'Learning Together'[1] strategy) and to comment on the accomplishments of some of the students: 'Did you notice how confidently they're reading now? They are doing this because they've learnt more sight words.' She gave adults in her students' lives access to strategies that might assist them to improve their reading. She described one afternoon when she had intentionally waited for a particular mother to come to the classroom so that Suzy could highlight how her son, Toby, was reading. Suzy explained to Toby's mother that he was going to read a familiar book, telling the story through the illustrations. On two or three occasions as he read, Suzy commented on his 'really good ideas' and said: 'What a terrific idea. I bet you visualised that!' At the end of Toby's reading, she said that he could take the book home that night so that Mum could also 'picture read'. In Suzy's words:

> I said it so nicely, but it was said in front of other parents, and the children, and I proceeded to ask her in front of other parents and children: 'Have you had the chance yet?' And I will do that, and if she says, 'No': 'Oh, never mind, there's always tonight.' Yeah … I do, I really try and push literacy without undermining them.

One of the effects of this kind of informal, but deliberately purposeful, teacher–parent–child literacy work is that the parents also take up the offer of 'noticing and naming' what students – other than their own children – can do. For Suzy, this recognition was crucial to teacher, parent and child learning with and from each other.

> I do notice that parents come in and greet lots of children within the class and I think that whilst we are a school, and an institution as such, I do actually like the notion of that family concept: 'We're all in this together; we're learning together.' And I think we travel through this journey like a school community family.

A classroom literacy event videorecorded by Suzy further highlighted the importance of knowing families and community. In her commentary on the video, she explained that, when teaching phonics, she invited the students to contribute words that begin with the sound that is the focus for the day. For one student, 'p-p-p-parole' was a meaningful connection. In Suzy's words:

> Rather than discard that as a word that wasn't feasible in this vocabulary, it was OK, so I wrote 'parole' up on the board and acknowledged that the beginning sound we hear in 'parole' is 'p'. And that obviously pertains to his life at the moment. Because his dad is on parole, it's a word he's hearing, so it's in the context of his life.

In Suzy's classroom, tough topics were not taboo. Early childhood pedagogies often repeat the mantra of working with 'what children bring', but teachers frequently act as gatekeepers for what is considered appropriate for children to know and to bring to the classroom, as we will discuss in later chapters. Suzy listened carefully to what each student offered and worked to incorporate these ideas and experiences in her teaching. She believed that students are better able to sustain the connection between the letter and the sound, and then transfer that sound–letter combination to other learning, if the word in question is significant. Suzy enabled children to make use of their prior knowledge in new situations, without excluding some forms of knowledge.

## Alicia: mobilising collective reading resources

When we first met Alicia, she had been teaching for three years and was teaching a mixed-ability Year 6/7 class at Highfield. The principal in her school had invested considerable teacher professional learning resources in *Accelerated Literacy* (AL), an approach to the teaching of reading originally developed by Brian Gray, and subsequently adapted as a resource for teacher professional development by David Rose (Acevedo & Rose, 2007; Rose, 2010). One of the features of this approach is that the teacher leads students to study a book in depth and deconstruct it in order to understand the way the language works to convey complex meanings. The teacher reads, re-reads and discusses the book a number of times with the class, over an extended period (for example a month). We often encountered classroom practices informed by the principles of *Accelerated Literacy* at Highfield and in other schools in our study. However, how Alicia put these ideas to work stood out from her colleagues' use of similar ideas.

Alicia's class had read the book *Tanglewood* several times. This award-winning Australian picture book was written by Margaret Wild (2012) and illustrated by Vivienne Goodman. The story is promoted as suitable for preschoolers, so what might be the rationale for Alicia's selection? And why read and re-read it? In the following description of Alicia's lesson, we hope to show that repeated close readings and discussion of this book afforded a number of rich opportunities for these Year 6/7 students to think about life, loneliness, relationships, hope and never giving up.

Alicia was one of the teachers we invited to make a digital recording of an example of their classroom practice that illustrated an approach to teaching literacy. Alicia chose to record one of her lessons in which she worked with *Tanglewood* and drew upon principles of *Accelerated Literacy*. We also recorded a conversation with Alicia, during which she described in detail the sequence of the lesson and the rationale that underpinned her pedagogical choices. The themes explored in the book connected strongly with the qualities Alicia valued and encouraged in the learning community she was co-constructing with her students. Her intentions are reflected in her description of the moment she found the book.

> The librarian had all the books out. I was just flicking. I just happened to be there at the right time, and this one ... [*Tanglewood*] ... it's about hope and family, and I'm just like: 'Oh, that's mine' ... because that's a big theme in my class, like always every year. Just that never giving up, just that moral, and helping each other out.

The lesson included a three-phase sequence through which she orchestrated students' complex engagement with the text. In the first phase, Alicia invited the students to contribute thoughts and opinions about the story of a tree called Tanglewood. The second phase involved the sequencing of colour photocopies of the pages of the book and, in the third phase, the students were organised into guided reading groups (five or six students) to practise group oral reading of five or six pages that told a section of the story.

The lesson began with Alicia scribing students' responses to the text – the facts they could recall and their opinions about the setting, character and theme. Two headings were written on the electronic whiteboard: 'What the text is about' and 'What the text makes you think about'. As Alicia noted down the students' responses, she acknowledged them with comments such as: 'Say your wonderful thought again', 'Can you add those lovely adjectives?' or 'I like the way you put that in a sentence'.

Alicia expected every student to contribute. She recorded students' initials next to ideas as she scribed. Towards the end of the first part of the lesson, she asked those who had not yet shared to 'have a think, because I might ask you shortly'. The multiple purposes embedded in this introductory activity gave the students an opportunity to: recall details of the text; engage deeply and personally with its themes; and express in their own words the nature of the relationships explored in the book. Scribing the students' words on the electronic whiteboard was useful both as documentation of the content of their ideas and a resource for extending and clarifying them. It also demonstrated to students how closely their teacher was listening and provided a kind of 'audit trail' (Vasquez, 2004) for their emerging insights about the book. When completed, it offered a resource that had been co-constructed and could be shared, thus deprivatising the practice of reading and making a range of meanings from a single text.

The range of responses from the students, ranging from literal to interpretive in relation to self and life experiences, is indicated in the following examples:

*Raelene:*  A seagull, a seagull that helps the tree ... [it] brings families to the tree.
*Student:*  I was going to say, like, it's about trust.
*Alicia:*  Ah huh, yes, trust, and I think that's what, when we read it the first time, Andy was saying, about keeping your word.
*Lily:*  This text is about like when Seagull goes: 'I'll come back.' You have to have hope in yourself, like, when she's going to come back.
*Tanya:*  This text is about a tree on an island.
*Alicia:*  A tree on an island. Do you want to give any more ...? What kind of tree, on what kind of island? Anybody? More detail?

| | |
|---|---|
| *Tanya:* | A green tree on a small island. |
| *Alicia:* | Sorry, who was helping out then? |
| *Student:* | Diane. |
| *Alicia:* | Diane, can you add in those adjectives? |
| *Diane:* | A lonely tree on a small island. |
| *Alicia:* | A lonely tree on a small island. There we go, good. Now we've got more description, and I like the way you helped each other out. |

In these brief interchanges, Alicia focused on listening to the students and capturing their ideas on the whiteboard. Because her back was turned, she asked who was 'helping out' Tanya and she duly recorded the adjectives and gave credit to Diane and all the students who helped each other out. The processes of remembering and recovering the book vocabulary became a shared responsibility. The next contributor signalled that she also wanted to add to the 'what the text is about?' column and she also added what it made her think about.

| | |
|---|---|
| *Elly:* | I've got two things, but both for what this text is about, um, um, from sports day, um, 'every face has a place'. |
| *Alicia:* | Oh yeah, yep, absolutely. |
| *Elly:* | And my Nanna always says: 'Always have trust in yourself.' |

Alicia's positive response and recording leaves space for Elly to refer to her Nanna's advice and enables Elly to make a significant connection with one of the themes in the book. Through immersion in the ideas, themes and characters in this story, Alicia's pedagogy encourages 'deep literacy' (Winch, Ross Johnston, March, Ljungdahl, & Holliday, 2014, p. 546).

A short time later, the following exchange highlighted the high level of trust between students and teacher:

| | |
|---|---|
| *Karen:* | This text makes me think about when, if you know that, you can't just know that you're ugly when you're actually pretty, or something. You can't actually say that about yourself. |
| *Student:* | Don't judge yourself like … |
| *Karen:* | And have trust in yourself. |
| *Alicia:* | Yep, so have trust in yourself and believe in yourself. Is that what you're trying to say? |
| *Karen:* | Yeah. |

This snippet of conversation about not judging yourself as pretty or ugly demonstrates how, in Alicia's classroom, opportunities were created for students to work with literature in ways that allow exploratory identity work.

During this introductory activity, the students took up the positions that Alicia made available for them as thoughtful participants in a community of learners who support each other to be successful readers and speakers. Unlike the more typical teacher-dominated Initiate–Response–Evaluation pattern of classroom interactions, this lesson was an example of classroom discourse in which the teacher and students negotiate meanings and build shared understandings through extended talk about the text. The students made sense of the text by drawing on previous discussions and appropriating vocabulary learnt in the context of exploring its themes. These are not insignificant accomplishments in themselves. The students also demonstrated a great deal of trust in their teacher and in their peers as they shared personal and family connections in their interpretive work, exemplified in the comment about Sports Day and an oft-heard saying of a grandparent. Moreover, rather than competing for the floor and being acknowledged for providing the right answer, they elaborated on each other's comments and helped each other to gain clarity.

In the following paragraphs, we draw attention to the ways in which Alicia enabled the students to collaborate on sequencing the story in the second phase of the lesson. At first glance it may appear to be a straightforward task of ordering photocopied pages of the book. Our first interpretation proved superficial when we witnessed the affordances of this activity for students to talk about text in productive ways. The task actually required students to negotiate the ordered spatial arrangement of the pages and to check and re-check the story sequence.

Alicia distributed the pages randomly to the class and, as the students moved amongst each other, looking at the pages in their hands and the pages of other students, talking about whether they might go alongside each other, the teacher remained seated at the front of the class. Gradually the students started to form a line, placing themselves in order. Alicia circulated amongst them, noticing what they were doing and saying and quietly acknowledging the ways in which the students were conducting themselves in order to complete the collective task.

Of the many interactions that occurred, we select a few short interchanges to illustrate the kind of talk that went on between students and teacher.

*Example 1:*

| | |
|---|---|
| *Anton:* | Mine [My page] is the last one, like the writing. |
| *Student:* | I've got Seagull. |
| *Lily:* | Is this yours? |
| *Belinda:* | Yes. |
| *Lily:* | Well then go, go back then. |
| *Alicia:* | Okay, well done Lily, I like the way you are directing. |
| *Alicia:* | [Speaking to Ky] Okay, so that's the seagull, so that's got to be before …? |
| *Ky:* | [Pointing to a space on the floor next to the pages he has been straightening up] I reckon it goes here. |

*Example 2:*

| | |
|---|---|
| *Student:* | Wait up, where's the storm? |
| *Student:* | I don't know. |

*Ky:*       We need more room. We need more room.
*Alicia:*   Okay, if we need more room, how about we bring some down, make a second row.
*Student:*  Where does yours go Kate, where does yours go?
*Alicia:*   Okay, Kate, okay, let's help her out. Where do they need to go?
*Student:*  Isn't that before the storm?
*Student:*  Yeah, it's before the storm.

*Example 3:*

*Alicia:*   Tess, can you please read out what Kate's got there and we'll find out what part of the story it is … Ssshh. Hang on, listen to her read it out.
*Tess:*     'Deep in the ground Tanglewood felt its roots would stop searching for water. Its bark began to curl and its leaves turned yellow. Is it possible to die of loneliness it wondered?'
*Alicia:*   Okay, Frank, you've got your hand up, what do you think?
*Frank:*    I think it's right before the storm hit.
*Alicia:*   You think right before the storm hit. Anyone want to differ? No? Alright, let's put it there and we'll have a look. Okay, so let's sit back so we can all have a look.

Here we read exchanges that took place between students as they claimed a space for their page on the floor. The actual physical movement of students around the room required them to be aware of their presence in relation to each other and emphasised the social and collective nature of the task – a stark contrast to conceptualising the task of sequencing a story as solitary and individual work. Of particular interest in the third example above is the support offered to Kate, who could use the cues in the illustrations, but had difficulty with reading the words on her page. Alicia's strategy of asking a nearby peer to read the page enabled Kate to be included in the task and emphasised that reading was both a social practice and a responsibility shared by the whole class.

The third phase of the lesson involved gathering and redistributing the sequenced pages to the students once they were organised into their guided reading groups (four or five students per group). The group task was to take responsibility for that section of the book. Alicia emphasised the importance of practising the reading:

> [and to] know the pronunciation of all the words, remember the intonation, okay. If someone is speaking, or if it's a sad part of the story, make sure your voice reflects that … And then we're going to come back together as a whole class and read the story, but obviously your groups will read your sections. Okay! Are there any questions about what it is that you have to do? … Next time we do it we might do it more individually. This time I want the group to read it as a group, okay, just like we do in AL [*Accelerated Literacy*] when we all read together.

In arranging the groups in this way, Alicia provided a differentiated task that would enable each student to understand the text and to read it as fluently as possible. She grouped the students so that those who might struggle to read independently could be supported, while others were given sections of the book that had more challenging vocabulary and sentence structures. For Alicia, such differentiation contributes to the academic learning in the class as well as 'emotional learning, self-esteem and confidence' that is engendered at the same time.

Reading and re-reading *Tanglewood* gave the students opportunities to notice, both in the illustrations and the text, details that they had not noticed on previous occasions. Such purposeful and repeated readings are characteristic of AL, a school-wide approach to literacy teaching. Indeed, Alicia's explicit reference to AL reminded the students that they are building on learning they have accomplished in previous lessons. It is also indicative of principles of practice that guide Alicia's pedagogical moves. In contrast to strict adherence to more scripted versions of literacy teaching explored in Chapter 5, the practice we observed in Alicia's classroom suggested a teacher whose respect for the students – individually and collectively – engendered mutual trust, an openness to genuinely learn with and from each other, and a desire to engage in complex and intellectually demanding tasks for an extended time.

Alicia's pedagogy took account of long-range consequences of what and why she teaches. To return to the question about why and how a teacher might use with a Year 6/7 class a picture book that is marketed towards four-year-olds, we can see how the application of *Accelerated Literacy* as part of Alicia's pedagogical repertoire allows for deep engagement with a text that enables complex and sensitive matters to be discussed. At the same time, it allows all students to participate in the successful reading, where reading includes decoding, fluent choral performance, inferring, intertextual referencing, analysis of language and image and more. Alicia's pedagogy deprivatised meaning-making and reconstituted reading as a collective, participatory practice, not unlike what happens in out-of-school book groups.

## Jason: producing texts with currency

Jason, a Year 6/7 teacher at Riverview, caught our attention because he was highly regarded by his peers for designing challenging, open-ended problem-solving tasks that connected with his students' interests. He resisted deficit assumptions about what his students were capable of achieving and incorporated aspects of 'turn-around pedagogy' into the learning tasks he designed. When describing his approach, Jason outlined a set of principles that allowed him to 'invent millions of variations on a theme'. He believed that his students needed 'to control their own learning'. He facilitated this by incorporating opportunities for them to negotiate learning tasks.

Jason conceptualised his teaching in terms of 'learning intentions'. He emphasised the development of students' research skills, describing it as a 'core' aspect of his practice. Engagement with content was important, but finding, organising, analysing, interpreting and presenting information were for him *the* most important cross-curriculum skills. As an example, when reflecting on his teaching exposition early in the year, and partly because persuasive writing would be included in the NAPLAN writing test early in Term 2 that year, Jason explained the relationship between literacy and subject-specific knowledge:

> I'll weave that content in with what I am doing … merge the science component [which] becomes my content, but my learning intention is still making sure that the students know how to create a hypothesis and construct a proper report and create a fair test and that kind of thing, and I suppose within all those things there are literacy components.

Jason's description of his pedagogy is reminiscent of researcher accounts of 'weaving' (Kwek, 2012), a process 'whereby teachers and students shift and establish connections between different kinds and levels of knowledge within and across lessons' (Kwek, 2012, p. 335). Often this is achieved through talking. The key thing here is that literacy was not taught as a separate skill, but put to work in the service of ambitious learning goals that were appropriate to a specific subject area.

However, Jason indicated considerable flexibility in how he designed and redesigned literacy tasks in order to win student interest. Jason's account of how he introduced students to writing film reviews (persuasive texts) is a productive example. To write a review, usually his class would first read a text or watch a film. Jason suspected that amongst the 28 students, some would be interested in the film, but fewer were likely to find reading the text appealing. Nevertheless, his class spent a lesson on familiarising themselves with the structure of a review. Instead of insisting on a review of a book or film, Jason turned the task into one that would require the students to write a proficient review 'without beating them over the head with a rubber mallet' and 'not really engaging them'. He explained how he changed tack and asked them to focus on something they really enjoyed, were good at and could teach him about:

> To write a good review, you need to know the subject matter pretty well. You can't fluff a review on something like that … and that's why, if you're reading a book and the kids are switching off and they miss the whole point of the story, or whatever, they're not going to be able to do the review well. So I said: 'Just do a review on what you enjoy' and they just switched on. And this strategy had a significant success. A little lad in my class, I couldn't get him to pick up a pencil, couldn't get him to do it … couldn't do it. As soon as he knew that he could write a review about Pokémon, he was the first one finished.

Another task Jason created for his Year 6/7 students had them working on a 'school fundraiser'. The students were asked to work collaboratively on a small-group project and to make equal contributions to their group's discussion and decision-making. In the introductory lesson, the students were given a rubric that highlighted group processes as well as problem-solving skills and mathematical knowledge. Jason provided examples of how to calculate quantities and costs of ingredients and worked with the students specifically on working as a group. As the groups selected their recipes, he worked with small groups to question and guide their problem-solving. They were required to use key words for an Internet search for four recipes that would be suitable for food for a school fundraiser, work out quantities and costs of ingredients, produce a poster that displayed their wares and show their mathematical workings. One group produced a poster including the four recipes (Jelly Cakes, Rum Balls, Sushi and Scones) neatly typed and displayed on the top left; beneath these was a detailed 'shopping list' of items and costs (e.g. 1250 grams self-raising flour / $1.18; 3 packets raspberry jelly crystals/$3.81; 1 litre light soya sauce/$2.50; 50 nori sheets/$5). Photographs of the end products and their prices were placed on the bottom right of the poster. Above the photographs was a hand-written explanation of how the students had calculated the selling price for their wares based on the cost of ingredients and their goal of raising funds.

The learning tasks Jason set his class enabled his students to produce texts that were meaningful. In other words, he taught a 'literacy curriculum with currency' (Comber & Kamler, 2005, p. 12). Such tasks also gave him insights into the resources his students brought to the task of writing and responding. Open-ended tasks presented opportunities for Jason to respond skilfully to the learning needs of his students by 'going off on tangents':

> I think sometimes people are scared of going off on tangents, but sometimes tangents are those learnable, teachable moments that the kids get the most out of. … I just tend to go off wherever I think the kids need to go. I know there's a curriculum that we need to follow, but sometimes kids just learn what they need to learn as well, and sometimes questioning and things like that sort of dictates where that goes as well, because I don't want to say: 'Sorry, we're not talking about that. We'll talk about that in Week 4.'

Jason's approach aimed to think past 'deficit views that [often] undergird interventions for students "at risk"' (Gutiérrez, Morales & Martinez, 2009, p. 216). 'Such approaches are organised around varying views of how to remedy students' literacy skills, including "fixing" individual students and their home literacy practices to help ensure their success in school' (p. 216). Jason's strategy rejected the logic of remedial education that argues for 'quick-fix approaches organised around generic forms of support' (p. 223) with an 'over-emphasis on basic skills with little connection to content or the practices of literacy' (p. 225). Instead, Jason's approach favoured re-mediating 'at-risk' literacy learners through positioning them as experts in particular areas.

Jason's open-ended tasks were designed to enable students to sharpen their problem-solving strategies and to learn in context the skills and content they needed to be successful learners. In his experience, when learning was purposeful, and when the students could 'control their learning', they tended to be much more engaged.

Unfortunately, this insight is often forgotten when working with students who have 'trouble' with learning at school.

## Carrie: making spaces for children's perspectives and explanations

Carrie was an early-career teacher at Sandford who had previously worked in another field and as a full-time parent to her children. Her capacity to integrate information and communication technologies (ICT) into her classroom practices made her stand out from her peers. Drawing upon everyday life experiences, she designed rich learning tasks that challenged and extended her students; she encouraged them to think creatively and to communicate their ideas effectively.

In Carrie's classroom, students were provided with opportunities to learn from her and from each other. In one lesson, she invited her six- and seven-year-old students to solve an open-ended mathematics problem and to explain the strategies they had used. Our field notes explain her approach.

The lesson began with the students counting by twos to 30, by fives to 100, and by tens to 100. Then Carrie posed a problem: 'I'm thinking of a number – I don't think you'll be able to get it! What's a good question to ask me?' One student guesses 60, but Carrie wants the students to think of questions that will help them to narrow the possibilities. One student suggests 'Is it odd or even?'

| | |
|---|---|
| *Carrie:* | Good question – it's an even number. Another question? A larger or smaller question? |
| *Student:* | Is it big? |
| *Carrie:* | I don't know what to compare it to – I need a number. Pick a number for me. |
| *Student:* | Is it bigger than five? |
| *Carrie:* | It's not bigger than five. |
| *Student:* | Is it four? |
| *Carrie:* | Yes, not bigger than five or smaller than four. |

Carrie moves on to set the scene for the next part of the lesson: 'Do you know why I picked four? I've been thinking about animals this morning and how many legs they have'.

Several students offer ideas such as: a zebra has four legs, humans have two legs, a dog has four legs. She asks three students to stand in front of the class, two next to each other and one by herself.

| | |
|---|---|
| *Carrie:* | How many legs are there? |
| *Students:* | Two and four. |
| *Carrie:* | How many altogether? |
| *Students:* | Six. |

Carrie used students' everyday knowledge to introduce what she wanted them to consider. Inviting them to guess introduced an element of fun. Playing with the invitation: 'What's a good question to ask me?' also opened up a space for children to contribute. Having three students come to the front made concrete the ways in which numbers could be arranged – in this case, pairs or twos. We want to draw attention to the way the teacher opened the floor for talk.

After this sequence, Carrie told a story about driving along the highway with her daughter and seeing a circus truck ahead. As they got closer, they could see the legs of a lot of animals and as they were passing the truck her daughter counted 18 legs. Carrie wrote: '18 legs' on the whiteboard. She explained that they were not sure how many different sorts of animals were in the truck, since circus animals could be all sorts of animals, including the kinds of animals you might find in a zoo or a farm. There might have been a lot of one type of animal and pairs of the same kind of animal.

Carrie asked her students to predict: 'What different animals made up the 18 legs?' This question was made intriguing and accessible to all the students through the narrative in which it was embedded. It required her students to use their skill of counting in multiples of four, but also invited creativity and imagination to solve a number beyond a multiple of four.

Carrie handed each student a large, blank piece of paper and stated: 'Write "18 legs" at the top.' She repeated her instruction by saying: 'Show me what animals are on the circus truck.' On the whiteboard she portrayed some examples of what she might see on their page – an outline of a four-legged animal; a tally 1111, or the addition 2+2 (a reminder that they had used this method previously). The students quickly organised themselves at their tables and began the task and the room buzzed with quiet chatter as they started to work in different ways to solve the problem.

Carrie moved from table to table, stopping to ask each student to explain how they were going about solving the problem and making a digital recording of their in-progress solutions on her iPad. She commented on, and questioned, the different strategies the students were employing.

When she arrived at a table where Matthew was working alone, she noticed that he had drawn a hydra-like creature with many 'legs'. She asked him how many legs he has drawn:

*Matthew:*   It's got 14.
*Carrie:*     Mmmm. I thought the number we were working on was 18.
*Matthew:*   I haven't finished yet.

He began to draw another 'leg' and Carrie moved on to the next table.

After about 20 minutes, Carrie called the students to sit on the floor in a circle with their pages in front of them so that they could see each other's work. 'Look with your eyes at everyone else's work' was the instruction.

Carrie then invited individual children to explain how they solved the problem of '18 legs'. Leon explained that he drew one four-legged animal first and then worked out he had to draw three more animals, but he hadn't quite finished yet. Another student drew 18 legs first and then added animal bodies. George had drawn four horses and couldn't decide what to do next. Matthew's hydra now had 21 legs. (Recall that earlier he had drawn a hydra with 14 legs when Carrie had come to his table.)

> Carrie looked puzzled and commented that she thought they were working out how many animals would have 18 legs.

> *Matthew:*   Well, it does have 21.
> *Carrie:*   How could I see 18 legs in the truck then?
> *Matthew:*   It was using its other three legs to eat its lunch.

> Matthew's inventive response and imaginative application of knowledge showed that he had extended the possibilities, much to the enjoyment of Carrie and his peers!

To draw attention to how the students had attempted to solve the problem, Carrie asked the students to recall key words heard as they were listening to each others' explanations. Someone suggested 'strategy'. Carrie affirmed that many of the students had used a 'picture strategy' to solve the problem. In the next phase of the task, she wanted everyone to use a different strategy – a tally strategy. She rehearsed one first with a student, making explicit the ways in which a tally is recorded. The students would have five minutes for this task.

At the end of the session, Carrie invited students to watch the digital recordings while they ate their lunch in the classroom. She asked for permission from each student, noting which students preferred not to have their part of the recording shown.

The digital recordings were used for multiple purposes: for Carrie's records of students' work in an e-portfolio to be shared with parents and other teachers, as well as for showing (sometimes more than once) to the students to encourage shared and reflective learning. Carrie felt that students' observations of how their peers practised problem-solving strategies may have had more weight than her suggesting: 'Why don't you try this?'

Carrie was critical of classroom interactions that required students to solve closed problems, since they did not provide opportunities to draw on either their imagination or creative use of knowledge and problem-solving strategies. She demonstrated problem-solving strategies for her students. She worked at creating a classroom culture that enabled students to share their problem-solving with others, shifting the power–knowledge relations from teacher to student and making spaces for children's perspectives and explanations in the official world of the classroom.

Carrie's open-ended task offered all children opportunities for participation and challenged them to think for themselves. They did not work alone, except by choice, as in Matthew's case. Collaboration and discussion occurred as the students were working on the task and more formally when they were asked to share their problem-solving strategies. Carrie's pedagogical repertoire also included elements of game playing and narrative. By asking them to guess a number that was in her head, she opened the possibility for all children to participate. As she narrowed the possibilities by giving them more clues, she required them to use their knowledge of numbers to inform their guesses. She then used an imaginative recount about driving to school to engage the children in what became their next task. Carrie's digital recording of her students' explanations of their problem-solving strategies was a novel use of ICT and captured their learning experiences in the classroom in a way that could easily be shared with multiple audiences.

Indeed, Carrie enjoyed experimenting with ICTs and happily explored the potential of XOTablets with her early-childhood class to see what they could do with them. Hence, she continually modeled an openness to learning new things and enjoyed demonstrating to children how they could learn together as a collective. Her language indicated puzzling, inquiry and possibility, rather than fixity and correctness.

## Lara: designing complex curriculum

Lara was an experienced teacher who had worked in the northern region for 17 years. Her class at Sandford comprised 24 Year 3 students of mixed ability. Her pedagogical practices stood out because of how she worked with her students to read and produce complex texts in different genres. She and her students engaged deeply with a range of literatures in a classroom culture characterised by learning and enjoyment. Another feature of Lara's pedagogy was the frequent incorporation of humorous texts and elements of popular culture alongside literary culture. Lara readily used film and multimedia and explored the Internet for specific science information and practices. She explicitly focused on building students' field knowledge and conceptual understandings. At the same time, she tapped into their interests in popular culture and designed challenging and open-ended tasks.

In what follows we focus on the ways in which she read to children and introduced a rich vocabulary of terms, as well as how she modelled undertaking scientific research using the Internet and creative story writing.

Drawing upon our field notes, we begin by relating how she spoke to her class in the first lesson we observed.

> When the children enter the classroom Lara is organising a range of things. They automatically sit on the carpet and chat quietly. She tells them that she is going to send home some books for them to practise their reading: 'Every single person I tested is going really, really well.'
>
> She then tells them she's dealing with 'a couple of issues' and so they should 'do five minutes' of free story writing with 'no talking at all'. While Lara follows up a few problems that appear to have arisen at recess time with a phone call to the front office, the children write quietly and Lara writes on the white board:

C–Characters
S–Setting
T–Trouble – 'complication'
A–Action
R–Resolution

Students seem not to notice the time has gone beyond five minutes and Lara lets them keep writing until she interrupts them with: 'Hands on top.' Students put down their pens, put their hands on their heads and chant along with Lara: 'That means stop.' She draws their attention to what she has written on the board and says: 'Today we are going to do some creative story writing.' She asks them about whether stories have more than one setting or more than one complication. It becomes obvious that this metalanguage has been used before.

She invites them to recall the book she has been reading to them – Roald Dahl's *Charlie and the Chocolate Factory* (2008) – and to identify the complications that occur in that story. She gives them an example of Violet turning into a blueberry. Then she asks a series of related questions to get them to recall that complication:

Lara:       What was his action to solve the problem?

[Students respond and she joins in.]

Students:   *De-juiced her!*
Lara:       What do you think they thought about having a purple daughter?

[Students offer responses.]

Lara:       What was the complication with Mike?

This high-paced collective recollection continues with different students invited to recall the problems and whether and how they were solved. The students appear to enjoy recalling the zany humour of the story. The conversation continues until Lara states:

Lara:       The cool thing about narrative … you can do what you want, even if it's a bit of nonsense. Gob-stoppers that never end! Who wishes that we did?

[Hands go up.]

Lara:       Can you beautiful people do some silent writing for ten minutes? Ready, set, go!

Our observations of the first part of this lesson indicated common features of Lara's practice that were demonstrated on numerous occasions. In terms of literacy pedagogy, there are a number of points to note. Lara used her reading aloud of shared novels to introduce children to how stories work and she offered them a meta-language for this. While this practice was very common in early versions of literature-based reading programmes, we rarely saw connections between children's literature and children's writing being made in other classrooms. In fact, with the exception of Lara's room, we saw very little extended writing done in classrooms at all, and almost no creative story writing. We discuss this absence in Chapter 6.

Another aspect of Lara's pedagogy that made it stand out was reading over an extended time, such as serialising a novel. We had mostly seen short tasks assigned to children that were typically done (with varying degrees of success and completion) within a lesson block. This transition to more complex tasks conducted over time typically occurs around this period of schooling, during Years 3 and 4 (Comber et al., 2002). This change of the organisation of literate practices presents both challenges and opportunities for teachers and students. In Lara's classroom we observed many children flourish with these extra challenges. However, we also saw children, who were still struggling to crack the code and make meaning, flounder in the face of these heightened expectations. The issue of the great range of children's capabilities evident in classrooms appears to increase exponentially during this period. This is critical, as it is also the period when children are expected to engage in academic literacies – that is, reading and writing to learn and show evidence of learning.

While Lara offered regular time for 'free writing', she also consciously worked to build students' knowledge and strategies for producing texts in various media and genres. We witnessed coproduced texts authored on iPads, posters of rides at the fair, Halloween tales, accounts of science experiments and more. The variety of texts explored highlighted the relative lack of text production in other classes.

## Andrea: making connections with substantial ideas

Andrea was an early-career teacher who had been teaching at Easton Primary for three years. Previously, she had been teaching in another part of the city at Hilton, a school attended by children from more affluent families, but she had subsequently accepted a position at Easton Primary, located near her childhood home.

> I was lucky enough that Hilton offered me a contract, and so did John (principal at Easton), and I thought that I could stay at Hilton in a nice, easy school, or I could come out here and challenge my learning, and I'm so glad I came out here because I have learnt. I learnt more in six months [here] than what I did in 18 months [at Hilton] … I went to [a school near Easton] … I had a teacher there say to me that no one from the north would ever go to university and so that kind of stuck with me and my friends, yeah, just to kind of prove a point in some ways, and then coming back … lots of people I went to university with were private school students. I was probably the only public school student from the northern suburbs, the other ones would be from the eastern suburb schools, so yeah, just making them aware that just because there's this stigma, doesn't mean anything really. Life is what you make it … If I can make a difference for one student in my class each year, then I've done my job. So if I can encourage them enough to make better choices in life and realise that they've got the world as their oyster sort of thing, that just because you're from the north doesn't mean anything.

Andrea's motivation for 'making a difference' for students from backgrounds like hers was in part shaped by her experience of living with the 'stigma' of growing up in a community where there were high levels of poverty. For her, 'making better choices' was a strong storyline in her personal narrative. Nevertheless, she also recognised the long-term effects of structural inequality on communities in the north and the importance of expanding her students' knowledge of local history so that they might be better equipped to withstand the 'stigma' she had faced, which blamed people rather than their circumstances for their low socioeconomic status in society.

History was Andrea's 'thing' and, during an interview late in Term 2, 2014, she described how she was collaborating with two of her peers to plan a history topic for their students (around eight years of age). They had selected a topic from the recently developed Australian history curriculum for Year 3, which focused on 'how things have changed in the community'. This topic interested Andrea immensely. She was especially excited because one of her co-planning colleagues had borrowed a suitcase from the Council Library that contained old photographs, maps and old footage of Elizabeth as it was being established. These primary sources provided in-depth information, not only about the planning and the building of the city in the 1950s, but about the purpose for building the schools, shops, hotels and homes in specific locations. Andrea had learnt several interesting facts from browsing the materials:

> Everything is designed and made for a purpose, even to the street lights – in the streets, lights are horizontal because they were new technology back in the 1950s that created lights for the footpath, but also for the road. We were the first suburb in the whole of Australia to have underground power lines; the sewage is at the back of the properties instead of under the streets, so like there's lots of purposeful architectural planning that's gone into Elizabeth.

Andrea's decision to focus on teaching recounts and information reports in the course of this topic were influenced by the literacy agreements in the school concerning the genres to be taught at each year level. She described her literacy block as being based on explicit teaching of the two or three genres she incorporated into her programme each term. She provided guided reading, as well as shared and independent writing experiences, so that the students could write the genres successfully. Andrea considered that implementing the school's expectations about what should be achieved during the literacy block made it difficult to make meaningful connections with the literacy demands in other curriculum areas. Preparing students for the national testing regime, NAPLAN, was also a factor, since they needed practice in writing narratives or persuasive texts for the writing test.

The class she had taught the previous year had created information reports about their families' countries of origin. However, for the current project, Andrea was interested in exploring with her students how the local area had changed over time, directly linking this focus to the Australian history curriculum. Once the students had learned about aspects of the city's development, Andrea was considering having students interview their parents or grandparents to record their perspectives on how Elizabeth had changed since they had come to live there. Even though the new project afforded opportunities for different kinds of products, such as oral history or historical narrative or biography, Andrea was tentative about exploring these options because they were not genres specified for Term 3 in the school's literacy agreement.

We visited Andrea's classroom towards the end of Term 3, when the history topic was underway. Our observation notes recorded the four poster-sized pages of the many questions that the students had generated in the previous lesson after comparing old photographs in the suitcase with current photographs of the same sites and places. The plan for the lesson we observed was to continue watching a 25-minute video of old footage, pausing every two or three minutes to check if it contained answers to their questions on the posters. The questions included:

> How did people dress and do their hair when Elizabeth was first built?
> When was the first shop built?
> Where was the first police station?
> Where was the first hospital in Elizabeth?
> Was there a gaol when Elizabeth was first built?
> What was the first train station?
> Where was the first petrol station?
> What type of money did people use?
> What type of transport did they use to get to other places?
> Was there anyone against building Elizabeth?
> What was the first bus stop?
> What was the first cinema?
> How many people built Elizabeth?
> Did European settlers build Elizabeth or did the Australians?

In spite of the difficulties of watching old footage with poor sound and image quality, the students paid close attention and were able to offer answers to many of the questions they had asked. There was some discussion at times, as one of the students recorded answers next to the questions. Students discovered that answering questions is not always straightforward. For example, 'Did European settlers build Elizabeth, or the Australians?' drew the following response:

*Student:*  The European settlers.
*Andrea:*  How did you come to that conclusion? What did it say to make you think that the Europeans built it?
*Student:*  It was the visual text.
*Andrea:*  OK, I like that answer, but I think it might get further explained a bit later.

Andrea acknowledged that the student had been observant, while keeping open the possibility of exploring the issue further at a later time. It is, of course, a very complex question. She anticipates that the question will be answered more fully as they continue to watch the video. She demonstrates that she values the students' interests and contributions to understanding and interpreting spoken and visual texts as resources for information.

A photograph of a dust storm in 1958 generated a discussion about the planting of trees when the city was being built. The planners and builders were confronted with the problem of building the city on flat open farmland, which had minimal animal and bird life. When the north winds blew, dust storms swept over the land. Planting trees was the major strategy used to address this problem. Andrea shared with the students her childhood memories of climbing a tree in her front yard, and a tree in her grandmother's yard some blocks away, and realising they were the same type of tree. She invited the students to observe the trees in the neighbour-hood on their way home, because they now knew that the first 200 people who bought a new house in Elizabeth in 1954 were given three trees to plant.

After sharing a range of primary sources from the suitcase, Andrea invited the students to brainstorm questions about the planning and building of Elizabeth. As they watched the video and looked at photographs, they actively searched for answers. In these lessons, Andrea worked with the students' current knowledge of Elizabeth, expanded it and offered them new resources for literacy in the form of a range of visual and print texts. She also engaged her students in the first stages of an inquiry project. While she may have initially intended that the students would produce recounts and information reports, she was highly focused on engagement, valuing students' questions and interests in finding out about the history of their place. Indeed, in many ways Andrea and the students grappled, more or less con-sciously, with the commonly held view that Elizabeth was a place where only people without a work ethic, and without aspirations, lived. Although Andrea's project wasn't followed through to completion, for a number of reasons, the first lessons showed the potential for students to engage with questions that mattered deeply to them (and to their families). Even though the school's literacy agreement required a focus on recounts and information reports, the conversations and learn-ing that were unfolding in these early stages may well have led Andrea to explore less restrictive options.

## The standout features of uncommon pedagogies

In this chapter, we have attempted to describe the classroom practices of teachers who stood out among their peers. Their uncommon pedagogies included com-monly used approaches, such as various types of group work and specific tech-niques for teaching literacy. They also incorporated commonly used ICTs, such as interactive white boards and electronic devices. Even so, while observing them teach, it took very little time to realise that how they worked in their classrooms was likely to make significant positive differences for young people's participation in classroom events and activities and their engagement with learning. While the project design stops short of examining direct links between individual students and their teachers' pedagogies, the ethnographic observations and case studies do illuminate the kinds of practices in which different students became active participants and those practices which produced disengagement.

These teachers' pedagogical practices were palpably different from the majority of their peers because of what they noticed and how they commented on it. Another difference was how they interacted with students and adults – not just in terms of what they said, but what they planned for them all to do together. Their organisational processes also stood out, including how resources were arranged and made available. Perhaps most noticeably, how these teachers related to knowledge and how they worked with knowledge – both the knowledge that students brought into the room and the knowledge they anticipated that they would take out of the room – was more interesting, challenging and engaging than what we observed in the classrooms of their colleagues. In addition, these teachers frequently checked what their students could do, their understandings, and the connections they made. Many of them positioned their students as capable informants. Most importantly, they gave them strong messages about their learning potential and they conveyed their pleasure in the students' engagement. As with other literacy studies focusing on how this might be achieved (see Rogers & Mosley Wetzel, 2013), we recognise the importance of teacher talk in the pedagogical process. What students get to do in the classroom is inevitably contingent upon what they hear as the invitations, tasks, moment-by-moment feedback and so on. Beyond any particular literacy strategy or programme is what the teacher makes of it.

Most surprisingly, these standout teachers appeared unaware of how unusual and exemplary their practices were compared to their colleagues. They were generally under the impression that others were working in similar ways. Also, these standout teachers were keen to learn from, and share with, their colleagues; they were open to new ideas and opportunities and constantly on the lookout for ways to expand and improve their repertoire of teaching practices.

The teachers we describe in this chapter stepped away from scripted pedagogies and instead designed learning tasks that interested and intrigued their students (Carrie and Lara), connected with substantial issues (Alicia and Andrea) and engaged with the community in positive and educative ways (Suzy and Jason). We observed these teachers learning with, and from, their students. These teachers were not inclined to expect less of students from socially disadvantaged backgrounds. Although their students often entered their classrooms with nonstandard English, or 'ways with words' (Heath, 1983) that were generally not recognised or valued at school, these teachers considered these characteristics to be resources to be worked with, rather than deficits to be overcome.

These standout teachers responded effectively to opportunities to tailor their teaching to the moment, but their overall approach was informed by an expanded and expansive view of literacy. They resisted deficit naming of students and families and listened to them to find ways of building educative relationships and to learn about their literacy practices. On that basis, they provided better support for students to more closely approximate the reading and writing they need to be successful at school. They understood that learning to read and write are both collaborative and social activities. They provided multiple opportunities for students to engage in literacy tasks that connected to their life experiences – their hopes, fears, problems and joys. These standout teachers worked to develop and sustain mutual trust in their classrooms, openness to diversity and a belief in each student's capacity to learn.

## Note

1   'Learning Together' is a State education department programme for families with children aged from birth to four, which has operated in South Australia since 2003. Development of the programme took account of research highlighting the benefits of a preventative approach toward possible later difficulties for all children in vulnerable communities, rather than an approach where some children and families are targeted for intervention. See http://www.earlyyears.sa.edu.au/pages/HOME/learning_together_ parents/?reFlag=1.

## References

Acevedo, C., & Rose, D. (2007). 'Reading (and writing) to learn in the middle years of schooling'. *PEN* 157. Sydney: Primary English Teaching Association.

Bourdieu, P. (1990). *Sens Pratique*. (English: The Logic of Practice) (R. Nice, Trans.). Cambridge, UK: Polity Press.

Bronfenbrenner, U. (1979). *The Ecology of Human Development: Experiments by nature and design*. Cambridge, MA: Harvard University Press.

Clifton, D. O., & Harter, J. K. (2003). 'Investing in strengths'. In A. K. S. Cameron, B. J. E. Dutton, & C. R. E. Quinn (eds.), *Positive Organizational Scholarship: Foundations of a new discipline* (pp. 111–121). San Francisco, CA: Berrett-Koehler Publishers, Inc.

Cochran-Smith, M. (1991). 'Learning to teach against the grain'. *Harvard Educational Review*, *61*(3), 279–311.

Comber, B. (2006a). 'Critical literacy educators at work: Examining their dispositions, discursive resources and repertoires of practice'. In R. White & K. Cooper (eds.), *Practical Critical Educator: Integrating literacy, learning and leadership* (pp. 51–65). The Netherlands: Springer.

Comber, B. (2006b). 'Pedagogy as work: Educating the next generation of literacy teachers'. *Pedagogies: An International Journal*, *1*(1), 59–67.

Comber, B. (2012). 'Mandated literacy assessment and the reorganisation of teachers' work: Federal policy, local effects'. *Critical Studies in Education*, *53*(2), 119–136.

Comber, B. (2016a). *Literacy, Place and Pedagogies of Possibility*. New York and London: Routledge.

Comber, B. (2016b). 'The relevance of composing: Children's spaces for social agency'. In A. H. Dyson (ed.), *Child Cultures, Schooling and Literacy: Global perspectives on children composing their lives* (pp. 119–132). New York and London: Routledge.

Comber, B., Badger, L., Barnett, J., Nixon, H., & Pitt, J. (2002). 'Literacy after the early years: A longitudinal study'. *Australian Journal of Language and Literacy*, *25*(2), 9–23.

Comber, B., & Kamler, B. (Eds.). (2005). *Turn-around Pedagogies: Literacy interventions for at-risk students*. Newtown: Primary English Teaching Association.

Dahl, R. (2008). *Charlie and the chocolate factory*. New York: Puffin Books (original work published in 1968).

Dudley-Marling, C., & Michaels, S. (2012). *High-expectation Curricula: Helping all students succeed with powerful learning*. New York: Teachers College Press.

Dyson, A. H. (1993). *Social Worlds of Children Learning to Write in an Urban Primary School*. New York and London: Teachers College Press.

Gutiérrez, K., Morales, P. Z., & Martinez, D. (2009). 'Re-mediating literacy: Culture, difference, and learning for students from nondominant communities'. *Review of Research in Education, 33*, 212–245.

Hardy, I. (2014). 'A logic of appropriation: Enacting national testing (NAPLAN) in Australia'. *Journal of Education Policy, 29*(1), 1–18.

Heath, S. B. (1983). *Ways with Words: Language, life and work in communities and classrooms*. Cambridge: Cambridge University Press.

Klenowski, V. (2014). 'Towards fairer assessment'. *Australian Education Researcher, 41*, 445–470.

Kwek, D. (2012). 'Weaving as frontload and backend pedagogies: Building repertoires of connected learning'. In C. Day (ed.), *Routledge Handbook of Teacher and School Development*. London & New York: Routledge.

Lloyd, S. & Wernham, S. (1992). *The Phonics Handbook* (1994 onwards: *Jolly Phonics*). Chigwell, Essex, UK: Jolly Learning Ltd.

McNaughton, S. (2002). *Meeting of Minds*. Wellington, New Zealand: Learning Media Ltd.

MetaMetrics. (2004). *The Lexile Framework for Reading*. Triangle Park, NC: Metametrics.

Rogers, R., & Mosley Wetzel, M. (2013). 'Studying agency in teacher education: A layered approach to positive discourse analysis'. *Critical Inquiry into Language Studies, 10*(1), 62–92.

Rose, D. (2010). *The Reading to Learn Teacher Resource Package*. Sydney: Reading to Learn.

Thomson, P. (2002). *Schooling the Rustbelt Kids: Making the difference in changing times*. Crows Nest, NSW: Allen & Unwin.

Vasquez, V. (2004). *Negotiating Critical Literacies with Young Children*. Mahwah, New Jersey & London: Lawrence Erlbaum Associates.

Wild, M. (2012). *Tanglewood*. (Illustrated by V. Goodman). Parkside, South Australia: Omnibus Books.

Winch, G., Ross Johnston, R., March, P., Ljungdahl, L., & Holliday, M. (2014). *Literacy: Reading, writing and children's literature* (5th ed.). Sth. Melbourne, Australia: Oxford University Press.

# 5

# COMMON PEDAGOGIES

## Missed opportunities and unmet hopes

Each school day, the teachers in our study spent most of their time in class focused on improving their students' literacy. They worked in the knowledge that, in the past, their collective efforts had generally fallen short of their hopes to improve their students' results on literacy tests. They recognised that improvement was hard to achieve and to sustain across the years of schooling. They also worked in the knowledge that each year the results of their labour would be made available for scrutiny, when their students' performance was made public and compared to others on the national *My School* website. These teachers wore the yoke of responsibility for their students' success at school. They were acutely aware of the critical role they played in expanding these young people's future life chances beyond their current circumstances and contributing to their long-term well-being.

Despite the challenges they faced, the teachers and school leaders we talked to spoke with conviction about their ongoing commitment to improving their students' learning and their concerns for their well-being. We are grateful to these educators for allowing us into their classrooms, offices and workplaces. It is only because of their openness, honesty and willingness to provide us with access to these places that we are able to write this chapter about the effects of their collective and individual practices. We believe that they participated in the hope that our research might help them, and others teaching in similar circumstances, to improve the learning outcomes for young people from socially disadvantaged backgrounds.

Although the previous chapter describes some standout pedagogical practices, our observations of classrooms more typically uncovered what we call 'common pedagogies' that order the day's literacy teaching; they are common in the sense that most teachers include them in their literacy programme and they are unremarkable to the extent that they are the ordinary, everyday experience of teachers and students. Tragically, however, despite the efforts of the teachers and school leaders in our study to produce improved outcomes through high-quality teaching and learning experiences, these 'common pedagogies' were most likely to result in constrained and limited literacy outcomes.

To illustrate common pedagogies, we describe in detail the practices of three teachers – Tracey, Jody and Maureen – whose work exemplifies, in different ways, approaches to teaching literacy that we observed more widely throughout this research. Our accounts were drawn from classroom observations, described in Chapter 2, that were compiled from our fieldwork over a three-year period (2011–14). In all cases, the teachers were aware of our interest in literacy learning and they allowed us into their classrooms to observe them teach, often during the literacy block. During the study, we asked for volunteers to share approaches to literacy that they considered to positively support improvements in their students. To ensure that the conditions were as favourable as possible, the classes in which they demonstrated these approaches sometimes took place when we were not able to be present. In these cases, the teachers recorded the lesson on video. When we returned to the school, we watched each recording with the teacher who had made it and recorded their explanation of what was taking place. The descriptions of teachers' classroom practices below draw upon our fieldnotes, as well as videos and related interviews.

The selection of these three teachers for detailed analysis should not be taken as an indication that their practices were exceptional and in need, for that reason, of being exposed. Instead, these extended accounts of examples of common pedagogies are used because they enable us to compare and contrast what was achieved with what might have been achieved. It is the latter that we believe reflects the hopes and ambitions of educators for their students. Failure to achieve these hopes and ambitions was, in our view, an unintended consequence of their efforts to respond to the challenges that confronted them – challenges we discussed in the first two chapters of this book. Our hope is that this analysis will assist educators to better realise their goals.

## Tracey: sticking to the script

### Lost opportunities to connect literacy with children's experiences

It is mid-morning in a Year 1/2 classroom. Tracey is reading *Charlotte's Web* (E.B. White, 1952/2012) aloud to the class and then watching segments of the movie made of the film so that the students can compare different versions of the story. In the book, the character Wilbur asks Charlotte what the unfamiliar words mean. In Tracey's class, student Simon could be relied upon to ask: 'What does that mean?' He was interested in words.

On one occasion, Simon remarked that 'radiant' was a type of detergent for washing clothes. However, rather than welcome his contribution, Tracey seemed annoyed by the interruption, especially as Simon persisted in saying: 'That's what it said in the book, and it's for washing my clothes.' Tracey thanked him but did not acknowledge the connection he was making with the book and did not take up the opportunity to explore multiple meanings of the word.

Paramount was Tracey's requirement that the students sit and listen quietly while she read and answer her questions. In this situation, Simon's efforts to show interest in the story were neither acknowledged nor developed in positive ways. Rather they were interpreted as an unwelcome interruption. During our interview with her, Tracey reported that she had not focused on words like *humble* and *salutations*, which Simon and some of the other students were curious about. Nevertheless, one morning, Simon came into class and greeted her with: 'Salutations!' Instead of welcoming Simon's use of this word, Tracey reminded him that 'We say good morning here'. Tracey's response was a missed opportunity to play with and appropriate words from *Charlotte's Web* as resources for writing and speaking.

Ironically, even when Tracey expanded her literacy pedagogy to include reading a complex narrative – an uncommon practice in most of the classrooms we observed – she missed other opportunities to expand students' language and literate repertoires. She did not appear able to interact with Simon in unscripted ways about ideas she had not yet taught. In Simon's case, this is compounded by Tracey's assessment of him as a 'behaviour problem' and as 'probably on the spectrum'.

With the pressure to teach phonics and sight words that has coincided with the escalating importance of National Assessment Program – Literacy and Numeracy (NAPLAN) results, it is not surprising that literacy pedagogy for early-career teachers like Tracey involves a narrow view of literacy, often to the exclusion of learning words in the context of meaningful reading and writing. Unwittingly, Tracey has also reduced appropriate ways of participating in the literacy lesson so that Simon cannot contribute and is not seen as resourceful.

Early-career teachers may feel under particularly strong pressure to meet system accountability demands, as well as the requirements of school-wide literacy agreements, as we discuss later. Increasingly, the dangers of such pressures can lead to teachers' feelings of powerlessness and alienation, and even to them leaving the profession (Blackmore, 2013; Dover, 2013). A common effect of these practices is that teachers attempt less and students are framed as less able. Teachers, for their part, become frustrated when students begin to perform in accordance with low expectations. It seems unlikely that Simon's resilience in noting 'radiant' and greeting his teacher with 'Salutations!' will outlast her insistence on the planned scripts for lessons. Tracey and many of her colleagues were focused on bringing off the lesson as planned, rather than engaging pedagogically with learning opportunities as they arose. This can be understood in part as a response to the school emphases on literacy and behaviour agreements and the accompanying stress on consistency.

Interestingly, when Sandford students participated in their school's review, one of their suggestions for improvements that could be made was to have more difficult and complicated texts to read in classrooms and made available in the library for them to borrow. This feedback indicated that some students were aware to some degree of the kinds of decisions that were being made for them about what constituted appropriate texts. Engaging with complex concepts and ideas provides the motivation that readers need to undertake the work of reading and to enjoy the subsequent satisfactions. Removing the challenges may also remove any reason to bother.

## *Accomplishing the ritual of writing a recount*

By the time students are in Year 2, they are usually familiar with writing a recount. In and out of school, recounts are commonly the means by which we tell stories of our lives. For some teachers, the main purpose is to ensure that the students know how to structure a recount and how to make it interesting by adding more description or detail. What unfolds in the following account is a poignant incident that demonstrates how Tracey's frame of reference for the lesson, along with her assessment of Simon, resulted in another lost opportunity for him to accomplish significant identity work through writing at school. We recall that Tracey was also unresponsive to Simon's perceptive take-up of the vocabulary of *Charlotte's Web*.

Six-year-old Simon had arrived in the classroom that Monday morning with something to say to his teacher. He wanted to make sure that today was the day for journal writing and told her what had happened on the weekend. Tracey assured him that sharing time and writing a recount would happen this morning. However, sight words and spelling activities would be completed first. When Sunday is mentioned during the routine of naming the day and the date, Simon, almost inaudibly, tells everyone that he went with his family to scatter his Nanna's ashes in Port River. Tracey continued with her questions about days and dates.

In preparation for recount writing, the children have about 30 seconds each to share with a partner what they did on the weekend. Simon wriggles himself to sit cross-legged opposite Becky. His hands in his lap, he looks down for a moment before he speaks, somewhat slowly:

> 'On Sunday afternoon we went to Port River to – to (pause) to throw Nanna's ashes into Port River. That's what she always wanted.'
>
> He pauses, looks at Becky, then rubs his forehead. He rests his elbows on his thighs and puts his face onto his palms for a moment. He looks away from Becky as she tells him, 'On the weekend I went to see my Nanna.' Moments later, Becky has her hands inside her sleeves and shakes them about her lap. Simon smiles immediately and starts to play 'Scissors, rock, paper' with her.

Tracey asks the students to stop their sharing and look at her so she can choose five people to share with the class. Children put their hands up to be chosen, including Simon. When the fifth child, Becky, is chosen, Simon clenches his fists and hits them onto his thighs. He knows he will not be chosen to share his news. Tracey reminds him to 'stay calm'. Simon clenches his fists again, raises them head high and firmly drops them into his lap and, looking into his lap, says in an upset tone, 'I just can't.' He continues to look down and fiddle with his shoes.

Students must negotiate learner identities in the micropolitics of classroom life (Comber & Kerkham, 2016; Dyson, 2016; Wortham, 2006). When students bring their home lives into the classroom, they run the risks of negative evaluation or ignorance from teachers and peers. Further, when teachers have assessed a child in a particular way, such as Simon being 'on the spectrum', it may be impossible for the student to shift that judgement, even when their classroom behaviour and engagement with a set task is entirely appropriate. Simon's disappointment and anger on this occasion was not an unusual case in terms of his experience; it also occurred for other students in other classrooms at Sandford (Comber & Kerkham, 2016) and at each of the other three schools. When teachers come to see a student as a problem, as lacking ability or as inappropriate, these accounts can become enduring and come to be shared by others. Hence, Simon can be seen by Tracey, and perhaps by some peers, as inappropriately angry.

As the lesson progressed, Tracey reminded the students to rule a margin down the left-hand side of the page, write the date at the top of the page, copy the sentence starter ('On the weekend I …') from the board and put finger spaces between each word. She also reminded them that once the writing was done, they 'may draw your picture of what you did on the weekend'.

As the students organised themselves, Simon, who prefers to stand while writing, leaned across his book to write. Suddenly he squeals, drawing a sharp response from Tracey and the following exchange:

*Simon:*    He keeps teasing me.
*Jason:*    (Quietly) I am not.
*Simon:*    Yes.
*Tracey:*    Simon! Stop.
*Simon:*    (Quietly) He was (with hurt expression).
*Tracey:*    Simon. Let's get on with our writing.

Simon copies the date from the board. Then writes: 'ONThe weekend I'.

He rhythmically taps his pencil on his middle finger, quietly saying: 'Ow, ow.' He reads what he has written and realises he has forgotten the finger spaces. He looks for his eraser and starts rubbing out the 'N' of 'ON'. He repeats, almost to himself, but heard by Tracey: 'I forgot the finger spaces.' He starts to erase what he has written. Tracey tells him to: 'Just put finger spaces in now, from where you're up to.' Simon subvocalises as he writes 'I' and then asks Tracey, helping another student at the table, if she can spell: 'We gone to Port River.'

Tracey reads over his shoulder and asks what word he is up to. She reads: 'On the weekend I? W? What word do you need there? W–e?' [The sound suggests that she is thinking 'went', following the sentence pattern on the board.] Simon writes 'we'. Tracey adds: 'Went, went is the next word. Then get your dictionary.'

As Tracey writes 'Port River' in his dictionary, Simon rocks gently. He copies the words, checking letter-by-letter, then stands back and audibly reads the words 'Port River' twice. He leans across his book and writes OT (without a space after 'river'). Simon then asks Tracey for the word 'fro', which she takes as an opportunity to reinforce the difference between 'f' and 'th'.

He copies 'throw', writes 'Nanna's' by himself and starts tapping his pencil on the table. He puts his hand up to get Tracey's attention. He starts to ask: 'How do you write …?' and she interrupts with: 'Ashes?' Yes, that is the word he wants.

He fiddles with his pencil. Tracey writes in the dictionary as she 'sounds': 'a–sh–es'. He copies and, talking to himself says: 'Mmmm, full stop. Stop.' (Pauses) 'Now comes the picture.' He says quietly, but to the table:

Simon:     I don't want to write the picture because it might scare everybody else.
Jason:     It's alright. You can draw the picture.
Simon:     It might scare anybody else. (He closes his book.)

When Tracey comes to read his recount, she reminds him that he needs to draw a picture. Simon explains that he doesn't want to, 'because it might scare everybody else'. She insists that he draw a picture because 'we always draw a picture after writing'. She suggests: 'Something nice that you remember.' Simon is reluctant. Tracey suggests: 'Something to do with your belly.' Simon said that his Nanna only made spicy things, which he didn't like, and that he didn't want to draw his Nanna.

The photocopy of Simon's recount shows that he drew two figures with smiley faces.

Despite the fact that Simon had shared his significant news with his teacher before class began, and had attempted to insert his story when the teacher was discussing the day and date before sharing time, he was not permitted to share with his peers what he had done on the weekend. How are we to make sense of this sequence of missed opportunities to engage sensitively with a child's experience of the death of a grandparent? How is the teacher's insistence on following the established procedure for writing an illustrated recount to be understood? In this instance, writing a recount is an extended version of 'fill-in-the-missing-letter' activities that are commonly provided. The teacher provides the starting point, 'On the weekend', and is unprepared for it to lead to any communication that is deeply felt and meaningful to the students. The task is simply an exercise to enable students to demonstrate their knowledge of the structure of a recount. Tracey seems unable to expand the communicative context of the literacy lesson to include the lives and experiences of her students. There is no space for pedagogical innovation and responsiveness. How such sequences of noncommunication come to be regarded as acceptable pedagogy continues to haunt us as teacher educators. These missed opportunities highlight what Freebody and colleagues (Freebody, 2003; Freebody, Ludwig & Gunn, 1995) describe as 'interactive trouble'. Such repeated occasions make it very difficult for students, such as Simon, to develop positive learner identities at school.

The tragedy of Tracey's approach is that she saw nothing wrong in this incident. Her default position was to attribute the trouble to Simon. Tracey is not alone in making such judgements and responding accordingly. She does not turn to Simon or recognise him as resourceful, as we might wish (Comber & Kamler, 2004). Partly, her desire for students to abide by the rules for behaviour that she has set prevents

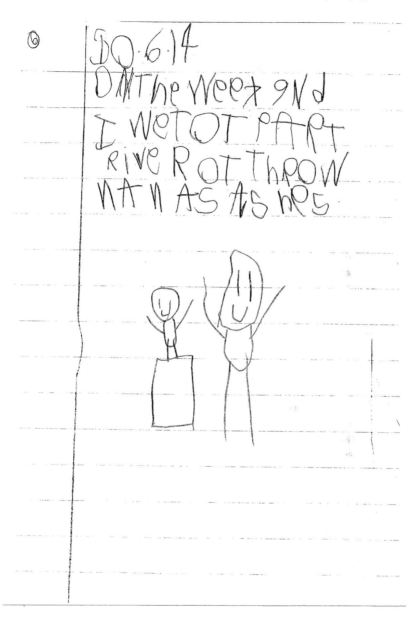

**FIGURE 5.1** Simon's text, 'On the weekend …'

her from noticing Simon's positive engagement with the tasks. We witnessed many similar occasions where students, who teachers had already assessed as problematic, were ignored, misunderstood or admonished for their efforts. It is not that Tracey does not care about Simon. It is not that her literacy teaching knowledge is impoverished necessarily; but her ability to see and recognise the resources that students bring to literacy/learning may be blinded by her misunderstandings of children's 'backgrounds' (Comber, 1998). Further, she remains unaware of the likely impact of her interactions and responses on different children. Hence Simon's anger, frustration and lack of compliance is seen as his problem.

## Jody: making shared reading routine

Jody had been teaching at Highfield for three years and, in that time, gained accreditation as an *Accelerated Literacy* (AL) teacher. AL was one of the key programmes in which the principal, Kathryn, had invested significant professional learning time and resources. Its hallmark is explicit teaching of the structure and language features of a text in order to support students to read at a level they may not be able to achieve independently. At the heart of AL is systemic functional grammar (Halliday, 1994; Halliday & Hasan, 1985), a model of language that is concerned with how language varies according to sociocultural context. Pedagogically, the AL cycle involves teacher-led introductory work to set the context, such as discussing the field or topic, giving a synopsis of the text, reading key passages and identifying specific vocabulary, and noticing sentence/clause structure. This orientation to the text may extend over a number of lessons. The second phase in the cycle is 'transformations', an activity designed to take the students from 'looking for meaning' to learning how the author uses particular techniques to achieve a purpose, including, for example, how illustrations contribute to the content of the text. It is also important for building common knowledge in the classroom and for developing students' abilities to infer and read a text critically (Cowey, n.d.; Custance, Dare & Polias, 2011). Jody used the AL cycle to introduce the students to fiction and nonfiction texts to support the students in successfully reading an unfamiliar text.

Jody chose to have a colleague video a lesson that she felt was a good example of putting the school's literacy agreement into practice and to demonstrate an AL approach. In this lesson, her Year 5 students were about to share in reading aloud a challenging text – an information report on childhood obesity. Jody began by asking students to volunteer to read the lesson goals displayed on the whiteboard. The lights were dimmed, so that the text on the smartboard screen was easier to see. One student read the learning goal: 'Students identify features of the report, using the information report.' Another read the reading goal: 'Read the text every day focusing on fluency and pace.' These are the goals Jody wanted the students to achieve 'today, by the end of the lesson'. She asked if any students 'want to read to practice their fluency' and the nine who volunteered 'have to remember [their] order' for reading the text. Before they start, Jody cued them to the genre and the topic – an information report that provides the reader with information about obesity in children. She asked if anyone could remember the discussion of the previous lesson:

Jody:     Who knows what obesity is? Does anyone remember from yesterday, before I tell them? Nigel.
Nigel:    Overweight people.

*Jody:* People being overweight, OK. And it's more than just being over-weight, it's being very overweight. OK.

[The students then take turns to read aloud.]

*Jody:* So Kerry's going to start reading. Remember, don't hold up the reading because we only want to read it once today. (She passes the microphone to Kerry.)

[The microphone is used so that all students can hear the reader clearly.]

*Kerry:* (Reads) The number of overweight children in Australia doubled in recent years with a quarter of children considered overweight or obese. Causes of obesity in children could be unhealthy food, processed (inaudible) eating habits.

*Jody:* Well done, Kerry. I like your reading. Amelia. (Jody passes the microphone to Amelia.)

*Amelia:* (Reads) The rise of the number of overweight children is disturbing because it causes health problems and can lead to social problems. Overweight children are more likely to be teased by their peers or to develop low self-esteem or body imaging, image, problems. Once children are overweight it requires a lot of effort and commitment for them to return, return to a healthy weight.

*Jody:* Next person.

*Georgia:* (Reads) Overweight and obesity in children are among the most important risks to children's long- and short-term health. Overweight children are very likely to become overweight adults.

*Jody:* Well done. Who's next? (Georgia passes the microphone to the next reader.)

This sequence is followed until the whole text has been read: a student reads a section of the text and Jody makes a brief comment on their reading or a strategy the student may have used (e.g. self-correcting or rereading when an unknown word has interrupted fluency), before passing the microphone to the next student. Jody is concentrating on the reading goal at this stage in the lesson and acknowledges that 'we've only just started reading the text this week, so in a couple of weeks' time we'll become much, much more fluent at reading.' The reading goal – 'Read the text every day focusing on fluency and pace' – is reinforced, as is the necessity of repeated readings in order to develop fluency and pace, which is central to the AL approach.

In the next phase of the lesson Jody asks two questions about the content of the report just read. The answer to the first question, 'What is the text about?', prompts Jody to ask another question of clarification related to who the text is about.

*Nigel:* It's about people that are obese and overweight, and they want to try and stop it.

*Jody:*    So what type of people is it talking about? Is it talking about adults? Is it talking about babies? Is it talking about children? Who is it talking about?

[No response from the students.]

*Jody:*    It's talking about kids.
*Georgia:*  And adolescents.
*Jody:*    Yep, so it's talking about children up until adolescence, OK. Up until 25 years old.

Jody's comment, 'It's talking about kids,' elicits the response 'And adolescents,' an accurate answer. She then suggests that people aged 'up until 25 years old' are included in 'adolescents', a fact that is neither explored nor fully explained. Instead, Jody comments immediately on two of several unfamiliar words the students had read in the report – *obesity* and *dietician*. These are categorised as words that need to be 'practised' in order to be read fluently.

*Jody:*    Now I know that you guys were struggling a little bit on the word obesity, so that's a word that we have to practise reading. And dietician is another word that you guys don't use in your vocabulary, so we have to practise reading that, OK.

In making this comment, she again inserts the particular reading goal of the lesson – to practise the reading of information texts. She verbalises her assessment about words they're struggling with, or which are not part of their vocabulary. Jody reiterates that the oral reading of unfamiliar words is required for fluent reading. By this time, almost 14 minutes into the lesson, several students are fidgeting, stretching or yawning.

Jody paraphrases the last paragraph that one of the students had already read ('This page has been produced in consultation with and approved by Royal Children's Hospital Nutrition Department') and explains that: 'The people that are a part of that department got together and collected research, and then wrote up this information report.'

Without further discussion of the vocabulary or content, Jody asks: 'How many parts does an information report have, before I tell you?' Some students are slumping over their table, rubbing faces, eyes, noses, or folding arms on the table and resting their heads, variously tuning out and in. Some raise their hands and offer answers, but even these students fidget and wriggle towards the end of the 20-minute lesson. Acknowledging a student's correct answer, Jody then points to the poster on the wall displaying the elements of an information report to reaffirm what the students have already articulated.

She outlines the task to be completed by the end of the lesson: use four coloured pencils to draw a key at the bottom of the page and use it to show that they can identify the features of an information report.

| | |
|---|---|
| *Jody:* | So what's our title, everyone tell me our title. |
| *Students:* | (Calling out) Obesity in children. |
| *Jody:* | Say it again, together. |
| *Students:* | Obesity in children. |
| *Jody:* | OK. You could underline it, you could do a star, it's up to you how you do your key, and I'm going to come around and just support people, especially the new students. If you need help, talk to the person next to you. |

The teacher's singular focus on the students reading the text aloud, and her literal questions about the structure of the information report, are comprehensible in light of the explicit lesson goals. The fading engagement of the students in the task of following the reading, and attending to the teacher, arguably occurs because there is an emphasis on following an oft-repeated routine. Such routines offer little challenge, especially when the teacher is the teller of answers. Questions such as: 'Who knows what obesity is? Does anyone remember from yesterday, before I tell them?' or: 'How many parts does an information report have, before I tell you?' invite students not to engage or make an effort. It is assumed that, if students do not remember the teacher's definition of obesity, they are unlikely to have this prior knowledge. Yet childhood obesity is a familiar and popular news story, frequently highlighted on television. Further, even in a 'low order' orientation (Cowey, n.d.) to reading the text, the teacher could have established a focus that intellectually engaged the students. As reading progressed, discussion could have involved not just recalling facts but challenging students to interpret and infer. Indeed, this topic of obesity is of considerable relevance to these preadolescent students. With no opportunities to offer their thoughts, knowledge or questions, the lesson is stripped of its social and academic potential. It becomes no more than a ritual exercise.

The concluding task for the lesson – to design a colour key and use it to colour the five parts of the report (a fact that had been stated more than once during the lesson) – underlines the constraints placed on this task by the teacher's apparent lack of interest in the language of the report and the vocabulary specific to the topic. Further, no attempt was made to open up a discussion of the content that might meaningfully connect it to the students' lives and experiences. The content is not simply 'stuff' to demonstrate a genre; it is the content that drives the genre. Even though the teacher may believe she has faithfully carried out key elements of AL pedagogy, her close reading of this text does not result in students developing an in-depth understanding of the text, the topic or the genre. Such a lack of student intellectual engagement with the substantive content in reading materials in the middle years of schooling is a major problem (Comber & Nixon, 2011; Luke, Dooley & Woods, 2011).

## Maureen: limiting experiences of being a writer

While writing may be included in teachers' weekly programmes, as required by the school's literacy agreements, its enactment does not look the same in every classroom. Further, teachers mean different things when they talk about children and writing. Here we examine how 'independent writing' lessons in two different early-years classrooms actually unfolded. Our concern is that what has come to count as writing in these contexts comes at the risk of limiting children's experiences of becoming a writer.

In the following account of writing in a Reception class, we draw attention to the ways in which the teacher initially structures 'learning to write' as a task of copying and practising 'sight words' before expecting children to copy or write a sentence.

## Cracking the code in the first year of school

Maureen was a teacher with more than 15 years' experience in early-years classrooms and had been at her current school for nine years when she agreed to participate in the project. Independent writing in Maureen's Reception class didn't start until mid-Term 2. During Term 1, before they were ready for writing, her five-year-old students experienced formal handwriting practice, tracing over words and writing beneath sentences scribed for them in their writing books.

Initially, 'writing' in this class involves a worksheet with two or three tasks that focus on 'sight words'. Tasks include: copying the sight word; reading three sentences with a missing (sight) word, then writing in the missing word using picture clues as a prompt; and creating an original sentence using sounds and letter knowledge, remembering finger spaces, and 'having a go' at spelling unknown words independently. The worksheets were developed so that the students could practise and use the first 20 sight words in the Oxford Word List (Oxford University Press Staff, 2008) that they were learning.

Later in Term 1, the children are organised into groups, each with a different task. More capable writers focus on writing, with support, the chosen sight word in their own sentence. A less independent group might contribute ideas for a simple sentence and each student attempts to write it, following explicit teaching about, for example, finger spaces. Other students would be given an activity practising recognising and writing their sight words.

In addition, writing a recount is a regular Monday whole-class activity. Maureen writes a short text on the board, usually about 'My weekend'. She models how to sound out the words to show the students how to apply their knowledge of sounds and letters. She also circles sight words and explains: 'I didn't sound this word out because I know it's a sight word.' She believes that modelling a short recount of her weekend motivates the students, because they are 'naturally interested in their teacher' and her 'life outside of school'. By way of demonstrating the kinds of writing the students produced, we discuss three texts that were written by Amira, one of the children Maureen chose as a case study.

## *Letters + finger spaces + full stops = writing*

Maureen had some concerns about Amira's oral language and her understanding of English, partly because five-year-old Amira didn't always seem to understand instructions, and partly because she didn't speak very confidently at sharing time or during class discussion. From Maureen's perspective, the highly structured days, as well as the visual timetable that listed the sequence of lessons for the day, helped Amira to 'learn how to manage herself in the classroom and understand what's being asked of her the majority of the time'. Observations of Amira suggested that she was having little difficulty keeping up with morning routine – the recitation of Jolly Phonics and singing along with the songs of the days of the week, the seasons and the months of the year. She organised herself, her books and pencils quickly and completed worksheet and writing tasks well ahead of many of her peers.

Characteristically, the tasks that were provided to prepare students to be writers focused on correct spelling of sight words; using a capital letter at the beginning of a sentence; accurate copying of the words scribed; and using finger spaces. Maureen's comments below are drawn from an interview where she discussed samples of Amira's writing that she had collected from early February until late July. Figure 5.2, 'Look at the family', was copied from the whiteboard. 'Look' was the sight word of the week.

Maureen scribed the sentence Amira told her and then Amira copied the words Maureen had written. Maureen noticed that the word *look* was written at the top and spelled correctly, and that Amira wasn't always using finger spaces between the words but recognised that she needed to use a capital letter at the beginning.

'Look at the family' imitates a language pattern of texts intended for children who are beginning to read. Such texts feature predictable and repetitive text, illustrations to support the text, consistent format and a layout that is easy to follow, and use of a range of punctuation. Amira's familiarity with such content-free texts is already shaping her writing and her teacher's interpretation of what she can do as a writer.

By mid-May, Amira was writing her own sentences independently. She had copied the first sentence, 'We went to the zoo', from the board, as expected, and added: 'I liked the crcsl' (I liked the crocodiles). She had correctly spelled the high-frequency words *the* and *I*, used a capital letter at the beginning of the sentence and used a full stop at the end. Maureen noted that Amira's attempt at 'crocodiles' showed that she was 'able to hear initial and final sounds and represent them on paper'. Her written feedback reinforced the purpose of the writing: 'Good copying' and 'Great sounding out'. Over the next month, Amira continued to accurately use the conventions that were the focus of Maureen's teaching. At this time, writing for Amira was an exercise in displaying her knowledge and her practice of spelling, capital letters and finger spaces. It offered few opportunities for communicating something meaningful.

When we talked with Maureen about Amira's response to a recount (see Figure 5.3), she again commented on her correct spelling of high-frequency words (*I, to, the*); her use of capitals for sentence beginnings and for people's names; and her use of initial and final sounds in words like *park* and *city*. The quality of this text is entirely different from Figure 5.2, even though its surface features might appear similar. Amira has attempted to include a narrative about what she had actually done on the weekend, using a familiar sentence starter ('I went to the') to structure it, and

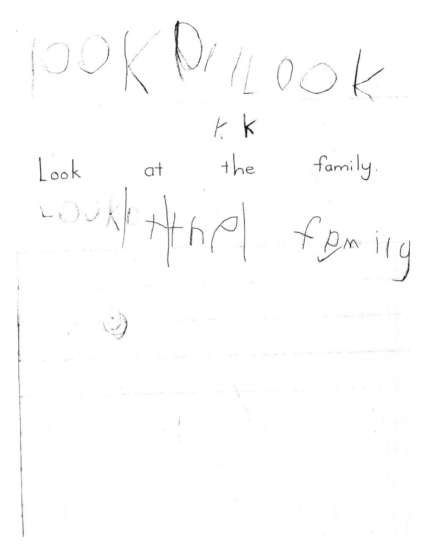

**FIGURE 5.2** Amira's text, 'Look'.

then embellished it with events and people in which she was interested. Maureen seemingly overlooked this aspect of Amira's text, having made no comment on it.

The writing goals Maureen recorded for Amira for the end of the year included: 'writing to construct two to three sentences independently, using capital letters and full stops; spelling, applying Jolly Phonics initial sounds to spell three-letter words correctly; transferring the ability to hear beginning, middle and ends sounds to being able to write/spell words; to spelling high frequency sight words correctly.' It is not surprising then that the ideas, the vocabulary and the structure of Amira's writing are not given attention. Yet the use of a writing assessment framework could produce a more holistic analysis of students' writing. Frameworks that could be used for this

**FIGURE 5.3** Amira's text, 'On the weekend …'

purpose include CAASR (concepts about literacy; attitudes to writing and reading; aspects of written products and reading comprehension; strategies for writing and reading; range of writing and reading purposes and forms [Education Department of South Australia, 1991]), or Spandel's (2011) domains of ideas, voice, organisation, word choice, sentence fluency and conventions – or even a modified NAPLAN writing assessment guide. Such frameworks provide insights into the range of aspects that a teacher might respond to as indicators of achievement in writing.

The discussion of Amira's texts is important for a number of reasons. It shows clearly how writing is conceptualised and practised in Maureen's classroom and indicates why one of the other students, who 'isn't retaining his sounds', gives her cause for concern. For Maureen, learning to write involves activating knowledge of sounds, remembering sight words, and using finger spaces, capital letters and full stops. Further, the concept of 'readiness' for reading and writing that underpins her teaching is grounded in a normative developmental model, the shortcomings of which have been recognised for some time (Comber & Kamler, 2004; Compton-Lilly, 2011; Dyson, 2013; Genishi & Dyson, 2009; Luke, 2005). At best, it affirms the notion of predetermined stages for learning to read and write that admits little room for students' curiosity or interest in playing with words. Moreover, the purpose for writing is to demonstrate competence with copying a title or sight words from the board, doing cloze exercises and then applying what is learnt to writing a sentence 'using your own words'.

Interestingly, Maureen reflected on how young Reception students 'recognise a sound when we do it as a Jolly Phonics sound on the board, and they can hear it, but actually transferring it into writing, for different students it comes at different stages'. While Amira's texts show she is making that connection, her writing also shows what she is learning about being seen as a successful writer in the classroom: she has learnt to copy accurately, to remember punctuation and to follow given sentence structures (like the ones she has seen written on the whiteboard or in the readers she is using in guided reading [Fountas & Pinnell, 1996] and the large-format books that Maureen uses in the literacy block). She is nevertheless beginning to use her knowledge of sounds, letters and words to write a narrative that does more than simply accomplish the surface features required by the task. In naming places and people, 'On the weekend' can be read as a genuine attempt by Amira to communicate something that is meaningful and of interest to her and to an imagined reader, not merely an exercise in demonstrating to her teacher that she can manipulate phonemes and accurately spell some sight words.

## Understanding common pedagogies and fickle literacies

The common pedagogies we describe in this chapter engendered approaches to literacy that were both limited and limiting, what Comber has previously termed 'fickle literacies' (Comber, 2015; Comber & Woods, 2016). These literacies operated in stark contrast to the smaller number of classrooms in the same schools where we observed teachers genuinely turning around to students and families, designing challenging curriculum and enacting pedagogies that connected in significant ways with students' lives and learning.

Our observations suggest that fickle literacies are not limited to rote learning and low-level tasks that require students to fill in missing words or letters, colour-code letter–sound relationships and match words and pictures. They also include tasks designed in the name of differentiation, genre pedagogy, explicit teaching, AL and so on. In other words, teachers are invoking the rhetoric of theoretically and ideologically underpinned contemporary literacy approaches in the service of fickle literacies. Our own practice as educational researchers is implicated in this analysis, as many of the pedagogical and organisational approaches that contributed to this situation were ones that had been previously identified by educational researchers as good practice – the kind that are likely to improve educational outcomes. However, there is an important distinction to be made between an espoused literacy practice and how it is implemented. The former accounts for what might be achieved. In reality, the process of co-opting these practices can involve a diminution of the original forms. As a result, only some elements of what is espoused are taken up and the 'whole practice' is not enacted as designed. When the substantive purpose is stripped away, what remains is a hollowed-out form of a more complex textual practice. Perversely, it is possible for students to complete the visible surface aspects of such tasks without any need to intellectually engage in the process. In such cases, learning is associated with producing surface features of a task and these features are reproduced again and again.

But how did these fickle literacies come to occur in classrooms where professional teachers were explicitly committed to high-quality literacy teaching, and in contexts in which they were enacting locally developed agreements about how to improve literacy? One reason appeared to be a recourse to 'safe' teaching in which students could be kept busy and their behaviour managed.

We recognise that many teachers have sought peace with a challenging class on a Friday afternoon by setting something easy for them to do. These kinds of tasks demand scant attention to content and minimal intellectual work. They are designed to keep students busy and occupied. Social interactions – usually conversations unrelated to the set task – surround this busy work and give the appearance of a relaxed and engaging classroom environment, as illustrated in the following extract from our fieldnotes in a Year 5 class at Sandford:

> Students were each given a text entitled 'How to make popcorn'. The students could choose to copy, or cut and paste, the instructions (provided by the teacher) onto a brown paper bag and then illustrate the text appropriately. During the completion of this activity, the students chatted amiably while remaining 'on task', and the teacher moved among the students talking with some individuals. There was no discussion about the topic, or the social purposes for procedural texts, or their structure and linguistic features. Rather, the focus was on capturing and illustrating the recipe on the bag (which presumably would later be filled with popcorn).

Our time in the four schools in our study suggests that this kind of work is commonplace, and in no way limited to Friday afternoons. Activities such as those described in the extended examples in this chapter – copying sight words, cutting out and pasting labels on diagrams, and matching words to pictures – can provide opportunities to practise perceptual and fine motor skills, but overall such practices do little more than accomplish the appearance of busyness and engagement in an activity of limited relevance to the development of literacy. Common variants include worksheets, sometimes copied from graded practice homework booklets of the type that can be purchased in local stores. While students are working with paper and pencils, and their focus is on print, the pedagogical goals of such activities are not evident; there is no obvious meaning-making required by such tasks.

These limitations may be recognised by teachers. Claudia, for example, taught the Year 5 class who were working on the 'How to make popcorn' procedural task. Like Tracey, she was an early-career teacher in her third year of teaching, when she agreed to work with us on the research project. Claudia was self-critical and keen to learn from others and regularly sought advice. She was also open to hearing about her students' lives. She treated them respectfully and listened actively. Claudia was seen as having great relationships with the students, and was given extra 'problem' students to deal with, because she showed potential in handling difficult behaviours. Students wanted to be in her class. However, by her own account, she found teaching extremely challenging in terms of managing the class and negotiating engaging academic tasks. Sometimes she admitted to abandoning her more ambitious plans and falling back on activities that would keep students busy. Claudia frequently voiced her disappointment in what she saw as her inadequacies as a teacher, and as a teacher of literacy, to the point where she felt she 'wasn't really teaching'. She applied for and won a job at another school after two years at Sandford.

However, many teachers will not recognise the limitations of their customary practices, attributing low achievement or engagement instead to the problems of students. Despite the obvious disengagement of her students, Jody maintained that AL 'just works really well. If you teach it properly you get the outcomes', while Tracey attributed Simon's frustration to his behaviour problems rather than to the limitations of her literacy pedagogy in enabling him to communicate important life events and emotions.

When we looked for explanations from teachers that might explain the widespread adoption of common pedagogies, we encountered localised accounts of what was possible within contexts where there were high levels of poverty. These accounts were frequently underpinned by deficit views of young people and their families, which are examined further in Chapter 6. Such deficit assumptions are well documented in the literature and have been attributed to 'widespread and resilient logic[s] of practice' that restrict the likelihood of students encountering, or being supported to engage in, an intellectually challenging curriculum (Johnston & Hayes, 2008, p. 110). These logics delimit what can be achieved by students in places where deficit ways of thinking about them, their families and their communities infuse teachers' explanations of what they are capable of achieving. Indeed, one principal reflected on the longer-term consequences of 'safe teaching' as a strategy for managing the challenging behaviour and social interactions that erupt when students are asked to do certain things. He questioned whether that had 'taken over our teaching approach as opposed to challenge and higher expectations to keep the kids progressing. So it's safe not to push the limits.'

However, safe teaching was not the only explanation for the common pedagogies we observed. Also implicated were teachers' understandings of literacy and their focus on embedding literacy at the expense of other pedagogical opportunities.

Teaching literacy is a complex process. Unquestionably, the systematic teaching of phonics and sight words does contribute to building students' knowledge of 'letters and sounds'. There is no question that beginning readers and writers need to recognise and use the alphabet, sounds in words, spelling, and structural conventions and patterns. Yet these are not sufficient in themselves (Luke & Freebody, 1999). If students are to develop a rich repertoire of literate practices, their understanding and use of decoding and encoding needs to be integral to composing and reading meaningful texts from their earliest experiences in the classroom.

However, our observations of teaching during the literacy block suggest that teachers frequently understand literacy as a set of autonomous skills to be learnt, rather than as a meaning-making, communicative social practice (Heath, 1983; Street, 1985). While we observed some contextualised explicit teaching (for example, comprehension strategies during guided reading, or the structure and language features of narrative and other genres), for the most part we observed the teaching of discrete skills, such as identifying and reciting sounds and letters, repeatedly writing 'sight' words, and the provision of worksheets for students to practise aspects of grammar and punctuation. In other words, we observed that a strong emphasis on the code-breaking function of language was dominant, in contrast to prevailing media reporting, which suggests that teachers are focusing on progressive approaches to literacy. It is expected that 'letters and sounds' are to be learnt before the students begin to write and, when they do begin, their writing is subjected to careful staging in an attempt to ensure that sight words are spelt correctly, capital letters and full stops are used accurately, letters are well formed, and handwriting is legible. It seems there is little room for young writers to put their knowledge to use to produce texts that go beyond copying words from the board, or the repetition of known words from readers and sight word lists. For what purpose can and do they write, apart from demonstrating their knowledge of surface features to the teacher? As Maureen's work with Amira demonstrates, when teachers forget that writing is a social process of meaning-making that involves identity work and see it only as a matter of scribing correct letters and sounds, the potential for pleasurable, intellectual engagement and serious investment in learning can be compromised.

The stripping back of meaning through a focus on the technical aspects of literacy was also evident in Jody's AL lesson focusing on obesity. Here, the teacher had chosen a challenging text about an interesting topic. She followed the suggested moves for this pedagogy in terms of making the goal for learning clear and pulling out the meta-elements of the structure of an information report for the students to notice. However, in focusing on the genre features of the text and fluency of pronunciation of the words read orally, in particular the potentially unfamiliar vocabulary, she has ignored the content. The students go through the motions of the lesson format, gradually disengaging from the matter at hand. In foregrounding the 'literacy', the substance has all but evaporated. We cannot know what the students may or may not have learnt about information reports as a genre, or child obesity as a social and medical problem, but we did observe them physically turn off as the lesson proceeded. Once again, in focusing on delivery of what the teacher has understood as the correct literacy pedagogy, the potential for complex learning and engagement is lost. The lesson is stripped of interest and many students appeared to decide that not only was the vocabulary not for them, but the problem was not their concern. In contrast to the high-energy AL lesson we witnessed in Alicia's class, discussed in Chapter 4, the point of reading is lost in sharing the text on obesity. One becomes an instance of working through the text, in contrast to the other, in which the teacher's moves open up the text for the students to make discoveries.

It is not that Jody embarked deliberately on such an approach. However, how she has been able to interpret and enact AL at this point in her teaching shifts the focus to the visible and audible moves of the pedagogy, rather than on its rationale to assist students to deconstruct texts in order to understand how they work and how meaning is made in various genres. The 'fickleness' here is in the translation of the literacy pedagogy to an empty set of practices, distilled as routines, rather than to meaning-making practices.

When combined with assumptions about students' knowledge or concerns about their behaviour, such pedagogical approaches may become doubly ineffective. Students are learning what they are doing (Nuttall, 2007), as well as the subject content that they are being taught. Often in these classrooms, they are 'doing' activities where typically there is little challenge or depth of engagement: reciting, copying, filling-in-the-gaps, using a sight word in a sentence, and following the rules for writing recounts and other genres. Through the teacher's repeated suggestions that they were not expected to know, students in Jody's class were learning not to engage with complex texts.

These kinds of practices ensure that superficial and technical aspects of reading and writing are learnt. Writing as a practice of making-meaning, and reading as stimulating imagination, raising critical questions, and encouraging complex deep thinking, are all sidelined. While these common pedagogies can have a positive difference on some NAPLAN results, namely, reading for students in Years 3 and 5, these results are generally not sustained over time. Although the tests focus on being able to perform simple technical tasks that are similar to those being taught, when students have limited opportunities to grapple with complexity, with finding their own authorial voice, with understanding the power of language, they are destined for limited outcomes. Such practices produce a double disservice to students: the fragmented literacy pedagogy on offer ultimately doesn't help students achieve the NAPLAN results teachers might wish for, nor does it induct them into the more sophisticated academic literacies they need to become a successful student in the long term. A downward trend in results for writing for students in Years 5 and 7 is arguably symptomatic of such limitations. (See Appendix for a brief discussion of NAPLAN results in the four schools.)

## Conclusion

In this chapter we have described the common classroom pedagogies that were most prevalent during our work in four disadvantaged schools. The examples used do not represent isolated instances and were not limited by any means to the three teachers whose work is described in detail. Despite the strenuous efforts of policy-makers and school improvers to embed high-quality teaching, avowed commitments of school leaders to improved literacy outcomes, the attempt to embed effective literacy teaching through whole-school literacy agreements, and the efforts of teachers to do the right thing by their students, what we commonly observed were limited pedagogical practices that were unlikely to achieve their desired goals.

Rather than being enhanced by these improvement efforts, pedagogy appeared to be impoverished. The irony here is that teachers shared a firm conviction that their job was to teach literacy. However, literacy was defined as a set of skills – 'basics', which, while necessary, are insufficient. The pressure on literacy assessment, and the faith placed by their school leaders in particular approaches, resulted in teachers often focusing on these skills in a decontextualised way and not being 'distracted' by other opportunities to extend children's learning, confidence, participation, trust and so on. The 'literacisation' of pedagogy (Comber & Hill, 2000) results in an overemphasis on the linguistic aspects of tasks, to the detriment of wider learning goals.

Moreover, many teachers, not only those who were early in their careers, operated as though their main priorities were for students to behave, to stay on task and to avoid annoying other students. In some cases, these priorities were combined with assumptions about students' lack of knowledge and capability. The emphasis on behaviour resulted in an overemphasis on the performance of literacy routines, not on their substance, and a turning away from the students and the resources they already had. Through this combination of circumstances, more expansive, critical and creative approaches to literacy were ignored, reducing literacy teaching to standardised practices that failed to take into account students' knowledge and potential. The result was a prevalence of low-quality schooling practices, similar to that described by Haberman in the early 1990s, and again, more recently, as the 'pedagogy of poverty' (Haberman, 1991, 2010). The larger aims of embedding high-quality teaching and high-expectations curricula were lost. Although, ironically, these practices have developed largely because of a concern about wide socioeconomic attainment gaps, we share the concern expressed by Comber and Woods (2016) that: 'A diet of low-expectations curriculum leads to little learning of value, so such an approach is unlikely to accomplish fairness on any grounds' (p. 205).

In the next chapter, we explore how different children responded to the literacy curriculum on offer over time and consider how they were seen by parents and different teachers.

## References

Blackmore, J. (2013). 'A feminist critical perspective on educational leadership'. *International Journal of Leadership: Theory and Practice*, *16*(2), 139–154.

Comber, B. (1998). 'The problem of "background" in researching the student subject'. *Australian Educational Researcher*, *25*(3), 1–21.

Comber, B. (2015). 'Critical literacy and social justice'. *Journal of Adolescent and Adult Literacy*, *58*(5), 358–363.

Comber, B., & Hill, S. (2000). 'Socioeconomic disadvantage, literacy and social justice: Learning from longitudinal case study research'. *Australian Educational Researcher*, *27*(3), 79–98.

Comber, B., & Kamler, B. (2004). 'Getting out of deficit: Pedagogies of reconnection'. *Teaching Education*, *15*(3), 293–310.

Comber, B., & Kerkham, L. (2016). 'Gus: I cannot write anything'. In A. H. Dyson (ed.), *Child Cultures, Schooling and Literacy: Global perspectives on children composing their lives* (pp. 53–64). New York & London: Routledge.

Comber, B., & Nixon, H. (2011). 'Critical reading comprehension in an era of accountability'. *Australian Educational Researcher*, *38*(2), 167–179.

Comber, B., & Woods, A. (2016). 'Literacy teacher research in high poverty schools: Why it matters'. In J. Lampert & B. Burnett (eds.), *Teacher Education for High Poverty Schools* (pp. 193–210). New York: Springer.

Compton-Lilly, C. (2011). 'Literacy and schooling in one family across time'. *Research in the Teaching of English*, *45*(3), 224–251.

Cowey, W. (n.d.). 'Accelerated Literacy Teaching Sequence: Department of Education, Science and Training & Northern Territory Department of Employment, Education and Training'. Retrieved 23 February 2016 from http://www.nalp.edu.au/verve/_resources/TeachingSequenceNEW.pdf.

Custance, B., Dare, B., & Polias, J. (2011). *How Language Works: Success in literacy and learning teacher development course*. Adelaide, South Australia: Department of Education and Children's Services (DECS Publishing).

Dover, A. (2013). 'Getting "up to code": Preparing for and confronting challenges when teaching for social justice in standards-based classrooms'. *Action in Teacher Education*, *35*(89–102).

Dyson, A. H. (2013). *ReWRITING the Basics: Literacy learning in children's cultures*. New York: Teachers College Press.

Dyson, A. H. (ed.) (2016). *Child Cultures, Schooling and Literacy: Global perspectives on children composing their lives*. New York & London: Routledge.

Education Department of South Australia (1991). *South Australian Education Department Literacy Assessment in Practice: R-7 Language Arts*. Adelaide: Education Department of South Australia.

Fountas, I. C., & Pinnell, G. S. (1996). *Guided Reading: Good first teaching for all children*. Portsmouth, NH: Heinemann.

Freebody, P. (2003). 'Studying educational interactions'. In *Qualitative Research in Education: Interaction and practice*. Thousand Oaks, California: SAGE.

Freebody, P., Ludwig, C., & Gunn, S. (1995). *Everyday Literacy Practices in and out of Schools in Low Socioeconomic Urban Communities*. (2 Vols.) Report to the Commonwealth Department of Employment, Education and Training. Melbourne: Curriculum Corporation.

Genishi, C., & Dyson, A. H. (2009). *Children, Language, and Literacy: Diverse learners in diverse times*. New York: Teachers College Press.

Haberman, M. (1991). 'The pedagogy of poverty versus good teaching'. *Phi Delta Kappan*, *73*(4), 290–294.

Haberman, M. (2010). '11 consequences of failing to address the "pedagogy of poverty"'. *Phi Delta Kappan*, *92*(2), 45.

Halliday, M. (1994). *An Introduction to Functional Grammar* (2nd ed.). London: Edward Arnold.

Halliday, M., & Hasan, R. (1985). *Language, Context and Text: Aspects of language in a semiotic perspective.* Geelong: Deakin University Press.

Heath, S. B. (1983). *Ways with Words: Language, life and work in communities and classrooms.* Cambridge: Cambridge University Press.

Johnston, K., & Hayes, D. (2008). '"This is as good as it gets": Classroom lessons and learning in challenging circumstances'. *Australian Journal of Language and Literacy, 31*(2), 109–127.

Luke, A. (2005). 'Normativity and the material effects of discourse'. *Critical Discourse Studies, 2*(2), 198–201.

Luke, A., Dooley, K., & Woods, A. (2011). 'Comprehension and content: Planning literacy in low socioeconomic and culturally diverse schools'. *Australian Educational Researcher, 38*(2), 149–166.

Luke, A., & Freebody, P. (1999). 'Further notes on the Four Resources Model'. *Reading Online.* Retrieved 19 July 2016 from http://www.readingonline.org/research/lukefreebody.html.

Nuttall, G. (2007). *The Hidden Lives of Learners.* Wellington, New Zealand: NZCER Press.

Oxford University Press Staff (2008). *My Oxford Word List.* Australia and New Zealand: OUP.

Spandel, V. (2011). *Creating Young Writers: Using the six traits to enrich writing process in primary classrooms* (3rd ed.). Boston, Ma: Pearson Education Inc.

Street, B. (1985). *Literacy in Theory and Practice.* Cambridge, MA: Cambridge University Press.

Wortham, S. (2006). *Learning Identity: The joint emergence of social identification and academic learning.* New York: Cambridge University Press.

# 6

## SUPPORTING CHILDREN'S LITERACY LEARNING AT SCHOOL AND HOME

### Analysing the effects of discourse

During conversations with teachers and others in the schools in which we conducted our research, they would often interpret the local conditions for us by describing the features of the surrounding neighbourhood and the kinds of families who lived there. Their explanations were based on their encounters with parents and caregivers, and their observations as they drove to and from work, and some had visited children in their homes. In these discussions, they revealed how they were attempting to make sense of the life circumstances of families living in poverty. The explanations were generally framed by the question: Why do children from poor families generally underperform and underachieve compared to their more affluent peers?

In previous chapters, we focused on the practices of educational leaders and teachers. We described how their practices took into account the local material conditions of poverty. We described the effects of their pedagogical and leadership practices. In this chapter, we pay attention to what is said about children and their families who live in poverty. Our purpose is to illustrate the power of words and of the knowledge conveyed by these words. We draw upon Foucault's (1991) understanding of discourse. We consider the effects of power and knowledge associated with what is said about children and their families, as well as what is not said about them. These discourses produce particular kinds of knowledge about children and their families. This knowledge is most likely to arise from the well-intended efforts of educators to make sense of circumstances that are complex, beyond their control and unlike anything they may have experienced. Nevertheless, it exerts power and the effects of this power are seen in the educational opportunities that are opened up, as well as those opportunities that are closed off to young people who live in poverty.

Foucault's (1991) often-quoted definition of discourse is particularly relevant to our purpose in this chapter. He described discourse as: 'the difference between what one could say at one period (under the rules of grammar and logic) and what is actually said' (p. 63). This difference is not simply a semantic detail; discourse also shapes what can be done, the questions that can be asked and the solutions that can be considered. Foucault moves beyond representation to claim that discursive practices systematically form the objects of which they speak (Foucault, 1972, p. 38). In this chapter, we describe how what is known about young people is constituted through discourse and emerges in a space of difference and tension – between potential and possibility.

We acknowledge that by recounting and critically analysing the explanations of teachers and parents, we risk being accused of taking part in blaming and intensifying anxieties about underperforming schools, teacher quality and disengaged learners. These anxieties are reflected in a circle of blame that swirls around these places: teachers blame poor families; families living in poverty blame uncaring teachers and inflexible school processes; politicians blame poor-quality teaching; and so it goes. At the same time, we feel obligated to make available the observations and insights we gained while undertaking our research. While the explanations provided by some of the teachers in this chapter make for difficult reading, because of the demeaning way in which they depict children and their families, we claim that it is necessary to 'denaturalise' these discourses and their often taken-for-granted effects in order to improve the outcomes of schooling for young people living in poverty. Other discourses are possible and visible, albeit in much smaller supply, elsewhere in these schools, as illustrated in Chapter 4. By drawing attention to the effects of discourse, we hope to show that it is a powerful determinant of the opportunities made available to children in school.

In the final year of our research, we invited teachers in the case-study schools to share their experiences of supporting the literacy learning of up to three students. We asked them to identify children who were not performing at the same level as their peers; children who challenged them to respond differently because their standard pedagogical repertoire did not seem adequate for addressing their literacy learning needs; and children who confounded them, whose learning needs puzzled them and who challenged them to think differently about their own practice. Our invitation may have unwittingly generated some of the judgemental accounts that teachers produced as they responded to our invitation to focus on children who in some way or another were understood as a problem. Yet in an earlier study, the focus on redesigning pedagogy in the interests of children about whom they were most concerned had provided a breakthrough for many teachers (Comber & Kamler, 2004), one which we came to understand and name as 'turn-around pedagogies', and which informed our research design for the study reported here. However, it may be that the temporal and policy context of the earlier study resulted in a very different set of conditions for teachers' work and what they believed was possible for them to change. The increase in poverty, intergenerational unemployment and the increasing emphasis on measurable standards for students, for teachers and for schools, positions teachers in new grids of accountability.

For the most part, the teachers were concerned about the literacy learning of boys. In some schools, we had to ask if there were any girls they were concerned about. As Walkerdine (1990) and Epstein (1998) have observed, the literacy learning of girls does not trigger the same concerns as boys, since they tend to slip below the radar in classrooms by complying with behavioural expectations and co-opting the support of their peers to complete tasks. When they do draw the attention of their teachers, it is often due to the fact that they are not behaving 'as girls should'. One of the ways in which teachers make sense of low literacy achievement, particularly in boys, is to blame poor behaviour. Improvements in literacy are seen to rest upon improvements in behaviour. The teachers we talked with were not concerned about the quiet girls in their class. The prevailing discourse is that these girls at least have what it takes to improve their literacy – they work quietly. What they are working on, or what they are avoiding by working quietly, is generally not an issue of concern.

We provided teachers with resources that might assist them to pay close attention to the literacy learning of the children they chose as participants in our study. These resources included descriptions of *turn-around pedagogies* (Comber & Kamler, 2005) and *funds of knowledge* (Moll, Amanti, Neff & Gonzalez, 1992), which describe in detail examples of how some teachers have successfully responded to the needs of individual literacy learners. We recorded conversations with the teachers on more than one occasion. During these conversations, they traced their efforts to respond to specific literacy learning needs, evaluated their success and outlined what they planned to do next.

We interviewed some of the parents of the children the teachers identified. These parents expressed a range of concerns, some of which matched those expressed by their child's teacher. Importantly, they gave us a different insight into the problem of supporting literacy learning and the particular issues they faced as primary carers in accessing services and being included in decisions affecting their child's welfare. All the parents we talked with were actively mobilising the resources available to them to support their child's literacy learning. They provided a bigger picture of their child's life beyond school. They also provided their perspective on their child's experiences in school, including the impact of the allocation of classroom teachers, interactions with peers and changes in the curriculum related to literacy.

We talked one-on-one with some of the children and observed some of them participating in classroom activities. This provided us with a first-hand opportunity to get to know them a little and to see their perspectives on their experiences at home and school. Principals with responsibility for supporting literacy learning across their schools, providing relevant professional learning, and data tracking and management, provided overviews of what was known about these children by other adults apart from their classroom teacher.

This chapter draws upon these recorded conversations, the notes from our fieldwork – which included classroom observations – and conversations with others tasked with supporting literacy learning, such as Accelerated Literacy (AL) consultants. We also include a small number of images of students' work samples, learning spaces and literacy resources. We have selected three students to discuss in detail – Gus, Brendan and Camilla. Their experiences of literacy are mediated by a number of adults who each have varying responsibilities and commitments to them as learners. We trace the experiences of these children over two to three years. We introduce some of the adults in their lives and note how they describe their roles as teachers, school leaders and caregivers. We trace how these adults understand each other and the cumulative effects of their collective efforts that occasionally work in the interests of young people. These complex webs of relationships play out in nearby communities. All three students attended the schools in our study, located in the northern suburbs. Brendan and Camilla attended Highfield, while Gus attended Sandford, except for a period of ten weeks (one school term) when he was excluded and attended school at nearby Easton.

In previous chapters, we described a range of features of these schools and of their neighbourhoods that are likely to have impacted on the literacy learning of these children. In this chapter, we briefly mention some key relevant contextual features. In more detail, we explore the impact on the children of transitions between schools and across primary school years. We describe the efforts of their parents to be respected, listened to and included in decision-making related to their child's schooling. We compare ways of representing these children as learners when they are displayed as coloured data points on charts of performance, attendance and growth against standards; as monitored learners assigned to interventions, peer groups and teachers; and as learners assigned acronyms as a shorthand for features of their identities, diagnosed disabilities and designated behaviour issues.

## Gus: from Sandford to Easton and back again

During the time in which Gus attended Sandford, the teachers and educational leaders were managing a human resource crisis due to the principal working temporarily in a system-level position. Consequently, the leadership team was made up of people 'filling in' for those who had left, including the principal and the school counsellor. In addition, a number of teaching positions were filled by teachers on short-term contracts. Students like Gus were not on anyone's radar in terms of learning support. His learning difficulties were not serious enough to warrant extra support; only his misbehaviour drew attention.

Gus was one of six children in Heather's Year 1/2 class whose progress she would map closely and discuss in her literacy chats with Lena, the senior leader for curriculum, literacy and numeracy. With parental consent, we started to observe Gus unobtrusively in 2013, when he was in Year 2, along with several of his peers in that class. In order to get a sense of Gus's school history, we spoke with each of his teachers and with Gus himself. These accounts are provided in chronological order. Our observation and interview data were supplemented by school records and reports.

### *Preschool and Reception: Natalie's Gus*

We were introduced to Gus through the recollections of Natalie, an early-career teacher in her first contract appointment following graduation. Natalie had taught him when he attended the on-campus preschool. When Gus started school, Natalie moved to teach a Reception class and Gus was placed with her. This placement was intended to facilitate his transition to school. Natalie recalled Gus in both contexts and volunteered her perspective and she referred to the notes that she had made at that time.

> I wrote that: 'He's a task avoider. He has had significant emotional issues at preschool. He did not cope with school transition.' In fact, I think he never turned up in the end, he was so stressed out about it … I've got here that: 'He will not look at readers or sight words. He cannot find an activity when he's asked to, or pack up.' He would just literally sit there, and kids like that, you can tell there's no stimulation at home. It was almost like he had no idea … that he actually could pick something up, and by him picking it up, he's causing an effect to that toy, do you know what I mean? He doesn't follow instructions, so he was one of those students that you have to explicitly – which you have to do in Reception anyway – but, give him that extra, repeat it one more time, type instruction. I've got here that I did discuss this with his Mum and Dad.

Natalie remembered vividly that Gus often appeared stressed at preschool, particularly with respect to food.

> Well he didn't have a great attendance, and that started right from preschool, and he was very stressed, very stressed, very worried about a lot of things, and he would actually work himself up to the point where he would be dry-retching, and we'd have to send him into the toilets.

She reported that by the time he started school, he 'wouldn't eat anything except if he brought it from home pretty much'.

> Everything he did bring from home had chocolate in it, so he'd have a muesli bar with chocolate chips, he'd have a Nutella sandwich, he'd have a chocolate bar; everything that you can buy with chocolate, he would have it.

Natalie also recalled that she suspected that Gus might have been at risk at home. She had an 'over-hanging doubt' in her mind about drugs being in the house and had put in a report to the child welfare authority.

> Well you know, potentially he could be at risk if they're manufacturing drugs … I think I might have only reported once on that. His sister, she's a couple of years younger than him, I'm not sure whose class she's in, and there's also like an aunty that's quite involved in the family as well, and her son comes here, and went to school, he went to preschool with Gus … and she, like would often pick him up. Mum is very thin. I haven't seen Mum for

ages, so very thin, I don't know, it sort of went with the drug kind of persona type thing. Dad didn't see him very much but I'm pretty sure he was still on the scene somewhere.

Natalie's account of Gus's family life suggested suspected health issues. It was known that Gus's father had left the family home and had a new partner. It was reported that Gus lived with his mother, sister and at times extended family, including an uncle and grandparents. Several teachers reported him being dropped off at school and collected by his aunty or grandmother. Natalie reported that 'the aunty probably would have been in a special class when she was at school'. Despite Natalie's concerns about the family situation, she was pleasantly surprised about Gus's appearance and clothing.

> This is where like it flies in the face of some things because he was never dirty, he always had his food, and his clothes were always washed and not ripped and, you know, all that kind of stuff.

Natalie's account is her attempt to make sense of Gus's transition to school and the glimpses it provided into his family over this time. It is important to recognise that the conclusions she draws are chosen from a range of possible explanations. Gus's lack of familiarity with literate practices ('He will not look at readers or sight words'), and school routines more generally ('He doesn't follow instructions'), led Natalie to conclude that there is no stimulation at home. These are not the only conclusions that might be drawn from this observation, but there is a certain naturalness, or taken-for-grantedness, about these conclusions within the context of this school. Another explanation might be that Gus has experienced different kinds of stimulation at home (Lareau, 2011). The need to provide him with explicit instruction, 'which you have to do in Reception anyway', adds to Natalie's assessment of what Gus lacks. Natalie acknowledges that explicit instructions are routinely required for Reception children, but this does not ameliorate her already-firmly held views about why Gus is experiencing difficulty at school.

In terms of his literacy learning, Natalie's notes indicated that, by the end of Reception, six-year-old Gus could recognise only two sight words and had difficulty writing recognisable words.

> So I've got him down here as at the end of his Reception year he knew two sight words … *Look* and *a*. It was just like pre-drawing. It was just, you know, scribble. It wasn't anything. He would tell you what it was, and so then I'd write it down, but there was nothing recognisable. I don't think there was much colour in there either … he'd just pick up one colour and not think, 'Oh, I'd better change …' He wouldn't even try, he'd often just sit there with his book in front of him at the table and do nothing, and he sat next to another boy who's got very good fine motor control and is a very neat writer.

Recollecting her frustration at Gus's lack of progress, she recognised his confidence in oral language, but that he 'just had no confidence to use it as much as he could' when it came to writing.

Natalie explained that she had tried to discuss various issues with Gus's family, but that 'they'd just clam up straight away'. Her files and her memories imply that Gus's school problems may result from his family life – drugs, inappropriate food, lack of attendance, lack of mothering, are all mentioned as possible causes for Gus's lack of effort, lack of self-regulation and inability to read and write after two years of early education.

Noticeably absent from Natalie's account is a description of how she is attempting to help Gus to overcome the difficulties he is experiencing at school. The potential of her pedagogical practices to support Gus are not mentioned. It seems that his best chance at improvement is sitting 'next to another boy who's got very good fine motor control and is a very neat writer'. Denaturalising these kinds of explanatory discourses requires noticing what is not said, as well as what is said. How might Natalie's pedagogies and the organisational processes of schooling be brought into these explanations?

### Years 1 and 2: Heather's Gus

When we first encountered Gus, he was in his second year in Heather's class. Gus was one student in a class where several were not yet making the progress in reading and writing that Heather wished. She created opportunities for one-on-one teaching from the very start of the day when students arrived with their reading books, and sometimes shared with a parent before they left the classroom. But the students could be difficult to settle and sometimes set out to disturb others and avoid a learning task altogether.

Heather had been recruited to the school because she had had six years' experience in teaching English literacy to students whose first language was not English. The principal had recommended that she participate in our study, because she had achieved some impressive results in terms of students' reading performance. She had nominated Gus as a potential case-study child because she was concerned about his reading and handwriting. But she was also concerned about Gus's social relationships and his difficulties in making friends amongst peers.

Her knowledge of Gus and his family complemented what her colleague Natalie had reported. However, she was more aware of the effects of the marriage break-up on Gus and what had been a close relationship with his father, especially with the arrival of a new baby in his father's life. Although Heather rarely saw Gus's mother, she noticed the close relationship between them and commented that 'because he's Mum's eldest and they were close I think, and Mum wants to be a friend rather than a parent'. Heather described Gus's Mum as 'having anxiety', saying that she was 'cleaning, constantly cleaning', and although she was quite attractive and seemed healthy enough, she was 'worryingly thin' and 'might have mental health issues'. Nevertheless, Heather remarked that 'Mum was quite with it' and the family 'were all pretty vibrant'.

Heather saw Gus as 'quite an emotional child' who lived in a complex multi-generational household, with 'too many people telling him what to do' and an uncle who played video games and watched movies 'that aren't at the right rating' for Gus. Heather's reading of Gus's family, and in particular his mother, is less negative than Natalie's. She recognises in more compassionate terms the impact of family breakdown and the closeness of the relationship between Gus and his mother, but she considers it inappropriate, more like a friend than a parent.

In contrast to Natalie, Heather was more confident that she could help Gus and that she was responsible for doing so. She recognised that the physical work of handwriting was making writing difficult for him and had requested an SSO[1] to support him to develop a firm pencil grip and improve his letter formation. She noted in his mid-year report that his handwriting was 'more legible' and 'appears easier' for him. She also set a goal for him:

> Next, it would be great to see you challenge yourself by beginning to write words independently using sounds correspondence. You are able to communicate your ideas in recount and narrative writing by drawing pictures that are increasing in detail, which are now also including some letters. Gus, you would benefit from more opportunities to trace and copy pictures to enhance your fine motor skills. (Year 1, mid-year report)

By the end of Year 1, Gus had learnt 83 sight words and had reached instructional Level 5[2] in reading. (The regional benchmark for Year 1 is Level 10.) Gus could instantly recognise 121 sight words by mid-year, although he sometimes forgot these and resorted to 'sounding out and blending', as Heather described in his mid-year report. However, handwriting was still an issue for Gus, who continued to receive extra support, and writing of any kind was still a challenge.

In his Year 2 end-of-year report, Heather summarised his achievements in reading, acknowledging that he had achieved Level 12 by the end of the year (the regional benchmark for Year 2 is Level 26) and had made good progress by learning 223 sight words (404 words in total to learn). She noted that when:

> [you] read aloud in guided reading and participate in class shared reading experiences, you confidently make connections to your life, school, to other books which shows engagement with the text and a higher level of thinking. (Year 2, end-of-year report)

Gus, however, remained less confident with writing.

> In spelling, you have improved your score in the Westwood Spelling test, and your results showed that you have a spelling age of 6 years and 6 months, which is currently below your birth age. You have developed some necessary skills in spelling, specifically being able to section words according to

the sounds that you can hear. You have learnt to spell three- and four-letter words based on sound recognition. Gus, you have made positive progress in literacy this year. You are however still working below your year level in literacy, including reading, spelling and writing. (Year 2, end-of-year report)

While Heather's comments about Gus and his achievements may seem strange to some readers, when students' learning is understood in terms of their attainment of targets, benchmarks, spelling and reading ages, Heather's report can be read as an explicit account of what Gus did achieve and had not yet achieved. That she addresses him directly suggests that Gus is as embroiled as she is in the discourses of accountability and performance that so strongly shape literacy pedagogy and assessment.

While Heather noted that Gus had achieved a minimum of what was expected at his year level, according to her assessment he had made a 'good' effort with reading and with listening and speaking, but he had given only 'partial' effort to writing.

Despite Heather's literacy programme, which provided a supportive mix of shared, modelled, guided and independent reading and writing lessons, Gus struggled with learning to read and write. In addition, records of being 'sent to the office', internal suspensions in a buddy class and eventual exclusions also told of a struggle with social relationships with peers and with teachers. Typically, Heather cautioned Gus over misdemeanours such as not following instructions or 'being persistent at those niggly, those low-level behaviours' because she felt it was important that he stay in the learning environment and she wanted to maintain the usually positive relationship she had with him. However, in the face of more violent behaviours, running away from class and mimicking the teacher, it was determined that there was little option but to remove Gus temporarily from the classroom. Throughout the two years he spent in Heather's class, Gus was removed from class almost on a weekly basis, sometimes more often, mostly for disrupting the class in some way and occasionally for violent behaviour.

Heather's observations of Gus in the playground were consistent with what she observed in the classroom.

> He just walks around like he's looking for friends … He doesn't really have very good social skills, and he tends to follow children … and will try and fit in, but it doesn't always work because of the behaviour … if a group leaves him out then he will look to see what he can do to get in, even aggravate them, and I noticed him taking someone's shoes, that's something that I've seen from Gus before, niggly things. He knows how to upset other children, and then the wrong child can get aggressive, so then he'll just be aggressive back.

By the end of Year 2, Gus had clearly made some progress as a reader but was 'still vulnerable', both as a writer and in finding a place in the social world of the classroom.

## *Year 3: another start*

Gus's Year 3 teacher, Lara, was new to the school, but had taught in the northern area for 17 years. She was passionate about children's literature, film and popular culture and drew on them to develop a literacy programme that stretched the students' learning, their imaginations, and their reading and writing. While she described herself as 'having a lot of structure in the room', she also responded enthusiastically to students' interests in 'what happened on the weekend, or something they heard on the news' that could be the focus of 'fantastic discussions'.

We had decided not to observe Gus during Term 1, while Lara established herself in the classroom. During that time, she worked at 'all the relationship stuff' and introduced the students to problem-solving resources, to meditation and to strategies from positive psychology that could contribute to a positive classroom environment. When we came to the school to observe Gus in Term 2, he was not there (Comber & Kerkham, 2016).

His behaviour management record indicated an escalation in frequency and intensity of verbal and physical outbursts that resulted in a number of 'contact parent' and 'take home' consequences. By the end of Term 1, his refusal to follow the school's behaviour code and persistent disruptive in-class behaviours had led to a ten-week exclusion and he was placed in another school for Term 2.

## *Gus: willing to please and wanting to try*

By chance, we learned that Sandford Primary had requested that Gus be placed at Easton, the nearest alternative primary school. Teacher Andrea agreed to have him placed in her Year 3 class. At a meeting with Gus and his mother, the principal and the school counsellor, Gus's teacher Andrea stated her 'quite high expectations' and explained that the class 'does not tolerate or put up with inappropriate behaviour'. She felt that she had 'a settled, structured, well-organised class environment that would help him' and she made it very clear that 'the students in [her] class are very mature and they'll just say it'.

As we had observed, when Andrea had to speak to a student about their behaviour, she focused on the issue that was causing a problem to make explicit why she was speaking to them. For example:

> I explain: 'This is the behaviour, this is why I'm talking to you about your behaviour. What are we going to do differently?' So I'm really thorough … I mean some days you do get snappy on the off chance but, with behaviour, I feel that it's important that I explain why I'm having to talk to them: 'I'm not picking on you. This is what's brought my attention to you, because you've been out of your seat,' or, 'You're not doing your work, so that's why I'm talking to you.' So not making him feel victimised, I guess, probably really benefited him.

Although Gus settled into the routines in his new class, within the first couple of weeks, Andrea noticed that he didn't make any friends. If she was on yard duty, he would walk and talk with her, just as he had 'hovered around' Heather. Andrea commented on Gus's lack of 'emotional resilience' and unwillingness to persist with tasks that challenged him, but when he was angry or upset over something he could not do, she 'put things in perspective'. For instance, he could in fact do something about his cutting skills:

> People having nowhere to live and things like that, that's something to get upset and angry about, whereas: 'Yes, you're having trouble cutting, but take some scissors home, here's some sheets of paper, practise cutting for homework.' And I told him that, and I think Mum did that with him, and eventually that emotional resilience got better.

Andrea described Gus as 'willing to please and wanting to try'. Apart from a couple of minor misdemeanours – such as sitting in a corner and not wanting to move when Andrea was 'pretty abrupt with him' and asked him to 'stand up and let's talk about it' – Gus neither disrupted the class nor engaged in inappropriate yard behaviour during the ten-week placement. For Andrea, what stood out was Gus's 'lack of self-esteem and not trying because he was worried about failing, about failure'. Nevertheless, Andrea felt that he 'thrived' and she recalled 'a few times where [Mum] had tears of happiness from some of the things that he was doing in class'.

Towards the end of the ten weeks, Andrea felt that Gus's mother wasn't entirely comfortable about him going back to Sandford, because he had been 'so success-ful' at Easton, and that Gus himself was 'a bit hesitant [because] coming here I got the impression he almost was able to start fresh'. Placing Gus in a class with students who Andrea described as 'academically minded' and 'focused on learning tasks' provided different expectations and opportunities for literacy learning for Gus, who could 'see everyone doing really well around him'. He had responded to the new school and classroom environment in positive ways, as had his mother. The concerns that Gus and his mother had about returning to Sandford proved to be justified, as outlined below.

### Back to Sandford: the new Gus

When Gus returned to Lara's class at Sandford, she reported that: 'We really looked at it as a clean slate: "This is the new Gus, a new start for you." And I think he really took that on board.' The 'new' Gus was more engaged and willing to 'have a go'.

> [H]e's putting up his hand, bless his little heart. It's nearly always wrong, bless him, and then he says: 'It doesn't matter if we get things wrong in this room.' I said: 'That's exactly right,' because that's something that's really important in my room, and it's really lovely, and the kids are fantastic, no one has ever commented, so that's been a real positive for him, the fact that he's just will-ing to give it a shot. That's significant for him.

Across four interviews, Lara made a point of noticing Gus's attitude to learning and his apparent internalisation of 'it doesn't matter if we get things wrong'. She mentioned giving attention to Gus and his 'talents', in one case saying to the class: 'We love how Gus helps people because he's such a kind person.' When a teacher turns to such descriptions, the student is recognised only in relation to his kindness to others, the implication being that if a child is not succeeding academically then a positive attitude will compensate. Gus's struggle to succeed remains problematic for him and his teacher in this context, especially since he had not yet consolidated his emergent reading and writing skills.

Lara's approach to reading and writing, as is common across Year 3 classrooms in most schools, required the students to be both more independent than they had been in Year 2 and more analytic in their reading (and viewing). We had observed in Heather's class that Gus was quite animated during shared and guided reading sessions and capable of verbalising connections he was making with his reading and with books being read by the teacher. Lara liked to 'really delve into text and really dissect it'. With a focus on Roald Dahl, she could include watching the movies based on his novels and critically analyse both the viewing and the text. She noted that: 'We draw comparisons – how is it different, what's different, why do you think they did this? – And we look at the bias of the author ... I really like pulling apart text, and to get them to really look at it deeply, and look at it from different perspectives, and I think that's facilitated a lot of their comprehension.'

She encouraged the students to develop reading strategies such as predicting, 'making connections about text-to-text, text-to-self and text-to-world', and noticing 'sophisticated' vocabulary. Words such as 'procrastination' and 'serendipity' were appropriated by the students and became part of the classroom discourse. Gus's return to this classroom context, and the hope for a 'new start' with a teacher who regarded him as lacking 'the intellectual capacity to delve into a text at such a deep level', proved to be challenging, especially when it came to writing.

Lara gave students regular time for 'silent writing'. She would turn on the timer and the students were expected to write as much as they could. Sometimes she gave them a topic related to themes they had been discussing in class or from their shared reading. Sometimes they could choose. If they got stuck, they could write that they were stuck, but they had to write. However, they were not allowed to speak to each other. Once writing was underway, Lara often busied herself with other tasks. After the students had been writing for some time, she would walk around the class, checking how much they had written. Sometimes she let the writing session go for 15 minutes or so if the class was quiet and writing. Gus was often very uncomfortable during these times. He took time finding his book and pencil, sharpening it, asking to go to the toilet and watching what others were doing. If a researcher was nearby, he sought our help. Sometimes we whispered spellings or wrote a word or two to show him how. This was difficult, as Lara preferred a totally silent classroom during this activity. During our observations, Gus was at a table with two or three girls, one of whom also had difficulties with writing, one who was independent and capable, and one who was often absent.

Gus may have initially 'taken on board' the notion that he had a 'new start', but within two weeks, he was being removed from the classroom for a range of behaviours. These included unsafe and antisocial behaviour, being off-task, screaming, being aggressive and threatening to bash a student. Lara explained that he was 'reverting to the same behaviours that [she] saw at the beginning of the year; defiant, silly, attention-seeking behaviours; some aggression in the yard'. Like Andrea, Lara felt that Gus lacked confidence and self-esteem and that 'if he [couldn't] succeed, even at a low level, he'd rather not try'. She was puzzled by his behaviour, but 'hoping it's just he's tired and nothing to be concerned about', because he had been 'great' and the class had been supportive of him. She thought that:

> It's his own inner demons sometimes. I mean we don't know what negative concept he's getting at home. Maybe Mum has no confidence, perhaps, because Mum's, you know, we don't know, and then maybe that's modelled behaviour, that maybe if family members are insecure, and they hear their parents doubting themselves, well, you know, your environment is very significant in your life. ... I mean we're not privy to that information, we can only make assumptions.

This somewhat common-sense psychological approach to Gus, as Lara admits, is based on assumptions. She does not see it as part of her remit to make connections with Gus's family in order to find out more. In the process, she implies an explanation for his lack of achievement at school as caused by 'his own inner demons', as a result of family modelling of 'no confidence'. The assumed insecurity and self-doubt are slated back to Gus's home life. In this reflection, although Lara acknowledges that 'your environment is very significant in your life', no consideration is given to the possible impact on Gus of the environment of school. It is Gus who must bear the responsibility for change. There is no suggestion that Lara might need to change her pedagogical practices to better accommodate Gus, and that no acknowledgement that being excluded from school for a term, the lack of friendships in his class, and his struggle to understand what it means to be a writer, may play any role.

In Gus's Term 4 report for Year 3, Lara wrote:

> It has been pleasing to note that Gus's reading level has continued to progress and he is currently reading at Level 11. Gus has found it challenging to create imaginative texts based on characters, settings and events. He has also experienced difficulty in creating texts and adapting language features when they involve characterisation, rhyme, mood, sound effects and dialogue. Gus is able to draw connections between personal experiences and text and enthusiastically shares his responses with others. His ability to comprehend text has continued to progress with an intensive level of support. With encouragement he is able to identify some inferential aspects of text. He is beginning to write procedures and requires support when elaborating his writing.

Gus has continued to experience difficulty with writing conventions. He continues to struggle to recognise high-frequency sight words and can currently identify 215.

Although this report produces a familiar account of Gus as a (non)writer, it also raises some vexing questions about records of Gus's development as a reader and writer. For instance, in his end-of-year report for Year 2, Heather noted that he knew 223 sight words (having learned 150 since mid-year), yet Lara's report suggests that he could identify 215. According to Lara, he was reading at Level 11, but Heather had recorded him reading at Level 12 the previous year. The point here is not to find fault with Gus's teachers, but to ask how it has happened that the data produced for a child who struggles with literacy can give very different information about his achievements from one year to the next. This is especially concerning given a comment that Gus made in an interview, when he stated that Lara thought he was in Year 2.

## *What have we learned?*

For some students, the transition into a more academically demanding Year 3 makes more obvious what they cannot yet do independently. If resources (such as an SSO) are not available to support a student who needs one-on-one support, even in decoding and letter formation, it is extremely difficult for them to make the progress their teacher might wish. By Year 3, few opportunities for extra help were offered to support Gus. He resisted the positioning offered by Lara as 'being kind'. Instead, he sought to become an accepted member of his peer group, sometimes trying to be funny or dramatic to attract the attention of fellow male students in particular. However, as he was seated far from the male students, with whom he had interacted in Heather's classroom, he remained quite isolated.

On numerous occasions his desire to receive positive attention from his classmates was observed. For example, around Halloween, he proudly wore his Dracula cape into class in the morning. He flicked and swirled it and a few students asked who he was. Other students popped Dracula teeth into their mouths as Gus moved around the room before Lara brought the class to the mat for morning routines. On another occasion a number of male students were told to write their names on the board for various minor misdemeanours during the morning. Each boy went to the whiteboard and wrote their name so small that it could barely be seen, rubbing it out and rewriting smaller and smaller. During that whole time, Gus had been attentive and was not one of the offenders. Later in the class, however, Lara noticed him do something and told Gus to add his name to the whiteboard list. Later they would lose points or stay in during a break, whatever Lara thought an appropriate punishment. Grinning widely, Gus approached the white board and chose a red pen (unlike the other boys, who had written in black). He wrote his name in huge letters across the whiteboard for all to see and returned, still grinning, to the mat.

In these instances, Gus was prepared to risk teacher displeasure to get a response from his peers. Unfortunately, no one was watching. As Nuttall (2007) has noted, if children have to choose between their affiliations with peers and pleasing the teacher, they will always choose peers. The double misfortune for Gus, however, was that neither his peers nor his teacher were paying attention.

In Lara's view, for students like Gus, making change for the best ultimately remained the child's responsibility.

> If they're just going to dwell on all the negative aspects, a lot of these poor children have got lots of challenges at home and in their lives, and I mean it's on them, they have the tools to dig themselves out of that situation in the future, and make their lives better … You know, we can't do it for them, as much as we'd love to we can't, so it's a matter of, you know, their outlook. And for one of my girls who's very negative, I've got her a Positive Journal, so she's only allowed to write positives in it, and even for something simple I say: 'That's OK, if that's your positive for the day, great, write it down', and I've noticed she's had more of a happy demeanour.

Lara theorises that it is the student's outlook that is fundamental to 'digging' themselves 'out of that situation in the future'. The 'challenges' of being poor are seen as subject to change by the individual. Self-improvement through one's own efforts is a core element of discourses related to social mobility and resilience. It is also an important component of psychological discourses related to mindset and motivation. These discourses have been criticised for blaming the poor for remaining poor and for suggesting that a way out of poverty is available to all individuals, if they choose to do so. According to these discourses, all that is required is for Gus and children like him to think more positively to 'make their lives better'.

## Brendan's experiences at Highfield

Each year, 30 to 35% of the children at Highfield moved out of the school and were replaced by about the same number enrolling in the school. This rate of turnover placed a drain on available resources, because teachers, school leaders and support staff were required to get to know and assess the needs of about a third of all enrolments each year. Like Brendan, the student described in this section, many of these incoming children required additional support; at the very least, their families were seeking a different schooling experience for their children. There were numerous other reasons why children with high support needs were likely to be well represented in the transitioning student population. For example, many families were housed nearby in temporary accommodation due to domestic violence, or because they had recently arrived in Australia, or as a result of homelessness. Other families were dependent on rental accommodation and experienced insecure housing tenure.

Brendan moved to Highfield from a nearby school because his father, Jeff, was unhappy with how his son was progressing. We were told that Brendan had experienced trauma at the hands of caregivers and that his school file was 'fat' with reports from a range of professionals. At an early age, Brendan's father Jeff was granted custody of him and he was placed under the care of a child psychiatrist. His Year 6 teacher, Diane, identified him as 'quite a complex student'. Diane was under the impression that Brendan was 'autistic'. She observed: 'When he talks with me it sounds like he's shouting or he's upset.' Diane reasoned that it was because he was rushing and he didn't want to disappoint her. Despite some behavioural difficulties, Diane observed, 'he's actually a really good boy, and he tries hard'. In her second interview, Diane hinted at her affection for Brendan: 'He's actually is a bit cheeky, but he's quite funny when he does it.'

We suspect that Diane's description of Brendan was tailored to match her perception of our sensibilities, perhaps out of respect for Brendan. Other sources were less measured and described Brendan's behaviour as at times 'bizarre'. His child psychiatrist described him as 'an extremely manipulative child'. We were also told that he would bang his head on desks, pretend to self-harm by biting himself – but not so hard as to do damage – threaten to take his own life, pretend to be experiencing wheezing and so on. We were also told that Brendan was asthmatic, and that he was often hospitalised for this condition.

In these settings, children are known by what is said about them. These discourses establish their reputations, which are often attributed to a range of pathologies and are sometimes viewed as a characteristic shared by their siblings or passed down from their parents – a family trait. Adults share information drawn from a range of sources. The reliability of these sources, or the evidence upon which information is based, generally goes unremarked and unquestioned. In contrast to what was 'known' about Brendan at school, Jeff had developed a different way of understanding his son's behaviour. He acknowledged that his son's behaviour had often concerned and puzzled him. For example, Jeff stated that Brendan had attention deficit hyperactivity disorder (ADHD), but he believed the reason that his son disliked school was because he had been bullied. He did not feel confident that Brendan's teachers would 'sort that out'. Jeff recalled how stressed he was when Brendan 'came home and said he wanted to kill himself, hang himself' because he was being bullied by a boy wanting money from him. Once the perpetrator moved to another school, Brendan settled down. Jeff said: 'He's a very sensitive child, but has his bad days, nearly every day.'

Jeff, a single parent, expressed many concerns for his son and these were refracted through his own experiences of schooling. He told us that he did not finish school and started work when he was 14. In his words: 'I never got an education, and then I got drafted into the army.' He described how he had to 'keep pushing' Brendan for an education and how he supported his son's learning at home – encouraging him to play games on his computer that helped him to read and learn in fun ways. Jeff's ambition for Brendan was 'to actually be able to get a job and work in amongst people'.

When we first met Diane, she had been at the school for four years. It was her first appointment as a teacher. She started as the Aboriginal education teacher, but did not identify as an Indigenous person. Brendan was in her composite Year 6/7 class.

She was a confident teacher; her classroom was well organised and she provided her students with explicit guidelines about how they were to behave and reinforced these expectations regularly, sometimes with just a look. The deputy with responsibility for student welfare described how Brendan was 'making progress' in Diane's class, because she 'didn't take any nonsense from him'.

Diane felt that Brendan 'put a lot of behaviour on'. However, the more she got to know him, the more she understood him. She explained how she was quite direct with him, occasionally telling him: 'Stop the attention-seeking behaviour.' Diane understood Brendan's difficulties with literacy learning as being the direct result of his behaviour. In Diane's view, improving Brendan's achievement in literacy was dependent upon his behaviour improving. In our conversations, there was no hint of a suggestion that the reverse might be worth considering – that Brendan's behaviour might improve if his literacy achievement improved.

Diane also noted that at times, Brendan 'will withdraw himself'. An example was when he did not want to visit the high school, which was part of a transition plan. Diane said: 'If that was going to cause too much of an issue for him, I didn't want him to lose sleep about it.' She noted that Brendan 'responds to change very badly' and sometimes gets frustrated. However, 'he doesn't actually get violent towards people, which is really good'. According to Diane, Brendan is 'not silly, he's actually quite intelligent'; however, because 'he's learnt a lot of behaviour to avoid doing work', she considered that 'his academic level is quite low'. The potential of Brendan's intelligence is viewed as inaccessible, almost irrelevant, because of his learned behaviours. What might it take for Brendan to learn other kinds of strategies – the sort that might contribute to his success at school?

When we first encountered Brendan, he was receiving additional support from an SSO because he was diagnosed as having a disability due to difficulties with his speech and language. Jeff valued the hour-and-a-half of one-on-one support that his son received each week. He believed that it helped him to gain confidence and to improve his reading and writing in an enjoyable way. However, Brendan's SSO support was discontinued. Diane explained that compared to other students in the school, Brendan was unlikely to be a priority for extra assistance in the future. Jeff viewed this as a loss: 'he was picking up really good, and then what happened here put him right back; put him back; right back, so he's going to have to build his confidence up again.'

The withdrawal of this resource, which Brendan's father at least considered to be having benefits, meant that Brendan had to rely upon the sole support of his classroom teacher to improve his literacy. Brendan's diagnosed disability did not warrant attention in an environment in which resources were rationed. At the start of each term, the school leaders met with departmental personnel who worked across schools in the area. They included a guidance officer, a disabilities coordinator, a speech pathologist and a behaviour support person. Together, they would consider teacher reports and school-level data to identify students for assessment by health professionals. The assessment process could take from two weeks to six months, depending on the type of problem. Once diagnosed, this team would allocate support for individual in-class support from SSOs for between five and 25 hours per week.

The adults in Brendan's life attributed his difficulties with literacy, and with learning more generally, to a range of causes – including having experienced trauma as an infant, suffering from autism, asthma, ADHD and a disability associated with a speech impairment. Brendan seemed to experience multiple and complex difficulties, but it was hard to assess the veracity of these problems and their likely impact on his learning. Diane acknowledged that her evidence for Brendan's perceived problem with learning was mostly 'anecdotal'.

The principal with responsibility for tracking and monitoring students provided an overview of his achievement levels. According to National Assessment Program – Literacy and Numeracy (NAPLAN) results, his reading proficiency was Band 5, below the target of Band 6 or 7. He scored 27 on his running record, indicating that he was not an independent reader. Indeed, he was below the target levels for his year level on all indicators, such as progressive achievement tests in maths, known as PAT-Maths (ACER, 2013). His score on this scale was 103.5, when the target level for his age was 125. The school was not able to estimate if Brendan's achievement levels had grown because he left the school before end-of-year data could be collected.

Jeff was keen to understand how his son was progressing, but this excerpt from our interview illustrates how difficult it was for him to understand the meaning of some achievement scales:

| | |
|---|---|
| *Researcher:* | So, do you know what reading level you're at, Brendan? |
| *Brendan:* | Thirty. |
| *Researcher:* | Thirty? |
| *Jeff:* | No, you're not. |
| *Researcher:* | Twenty-six? |
| *Brendan:* | Level 27. |
| *Researcher:* | Twenty-seven? |
| *Brendan:* | I am. |
| *Jeff:* | How do you know you're Level 27? |
| *Brendan:* | Because I saw it. |
| *Jeff:* | But what's Level 27 – good reading, really good reading? |
| *Brendan:* | No, I guess at Level 7, it's hard to read them. |
| *Jeff:* | At Level 7? Well, 27 is higher than 7. |
| *Brendan:* | No, and I read the whole book. |
| *Jeff:* | Yeah, well, what are you at? Do I have to ask Mr Chris [Brendan's current teacher], do I? Are you 3, 2, 4, 5, 6? |
| *Brendan:* | Seven. |
| *Jeff:* | You can't be at 27, you can't be at 27. |
| *Researcher:* | It depends what they use to … |
| *Jeff:* | Evaluate it? |

As previously noted, a factor that contributed to Jeff moving his son to Highfield was that he was unhappy with the reports he received on Brendan's learning from his previous school. He observed that the reports at Highfield were better, but still 'not good'. He stated that Brendan 'needs a lot of learning' in maths, reading, writing, spelling and pronouncing words properly, but he found the available means of communicating with the teacher unsatisfactory: 'You have the talks and you go: "Oh yeah, here we go, more bullshit," you know. That's how the parents are looking at it: "Oh, it's more bullshit," you know what I mean? Jeff wanted information about his son that he could understand. … all this new-fangled stuff I don't know crap about that, you know, they say: "Oh, he's …" What? What's that mean, what's that mean?'

Jeff wanted information about his son from the school that was accurate and in a form he could understand. In contrast, information was shared with us about the children's lives outside school. We were unable to determine the provenance of this information, or whether it accurately portrayed the lives of young people, their families and their communities, but it did indicate what the adults who talked to us believed, and what they relied upon to make choices about children's needs and future possibilities. Importantly, the flow of information in both directions passed through the 'school gate'. In other words, what parents and caregivers found out about their child's progress, as well as what educators found out about the life circumstances of families, was controlled by teachers and others in the school.

According to Diane, Brendan's father was 'quite illiterate'. She was concerned that he did not respond appropriately to Brendan's behaviour – she recalled an incident where Brendan 'got a little bit upset at Performing Arts, and actually threw a chair across the room', after which she had an interview with his dad. Diane believed that Jeff made excuses for his son's behaviour. Diane was also concerned that Brendan's diet was 'very unhealthy' and included 'food full of preservatives and additives'. She stated: 'He goes to sleep late.' This contributed to what Diane described as one of her 'biggest challenges', his moods and his behaviour, which 'are influenced so much by his food, his sleeping'. Diane was concerned that Brendan 'watches a lot of random YouTube clips, plays games until late at night'. She observed that Brendan 'actually looks quite unhealthy'. Part of this was his asthma, and Diane thought 'his dad smoking in the house' probably didn't help, as it 'doesn't give him time to actually recoup'.

Diane described how she spoke carefully to Brendan, but was 'still very direct with him'. She also tried 'to just have a bit of small talk with him' so that he would think '*Oh, she's actually interested in what I do*'. According to Diane, he 'thrives on encouragement, he loves being encouraged'.

Diane set up a system that enabled him to choose when to take a short break from class. Diane said that 'he is choosing that quite carefully'. She allowed him 'up to about three a day, if he needs them'. Diane had worked out that it was a better system if Brendan got to choose when to take his breaks, as opposed to her setting them for him.

The concept of choice was an important feature of relationships between teachers and students, and also between peers in the school. A noticeboard in Diane's class-room displayed behaviours categorised as 'above the line' or 'A choices', including: stay on task, smile, take pride in your work, be mature, use appropriate language, control your anger, respect the teachers and use appropriate body language. The board also contained 'below the line' or 'B choices', including: swinging on your chair, yelling across the room, swearing, fighting over a small issue, distracting others, back-chatting, giving up and refusing to do work. This way of understanding behaviour is a commonly used tool in business, human resource management, leadership, life coaching and other approaches to supporting individuals in competitive environments to make choices that are likely to advantage them. In Diane's class, it provided a quick reference for categorising the kinds of behaviour that were acceptable and those that were unacceptable. Behaviour was thus viewed as a matter of choice, something that could be controlled by each individual.

Diane explained that she and Brendan were working towards goals that they set together. Diane explained her expectations 'to Brendan as well as Dad, so they know that we're on the same page'. This was 'working well', because Diane could 'draw on it' and 'celebrate the small things'. Diane had 'high expectations of him'; however, she also 'tries to talk to him about what's going to work for him', saying that 'at that age especially … [students] know what is going to work for them'.

In our second interview, Diane noted that she had 'kept going on about him not doing enough work' in the first interview, but that this was possibly because she 'had to get to know him and his learning style a little bit better'. Also in the second interview, Diane commented that Brendan's handwriting and sentence structure had both improved. More than this, though, 'having him actually functioning as part of our class, sitting with the group, not screaming and shouting, actually following my instructions' is a 'huge success'.

When Diane started at the school, 'as the Aboriginal education teacher', she did 'lots of home visits'. She said, 'I'd always go with someone else from the school … and that's I suppose what opened my eyes up a lot to the community, just driving through the streets and noticing what actually happens there, when you're paying attention.' Since becoming a classroom teacher, she had continued to conduct home visits with the counsellor, though this had been mostly to do with attendance. She and the counsellor thought it was their 'responsibility to try and sight the child, to make sure that they're safe'.

Diane felt that this had given her a greater awareness of her students – for example, 'just making an assumption that a family has a dining table and a couch, just very basic things, that isn't possibly the case'. Diane stated that home visits helped her to 'understand why our children behave in certain ways sometimes', for instance, 'understanding the way some kids might come to school tired' and not allowing this to make you 'irritated'; or if they're late, accepting that 'they're just late, they've slept in, their home life is dysfunctional', rather than reprimanding them. Diane noted 'the fact that the child has walked through the door' is in itself worth 'celebrating'.

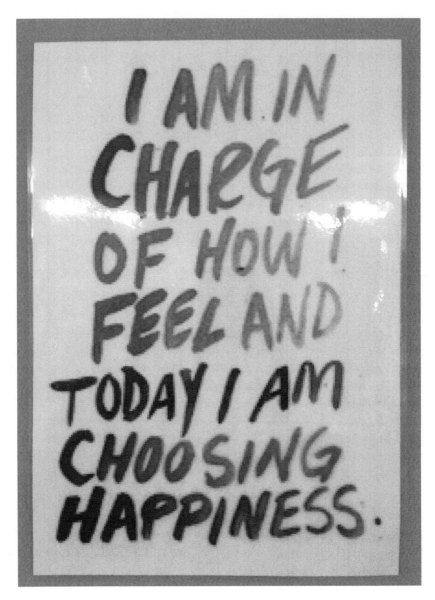

**FIGURE 6.1** 'I am in charge.'

During our final visit to the school, we were informed that Brendan had left before he completed Year 7. He did not go to high school. Instead, his father chose to enrol him in the Open Access College, which provides a blended approach of online, virtual classroom lessons in small groups, including face-to-face opportunities, and tailored support materials. Brendan's teachers advised against this option, because they were concerned that he would have less access to services and to his peers. Our description of Brendan ends in a similar place to where it began, with his father making a choice that he believed was in his son's interest. Despite the disapproval of Brendan's teachers, Jeff opted to educate him at home. For the time being, the school gate became something neither of them needed to negotiate.

## Camilla's experiences at Highfield as a learner for whom English was an additional language

As noted previously, students for whom English was an additional language or dialect (EALD) were not large in number in the schools in our research. Like Brendan, Camilla attended Highfield. When we first encountered her, she was in Year 1. Her teacher, Joanne, selected her as a participant in our study. Joanne was concerned, because Camilla was not moving at the 'same pace as other kids' in her literacy, but was 'so clever' at maths and 'really fascinated by numbers'. Joanne described Camilla as 'very much a girlie girl, so she loves her dolls and things like that' and as 'very visual and draws detailed pictures'. She liked to play 'electronic games' and was 'very creative, very artistic'. Joanne described her as 'an amazing little thinker'.

Joanne was puzzled, because she believed 'there's a smart little brain that kicks in there, but for some reason the literacy, it's just not clicking the same'. Joanne said that when she started working with Camilla, 'there were about five or six sounds that she knew' and that now she was recognising about 95% of her sounds.

Joanne assessed Camilla's reading according to her performance on running records. She looked for the strategies Camilla was using to make meaning of individual words and texts as a whole. When we first talked with Joanne, she was concerned that Camilla was only achieving Level 3 in running records, whereas she was aiming for Level 20. By the second interview, Camilla was 'nearly Level 7' and by the third, she was 'almost Level 9'. On her record, Joanne wrote such comments as: 'A lot of guessing, not looking at letters or sounding out.' Joanne also used the 'Monster Spelling Test' (Gentry, 2007) and noted that Camilla was 'moving much closer to being a phonetic speller'. Camilla took part in a MultiLit programme (Wheldall, 2006), in which she received 'one hour each day of intense reading, handwriting and spelling intervention'.

Camilla's first language was Spanish, which Joanne reasoned was why Camilla's difficulties with literacy related to 'grammatically how a sentence is structured and sounded out'. According to Joanne, her family did not speak English at home: 'I think they do a bit, but it's mostly their language at home.' Joanne also noted that they lived quite a distance from the school. Camilla's two older brothers were also 'struggling' with their literacy. There was also 'one little one at home, about two or three years old'. 'Dad works' in 'something sort of manual', but 'Mum doesn't work' and Joanne thought that 'Nanna, their grandma on the mum's side, has a lot to do with the family.'

Each time we met with Joanne, she expressed how puzzled she was that Camilla was making only slow progress in her literacy, given her cleverness in other areas of the curriculum. She did not seem to recognise the likely impact of Camilla's Spanish heritage on her literacy learning and did not seem to understand what Camilla might find difficult. Seeking to explain Camilla's difficulties with literacy as in her 'brain' sidetracked Joanne from recognising how she might support Camilla as a second language learner. Neither did she appreciate how Camilla's background might provide a rich resource and source of knowledge about language that she could draw upon to support her learning. This was a lost opportunity for Camilla, because Joanne demonstrated a willingness to adapt her teaching to better support her students' literacy learning. In Camilla's case, Joanne did not seem to know what to do, despite receiving one-to-one coaching in AL for an extended period during our research.

Camilla's parents, Veronica and Marco, were keen to support their daughter's literacy development. They recognised the importance of the relationships between teachers and their students and that this takes time to develop. Although they had moved to another area, a fair distance from the school, they continued to drive their three children to Highfield each day in order to maintain the relationships they had developed with their teachers.

Although Joanne was familiar with Camilla's parents, she questioned their interest in their daughter and their ability to support her learning. Joanne had little sympathy for their circumstances that impacted on the children's attendance at school – the family had one car, and when it broke down, or when Marco needed it to get to work, they were unable to get the children to school. The vast swathes of housing estates that make up the northern suburbs are not well served by public transport.

Joanne would send them the words she was learning in class and Camilla's mother and father would practise reading and saying these words with her. Joanne acknowledged that 'there is a bit of support from home there'. But it was Camilla's regular absences that had Joanne most concerned – she said 'sometimes it's Mum' and there is 'an excuse about the baby or something'. Over the course of our study, these concerns increased to the level that Camilla was missing 'at least' one day a week. Joanne was of the view that 'they're just too lazy to get out of bed sometimes'. She noted that 'if one doesn't come, none of them come'. Joanne said that 'there's not much more you can do, is there?', having already spoken to the parents about 'how important it is' that Camilla attends school and how being absent negatively impacts on her learning.

Joanne and Camilla's parents met regularly to discuss her progress. Joanne indicated that she had instigated these meetings to discuss their daughter's 'targeted learning needs'. Veronica and Marco told us that they liked to stay in touch with their children's progress at school, but their concerns did not feature in Joanne's description of these conversations. In particular, their concern that Camilla was anxious about not recognising words when she was reading did not feature in Joanne's recount of these conversations. These parents were concerned about how quickly their daughter would get stressed and anxious when she was not able to pronounce words. 'I think that's the main major thing with her, that if she can't say one word, she feels disappointed in herself, and she feels like she can't do it, and gives up really quickly.'

Camilla's parents were aware of their daughter's progress and of the targets that Joanne was setting for her. They stated: '... she tells us what level she wants to get her up to. So we work ... towards that kind of level.' However, they also noted that Camilla 'doesn't like reading ... She's a maths person.' Camilla's parents related that she would say, 'I hate reading!' Indeed, Veronica and Marco described how their three oldest children all 'hate, absolutely hate, books'. They feared that they had introduced books too early. Veronica said that their youngest child 'loves his nursery rhymes, and he loves me reading books to him, but they all did at that stage, because I used to read books to them when I was pregnant with them, but now I don't know if we introduced books too early or something'.

Even when they had done what might be expected of 'good' parents – supporting their children to read at home – Veronica and Marco feared that they had done the wrong thing. They too seemed anxious and stressed that they had failed to measure up to Joanne's targets and expectations.

Joanne's classroom practice included guided reading, but she said: 'You don't want to prompt them too much because then it's not their thinking.' She wanted to teach her students 'strategies and [to] combine strategies'. She stated her goal was not to be always 'rescuing' her students: 'I want their thinking instead of my thinking.' Camilla in particular, she said, is 'one who doesn't benefit from being rescued at all'. This was a recent change to her teaching, and Joanne wondered how much 'damage' she might have done in the past to students by 'rescuing' them too much. By the second interview, Joanne mentioned that Camilla was 'using a lot more strategies now'.

Part of developing this independence had been stopping the use of the 'hands up' strategy, because Joanne 'found it was always the same kids who put their hands up'. Instead, she used 'thumbs up' to see who had grasped each concept in class. She felt that she couldn't let Camilla 'quietly sit back', but perhaps needed to call on her 'a little bit more'. What Camilla needed to develop now, Joanne said, was 'her confidence with her spelling'.

Joanne had also been using Jolly Phonics, which she believed worked particularly well with Camilla, because: 'It's the visual, it's the action with each letter and sound as well, and she's really cottoned on with that; that's really helped her.'

Another strategy Joanne employed was hanging up the students' 'Oxford Words' in the classroom. This meant that students could come in, take down their words and read them in the mornings. The words had students' names next to them, to indicate who was working on what.

Joanne also kept detailed records of her students' progress, including use of a coding system to remember whether they had done a piece of work 'spontaneously', if they had been 'prompted', or if they had been given a 'scaffold'. She also took 'photos and videos' to 'see their real thinking'. She even used this in class, 'using other kids' examples of good learning to teach the kids'.

Joanne's main goal for Camilla was for her to learn 'to think of a strategy that she can use before asking the teacher, so teaching that independence'. Unfortunately,

Camilla and other children struggling to learn to read, especially children from backgrounds other than English, rely on their teachers to help them to develop the code-breaking skills they need in order to understand language. In this regard, expecting Camilla to be able to articulate what she needed to progress was perhaps an unrealistic expectation and may have contributed to the child's frustration.

Despite their interest in their daughter's progress, Veronica and Marco were not familiar with the literacy strategies used in the classroom and were unaware that their daughter was involved in the MiniLit programme that replaced the in-class support she had received previously. They expressed concern that their daughter no longer received one-on-one assistance with 'spelling, sight words, reading, all that kind of stuff, but that was back in Reception and Year 1. Now all she has is buddies, that's all that help her read'.

They were reassured that Camilla had developed a good relationship with her teacher, but concerned that she would need to start again when she moved on to her next teacher. Marco stated that Camilla and her teacher had 'got to a stage now where they like each other … I'm thinking next year if she got a different teacher, she's going to go back to square one, because she's not going to have that.'

Unfortunately for Camilla, her teacher's and her parents' shared concern for her to become a more confident and capable reader did not appear to accrue additional benefits that worked in her interest. Instead, their efforts remained largely independent of each other. Joanne's strategies and targets did not translate into something that Veronica and Marco understood, but they supported the stated purpose of these targets – to improve Camilla's literacy outcomes. Despite their stated interest in their daughter's progress, their regular meetings with Joanne and their efforts to support Camilla at home, they still fell short of Joanne's expectations and were largely described in deficit terms. Joanne too seemed willing but unable to meet Camilla's needs as a literacy learner. Her use of standardised scales to assess progress in literacy produced specified targets and informed conversations about students' progress and how they might adopt different learning strategies. Joanne missed the opportunity provided by this feedback to reflect on her pedagogical practices.

## Conclusion

The experiences of Gus, Brendan and Camilla demonstrate the problematic nature of parent–teacher interactions in high-poverty contexts when these relationships are framed by discourses that ultimately blame children and their family for being poor and expect them to bear the main responsibility for changing their circumstances. Parents rarely make the grade. They are considered too disinterested, illiterate, lazy and so on. Their concerns for their child's progress at school does not register, and are generally not heard. Their understanding of their child is generally considered irrelevant or unhelpful to the task of educating them.

Throughout the period of our research, the practices of Suzy, a Reception teacher at Highfield, provided an alternative to this dominant discourse.

Suzy, whose pedagogical practices were described in Chapter 4, drew upon a strengths-based approach in her interactions with parents. She 'turned-around' to parents and tapped into the resources and knowledge that were made available in each child's home. However, the kinds of practices that Suzy demonstrated were rare; a discourse of poverty was more common.

Suzy made a conscious effort to develop different kinds of relationships with children and their caregivers. However, in the absence of such an effort, what prevails is what is taken-for-granted; educators hold onto deficit views about families, even when presented with counter examples that 'fly in the face' of such views. The fact that educators, on a daily basis, make up these views and select them from a range of possibilities goes unnoticed, and largely unchallenged. Consequently, established relationships of power are sustained – teachers remain the experts, the gatekeepers of knowledge, the determiners of goals, and the arbiters of what is valued and considered relevant to children's learning.

Importantly, it is in the nature of discourse that this goes unnoticed. Hence, its effects can be attributed to other causes. The effects of schooling practices – namely, underachievement in literacy – can be attributed to the culture, mindset and aspirations of the poor. Recognising these discursive effects does not shift the blame from families to educators and it does not deny the impact of the material conditions of schooling in high-poverty contexts. Instead, it focuses our attention on what is said, as well as what is not said. The relationships of power and knowledge produced by these discourses generally do not operate in the interests of young people who live in poverty. The good news is that these discourses are not fixed, since they can be disrupted, as demonstrated by Suzy. The bad news is that this kind of disruption is rare, and hard to sustain.

The challenge for teachers and school leaders is to recognise the effects of these discourses and how they operate, at least in part, through their practices. We are convinced that most of the teachers and leaders we encountered during our research genuinely believed that they were making a difference and helping students to overcome – within the limits of what they could collectively achieve – the limiting material conditions of their lives. Yet it is unlikely that the outcomes for these young people will improve if existing relationships of power and knowledge go unchallenged and undisrupted. Signs of disruption might include when Gus's family no longer feels the need to 'clam up' in conversations with his teacher, when Jeff is acknowledged as the primary educator of his son, and when Veronica and Marco's interest in their children is listened to and respected.

## Notes

1   A school support officer (SSO) can provide intensive support for individual students, or small groups, who need to develop specific skills in reading and/or writing.
2   To determine a student's instructional reading level, teachers use running records to note their use of syntactic, meaning and visual cues. Instructional level refers to a text that is read at 90% accuracy, giving the teacher information about which cues the student is using successfully and which may need to be a focus for individual or small-group work.

## References

ACER (2013). *Progressive Achievement Tests in Mathematics* (PAT-Maths) (4 ed.). Camberwell, Victoria: ACER.

Comber, B., & Kamler, B. (2004). 'Getting out of deficit: Pedagogies of reconnection'. *Teaching Education, 15*(3), 293–310.

Comber, B., & Kamler, B. (Eds.). (2005). *Turn-around Pedagogies: Literacy interventions for at-risk students*. Newtown: Primary English Teaching Association.

Comber, B., & Kerkham, L. (2016). 'Gus: I cannot write anything'. In A. H. Dyson (ed.), *Child Cultures, Schooling and Literacy: Global perspectives on children composing their lives* (pp. 53–64). New York and London: Routledge.

Epstein, D. (1998). *Failing Boys?: Issues in gender and achievement*. Buckingham: McGraw-Hill Education.

Foucault, M. (1972). *The Archaeology of Knowledge*. New York: Vintage Books.

Foucault, M. (1991). 'Politics and the study of discourse'. In G. Burchell, C. Gordon & P. Miller (eds.). *The Foucault Effect: Studies in governmentality: with two lectures by and an interview with Michel Foucault*. Chicago: The University of Chicago Press.

Gentry, R. (2007). *A Viewer's Guide to Assessing Early Literacy with Richard Gentry*. Portsmouth, NH.: Heinemann.

Lareau, A. (2011). *Unequal Childhoods: Class, race, and family life* (2nd ed.). Berkeley, California: University of California Press.

Moll, L., Amanti, C., Neff, D., & Gonzalez, N. (1992). 'Funds of knowledge for teaching: Using a qualitative approach to connect homes and classrooms'. *Theory into Practice, 31*(2), 132–141.

Nuttall, G. (2007). *The Hidden Lives of Learners*. Wellington, New Zealand: NZCER Press.

Walkerdine, V. (1990). *Schoolgirl Fictions*. London: Verso Books.

Wheldall, K. (2006). *MultiLit (Making up lost time in literacy)*. Retrieved 18 June 2015 from http://www.multilit.com/.

# 7

# 'WE CAN MAKE A DIFFERENCE'

## Educational leadership practices for literacy learning

> There has to be someone that's going to be a champion for these kids, someone that's going to be there and support these kids. ... So we look at it as opportunities, how can we improve? ... it's still that belief here that we can make a difference, and it's maintaining that belief.
>
> *(Angela, Principal at Riverview)*

We begin this final chapter by summarising key features of our research and how we have presented it in this book to explicate what we have learned about leadership for literacy in schools located in communities where there are high levels of poverty. We then revisit the dilemmas we introduced in Chapter 3 to render accessible some insights from our research. We also discuss two other sets of findings that have emerged from the very heart of our research: the dampening of efforts to develop an intellectually challenging curriculum due to the adoption of highly scripted, ritualised literacy teaching; and, in contrast, the potential of some teachers whose practices stand out from their peers to teach 'against the grain' of these scripts and to support literacy learning. We conclude by discussing a number of other insights from our research before considering some implications for practice, policy and further research.

As noted in the Introduction, this study was designed from the outset to inquire into the practices of a careful selection of schools that had already demonstrated some success in improving literacy under these challenging conditions. We were keen to track the progress of these schools and to examine the extent to which their success was sustainable. In addition, we specifically inquired into the work of school leaders and how they work both with and against the logic of policy that presents one-size-fits-all solutions for their problems, whilst engaging in 'a cruel accounting' (Thomson, 1998) that undermines local school efforts to devise poverty-responsive curriculum and pedagogy. We investigated some of the ways that school leaders constructed opportunities for professional learning to enable their teachers to improve literacy learning and, specifically, the ways that teachers take up school-based reforms that inform the ongoing development of their classroom practices. Ultimately, we traced student experiences of classroom practices that enact school reforms in different ways.

The study reported in this book is based on our ethnographic case studies of four primary schools in south Australia; hence, this book reports examples of educational leadership in one state of Australia. However, the writers have all worked in schools around Australia and in England and we trust this book portrays a slice of life that resonates with the 'reality' of schooling in other parts of the globe, especially those countries now involved in what Ball (2012) refers to as *Global Education Inc.* and the influence of the Global Education Reform Movement (GERM). To take the demand for context seriously, we have attempted to provide an account of the social and policy contexts in which educators work in schools located in high-poverty communities. The detailed nature of these accounts over time, of life in actually existing schools, has required us to focus on a small number of schools.

In this book we have attempted to represent educators (both teachers and principals) as active agents who are able to make some, albeit limited, choices about their work. The people we represent in this book – principals, teachers, students and their parents – are neither victims, nor superhuman agents. However, their work and learning, in various ways, is shaped by both the translocal educational policy conditions and the material impacts of poverty in everyday life.

Throughout this book, we have treated the specific schooling contexts in which we conducted our research as key sites of educational change. These places have in common low performance of students on standardised tests of literacy. We have argued that too much policy in recent years has framed this problem in terms of individual teachers, who are constituted as free choosers and abstracted from the complex situations in which they work. We do not subscribe to the view that attributes responsibility to schools for standardised measures of learning outcomes whilst simultaneously reducing funding to public schools and effectively closing down autonomy through regimes of performativity.

This final chapter has two main sections. First, we summarise our findings across the book, including what we learned about poverty and schooling, and about school leadership and its effects on teaching and learning. Second, we propose some key implications for practice for those working in schools, especially school leaders and teachers, together with implications for policy and for further research.

## What did we learn?

### *Poverty does matter*

In the years 1972–75, a Royal Commission was conducted into poverty in Australia. The following is a quote from its final report about people who are poor and disadvantaged:

> They have been encouraged to believe that a major goal of schooling is to increase equality while, in reality, schools ... maintain the present unequal distribution of status and power. Because the myth of Equal Opportunities has been so widely accepted by Australians, the nature of unequal outcomes has been largely ignored. Thus failure to succeed in the competition is generally viewed as being the fault of the individual rather than the inevitable result of the way our society is structured.
>
> *(Fitzgerald, 1976, p. 231)*

Although these words were written over 40 years ago, they are still relevant today, and are perhaps even more salient given that, as reported in Chapter 1, the gaps in achievement between students from wealthy and disadvantaged backgrounds are widening. The claim of a myth of equal opportunities in Australia also seems to have some truth about it, and especially so for educators themselves. We all desperately want to believe that schooling works for social inclusion, but the facts continue to belie our best intentions. The way schooling functions to produce social stratification is complex but, in general, social policy – and that includes schooling policy – reflects the interests of those already doing well and those groups who have traditionally succeeded at school. We also agree with the Commission's finding that those who fail at school are positioned by the discourses surrounding poverty to blame themselves for their failure, rather than the way that schooling and other social policy fails them or, in the Commission's terms, 'the way our society is structured' (p. 231).

The shift in political philosophy since the 1970s, from a social-democratic welfare state to a neoliberal, market-driven one, has refocused the object of *all* blame onto individuals, given that one of the defining characteristics of neoliberalising policy is to render individuals as autonomous and responsible (Rose, 1999, p. 214). All of us, and that includes principals, teachers and their students, are now rendered as human capital and as entrepreneurs of ourselves.

> Poverty and many other forms of social exclusion are now thought of in terms of lack as regards the acquisition of adequate human capital, irresponsibility towards one's learning capacity or not being able to manage one's learning.
>
> *(Simons & Masschelein, 2008, p. 197)*

We find ourselves writing about educational leadership in schools situated in high-poverty areas at a time of serious dissonance between the logic of schooling policy and the social reality in which we now live and work. This dissonance manifests mostly around issues of inequality. In Australia, we have historically supported the rhetoric of egalitarianism, which assumes that schooling provides opportunities to get ahead if people work hard enough and are smart enough. While educators by nature claim good intentions, our descriptions of classrooms and our narratives of the experiences of individual students raised serious concerns about how the system (re)produces social stratification (Ashurst & Venn, 2014; Au, 2009; Brown, 2015; Duggan, 2003).

The impact of poverty defines school communities across large portions of every city. Certainly, in the four schools involved in our study, poverty appeared in myriad ways, including troubling and even violent behaviour, children not having had enough sleep or any breakfast and children not being at an 'age appropriate level' for reading or writing. Whilst educational policy might be silent on these kinds of phenomena, poverty was one of the most important existential realities for the principals and teachers in these schools. Poverty was not a background that could be separated out from other factors, nor a context that could be ignored conveniently, but a defining feature of the educational work being conducted in every part of these schools. Poverty was written into the bodies of children, their families, their neighbourhoods and their schools.

Poverty is both 'real' and an object of knowledge and, for us, can be considered a problem for educational policy and practice. Various 'regimes of truth' about poverty circulate in and around schools and these include 'poverty knowledge' (Peel, 2003, p. 28) from anthropology, educational psychology, sociology, political philosophy and 'poverty news' (Peel, 2003) portrayed in media culture. What is most disturbing though, is that essentialising, deficit and individualising 'truths' about poverty continue to promulgate, and dominate, policy and practice. Contemporary discourses quite literally shout deficit views about people living in poverty.

## Principals struggle with/against policy logics

Educational policy defines what leaders should be and do. As Ian Hacking (1986) puts it, policy 'makes up' school leaders by naming and framing the commitments, values, actions and objects of action that are important and 'right' in leadership practice. Leaders bring their individual histories and dispositions to the task of leading, but this is always framed by policy. Education policy differs in what it demands of those who lead schools; it is variously enabling and constraining. Some policy has encouraged leaders to be innovative through processes of school and community participation – the former Disadvantaged Schools Program in Australia, for instance, where teachers and often parents were routinely involved in designing school curriculum development projects. Meanwhile, other policy has left open a range of possibilities for action – Building Schools for the Future in England, for example, where architects, teachers and students sometimes worked together on designing their future buildings. Typically, today's testing-focused policy is highly directive about particular priorities such as literacy, and this leaves school leaders with a narrower range of choices than their predecessors about the priorities and processes that they institute and promote.

Leaders' choices are delimited by 'the stuff' they have to work with. System-wide directives largely determine how school budgets are spent, thus limiting local autonomy. Externally developed curriculum frameworks mandate what is to be taught, although schools still have some choice about how the curriculum is implemented. South Australia has not yet moved to scripted schooling, using preset textbooks or literacy hours for example, as has been the case in parts of the

United States and England. System-level human-resource policies largely determine which teachers are appointed to their schools, although leaders can shape role descriptions in ways that help them to get an appropriately qualified person.

Thus, any stories we might tell about school leadership are, from the outset, accounts of how discourses of power and knowledge that govern schools 'make up' leaders. These discourses work in ways that suggest that knowledge is outside of, or beyond, power relations. In addition, contemporary policy discourses are not entirely about enforcing rules and procedures, restricting people, or repression, but rather for 'determining how teachers and leaders should *think* and *feel* about what they produce (Willmott, 1993, p. 253). Importantly though, in this study, school leaders are also making up leadership in response to their own reading of their unique school communities (Kerkham & Comber, 2016). This requires ongoing analysis of the policy landscape in relation to the everyday contexts of their work, in order to see how leaders make continual adjustments in the face of competing priorities, narrowing spaces for discretionary judgements and the resources they can muster – human and material.

The school leaders with whom we conducted the research had different relationships with the community, had been at their schools for differing amounts of time and had different understandings of literacy and, therefore, leading literacy. The female school leaders at Highfield and Riverview had both been at their schools for some time. Both brought strong professional understandings of literacy theory and contemporary approaches. The principal at Sandford was a relatively recent appointment, with curriculum expertise in numeracy. He appointed a senior leader to address literacy improvement and also employed an external literacy consultant. He also worked overtly to recruit teachers with strong reputations for literacy pedagogy. The principal at Easton had a strong literacy programme, sustained by a literacy key teacher and inherited from an innovative and charismatic principal with expertise in special education. The literacy agreement documents in each of the schools provided traces of their different histories as well as their attention to current accountability demands. Hence, there are no simple, predictable relationships between the approaches taken towards enhancing student literacy and policy demands. In practice, each of the principals sought to analyse all the information they had about how students were responding to literacy programmes and pedagogies in operation in their school. This included regular classroom visits; closely monitoring a range of data (such as Running Records); talking with teachers, teacher aides, tutors and the leadership team; asking for feedback from consultants and key teachers; reading student reports; and so on.

In this book, we argue that improving literacy learning outcomes for students growing up in high-poverty locales requires confronting things we – and others – often take for granted. In other chapters, we have highlighted the problem of what truth claims are made about students living in poverty. A similar issue was raised in regards to educational leadership. How are school leaders defined in educational discourses and, hence, how are they being constituted or made up through discursive means? Put more simply, how are school leaders being *framed*? We think that school leaders are actually being framed in both senses of the term – invoking here the colloquial use of that term, they are being set up by policy discourses in ways that are potentially counter-productive to their work, especially for those leading schools serving high-poverty communities. Nevertheless, leaders, and teachers, still have some space to move.

The pervasiveness of global neoliberalising discourses now reframes policy and leadership in schools by reorienting the purposes of schooling towards market mechanisms based on consumer 'choice'. These forms of new public management (Griffith & Smith, 2014) assail school leaders and teachers with new textual prac-tices, sometimes referred to as steering-at-a-distance, and intensified demands for performativity. One of the challenges for educational researchers is to work out the changing nature of policy technologies and to ascertain how exactly neoliberalis-ing policy logics work as technologies of change and control. On this theme, Ball (1997) argues that the shift from welfare state to neoliberal governmentality has meant 'new structures and new technologies of control', as well as 'the transfor-mation of the values and cultures' of our institutions, but, most importantly, the 'concomitant formation of new subjectivities' (p. 259). This means that those who work in social institutions such as schools are directed to 'own' and 'become' what it is that policy wants them to be. In our research, school leaders had to work with policy regimes that involve substantial restructuring informed by marketising logic, renewing technologies of control that integrate coercion with self-formation and constitute new subjectivities. We needed to be attentive to these new forms of leadership.

Neoliberalised policies of devolution, choice and accountability demand the adoption of managerialist orientations to leadership that narrow and instrumentalise 'educational' leadership practices. In some parts of the world (e.g. England or parts of the United States), where learning is equated to performance on standardised tests, such a shift often leads to alienation of principals from their staff. Whilst such alienation was not evident in our schools, we can report that the principals them-selves reported alienation from the logic of policy and from the demands for policy compliance being made on them by the system. They worried about the constant demands for accountability using data that failed to account for the complex array of learning and value-adding that their teachers achieved with challenging cohorts of students in every classroom.

There are global variations in new forms of leadership, variations in the different state jurisdictions in Australia and variations between schools in each jurisdiction. In an early chapter, we argued that in Australian primary schools, unlike in England for instance (see Gunter, 2012), school principals were able to operate beyond mere demonstrations of compliance to demands for effectiveness and efficiency and, in fact, had some capacity to reform school structures, school culture and pedagogical practices in ways that were responsive to the unique communities that they serve; and also to enact, in part at least, the practices of an 'educational' leader.

This is also true in our research. We saw principals not predetermined by policy, but continually juggling what they needed to do in their local school with the demands of policy. They knew what they needed to do to meet system expectations in testing, because that was important for the school. And they were strongly committed to the importance of literacy as a key to educational equity – literacy unlocks learning across the curriculum. However, they were concerned to various degrees about the ways in which their overall commitments and policy requirements seemed to work together. The tensions between policy, local need, educational beliefs and pedagogical know-how created what we think of as a series of dilemmas. We turn to these dilemmas next.

## Dilemmas associated with working within/against the logic of contemporary policy

In Chapter 3, we introduced the concept of dilemmas to represent the complexity of the work of educational leaders. These dilemmas manifested in various ways in our study schools. Below, we revisit the dilemmas we introduced earlier to render accessible some insights from our research.

## Serving the local community

Some of the principals we studied rejected market-driven purposes for education and instead framed their leadership in terms of sustaining a hopeful educational project that aims to seriously interrupt the long-term educational reproduction of social stratification that was evident in the communities that they served. In such cases, being a school leader meant taking up the challenge of being a 'good' school for every child who enrols, not just those that are likely to bolster the school's ability to achieve and maintain a reputation as a good school, as determined by student performance measures. For the schools we studied, this meant getting a reputation for being able to handle the hard kids. The schools in which we conducted this study worked hard to become sites of learning for all their students and accepted young people who they knew from the outset had a strong history of trouble thus far with the institution of schooling.

Providing an opportunity for a good education for every child in the community often meant taking on students who struggled academically but who also brought their troubles to school. The principals in our schools reorganised and restructured people and resources in order to provide for such students. On the one hand, these principals argued that all mainstream classrooms needed to work for the complex cohort of students that populate every class. The professional learning approaches were focused on that assumption and demand. But the mainstream class just does not work for every child at all times and every school develops programmes that operate to augment mainstream classrooms. Such strategies are essential if schools are to avoid falling into the usual behaviour management techniques, such as internal suspensions, short-term exclusions from the school or longer-term placement at another school (Sullivan, Johnson & Lucas, 2016). A challenge for all schools working on this dilemma is to fashion an ecology for learning in ways that do not fall into the problem of remedial logics, as we outlined in our introductory chapter, and hence to emphasise basic skills. Instead, and borrowing from Gutiérrez, Morales and Martinez (2009, p. 227), such programmes can be informed by a logic of *re-mediation*, in which cases the key driver is reconnection (not responding to lack) through providing students with opportunities to work with their home and community experiences to expand their repertoires of literate practices.

However, as we have indicated, there were occasions when including and keeping every child became too difficult and suspensions and exclusions (if temporary) to other schools did occur. These decisions were not reached or maintained easily and leaders worried about the negative impact that exclusions and suspensions would have on the students concerned, as well as on their overall school philosophy in practice. The educational leaders in our study recognised that they *were* in competition for reputation and enrolments. Parents often choose schools based on potential peer group and they are influenced not only by published league tables but also by neighbourhood conversation. The risks associated with taking and keeping every child meant that school leaders had no choice but to continually monitor and match enrolment trends against their practices of inclusion.

## 'Democratically' changing school culture

For principals, enacting hopeful and expansive purposes for schooling required redesigning hierarchical school structures to become more democratic, transforming a culture of complaint and deficit to one focused on what teachers could do differently. Principals worked to shift the pedagogies of lack and isolated individual practice to pedagogies of engagement and whole-school agreements. The school reforms that our schools engaged in entailed forms of leadership that rejected straightforward managerial versions of leadership. Instead, educational leaders adopted more democratic modalities of leading schools through co-construction of practice. Our school principals demonstrated thoughtful and ongoing diagnoses of school-level problems, which then shaped their responses that were assembled into practice – including school planning, professional learning, performance management and development, and supporting forms of distributed leadership. However, they also knew that 'the buck stopped with them' and that the pace of reform was set by policy demands for improved test outcomes. The leadership dilemma sat in judgements about how much to let change occur at its own pace and how much to allow democratic process dictate directions for change. These decisions often sat uneasily with external pressures to demonstrate that change had not only occurred but had also led to improved results.

## Changing pedagogy through whole-school agreements

The reform projects of all the schools we studied were driven in part by a need to provide a more 'consistent' approach to teaching literacy across the school. Literacy-focused School Improvement Plans were intended to support this goal and to inform whole-school professional learning. In Chapter 3, we outlined in some detail some examples of such agreements operating as 'active texts' (Kerkham & Nixon, 2014; Smith, 2006), which guided and regulated teachers' and leaders' understandings of literacy practice. The rationale and development of such agreements can become problematic if they 'become ends in themselves divorced from the goals of transforming students' educational experiences' (Lipman, 1998, p. 296). In such cases, the shared and binding nature of the agreements often meant that teachers were inclined to 'teach safe' and to adopt specified approaches to the teaching of literacy that were overly constrained by narrow definitions of literacy – and mostly driven by aligning too strongly to improved National Assessment Program – Literacy and Numeracy (NAPLAN) scores – and/or were highly scripted. This kind of conservative consistency undermined opportunities for co-constructing learning with each unique class.

This is a classic equity dilemma. Difference and diversity are integral to labelling and stratifying students on the basis of their apparent learning, demonstrated in tests and exams. Yet simply standardising pedagogies and making them consistent can have exactly the same effects, particularly if the standard approach is narrow and limited. Designing differentiated classroom practices that support the learning needs of individual children, while also promoting pedagogical consistency, curriculum coherence and high expectations, is *the* dilemma faced by all teachers. This is especially true for teachers working in schools serving disadvantaged neighbourhoods, where the children are likely to have more diverse and deep learning needs. It is hardly surprising that we saw our schools and their leaders struggling to manage this challenge.

For the literacy agreements to work over a number of years, school-based professional learning needs to inculcate new staff into the agreements and the sorts of pedagogical practices that have been (re)designed. Support to develop these practices came from a range of sources, including locally developed resources, specialist trainers and coaches, targeted professional development, mentoring in various forms such as 'literacy chats' and modelling of pedagogy and professional learning teams. However, another 'reality' for our schools that informed professional learning was the high level of teacher turnover. Schools were thus always beginning again, inducting new staff members and ensuring that they knew the basics of the school philosophy and culture. This delimited the pace of change and created a kind of stop-start, stop-start rhythm. Because the educational capital in professional learning teams remains contingent on their membership and their opportunities to engage deeply with complex ideas, there were often strategic tensions arising from the desires of the more experienced staff to continue to innovate, and the need to nurture new staff and ensure consistency of approach across the school.

## Practising 'educational' leadership whilst responding to demands for performativity

Against the logic of marketisation, the principals in our schools demonstrated a commitment to 'educational' leadership with a focus on local needs, the particularity of place, history, enrolment and staffing. This often sat somewhat uneasily with demands for tangible signs of improvement. Principals often found themselves using the very categories of disadvantage and stereotypes of neighbourhood that they rejected in order to explain to line managers why they had not achieved as much as was expected – or to claim credit for the changes that had been made. External expectation of improvements in performance sometimes failed to account for the challenges confronting local leaders, as well as the slow and unpredictable nature of change that often scuppered improvement in performance. An unrelenting press for changes in output measures meant that our principals had to continually balance and mediate external and internal pressures. This is physically and emotionally as well as intellectually demanding work.

## Literacisation and the dumbed-down classroom

In earlier chapters, we referred to numerous prior studies that have reported on the 'actually existing pedagogies' (Lingard, 2007, p. 246) that seem to dominate in classrooms, particularly in the teaching of literacy. For example, Lingard (2007) refers to the dominant pedagogies as *pedagogies of the same*, which he summarised as being strong in care for students, but which mostly 'fail to work with and across differences' and also 'fail to make a difference in their lack of both intellectual demand and connectedness to the world' (p. 246). This view was confirmed by Hayes, Johnston and King (2009), who observed that classroom practices are mostly 'very traditional, following predictable routines, and are largely unsuccessful as far as formal learning is concerned' (pp. 251–2). Research by Hattam (Hattam, 2010; Smyth & Hattam, 2004) indicates that pedagogy, in normal(ising) school, is often characterised by: an over-reliance on worksheet pedagogy; low expectations of student learning, which is compensated for by high expectations for student behaviour; low levels of choice in classroom learning tasks and assessment; and little explicit teaching of school literate practices. Put simply, 'normal' curriculum and pedagogy are often uninspiring and even alienating.

In our research for this book, we observed what we call *common pedagogies* or *fickle literacies* (Comber, 2016), which order the day's literacy teaching. In Chapter 5, we described some examples of these approaches, such as Tracey's teaching that exemplified scripted teaching rituals in which students are required to sit and listen quietly while she reads to them from the selected book and to answer her literal, rather than interpretive, comprehension questions. Unfortunately, these kinds of scripted teaching rituals limit the potential for students to play with appropriate words, to offer alternative meanings and to connect up their lives to the content of the texts. These missed learning opportunities pass unnoticed, but they might have been resources for their writing and speaking. In the schools that we studied, most of the teachers had been involved in devising literacy agreements and certainly the original rationale for these was worthwhile – to provide a shared understanding of what was to take place in classrooms across the school. The agreements were sometimes devised during professional learning activities, or during other activities in which school leaders and teachers could discuss and negotiate their form. Despite the considered nature and scope of the pedagogies included in the agreements, we often encountered common pedagogies that undermined their realisation due to the following:

- Narrow views of literacy that get promulgated through overemphasising the NAPLAN tests. NAPLAN is designed as a test of functional literacy skills and does not pretend to do otherwise, but then, as an unintended effect, the working definition of literacy gets dumbed down in classroom practice. Too much emphasis is put on functional skills and the technical aspects of being literate, at the expense of those other aspects, such as participating in understanding and composing meaningful texts of various kinds, using texts for multiple purposes, and critically analysing and transforming texts (Freebody, 1992; Freebody & Luke, 1990).

- Narrow views of literacy also constrain the purposes for literacy teaching and learning. If the aim is to develop a rich repertoire of literate practices, then student understanding and use of decoding and encoding needs to be integral to composing and reading meaningful texts from their earliest experiences in the classroom.

- The problem is further compounded if teachers work from normative developmental models that assume that students need to have basic skills before they can do other, more demanding literacy tasks. Enacting such theories affirms the notion of predetermined stages for learning to read and write that close down opportunities for students' curiosity, an interest in playing with words and writing for purposes other than demonstrating competence with copying a title or sight words from the board, doing cloze exercises, and then applying what is learnt to writing a sentence 'using your own words'. Put simply, we witness a serious disconnect between reading the word and the world.

- Unreflective performances by teachers using commercial materials or system-supported models for literacy teaching. As an example, we described Jody's enactment of an Accelerated Literacy (AL) approach as part of putting the school's literacy agreement into practice. We do not want to be passing judgement on the efficacy of AL as a model, but to draw attention to the dangers in assuming that any model is a universal panacea, since success is determined by how such a model it enacted through teachers' practices in actual existing classrooms. When the enactment of models leads to mostly highly scripted rituals or routines, then students are often not afforded opportunities for challenging learning; and with no opportunities for children to offer their thoughts, knowledge or questions, lessons are stripped of social and academic potential.

- Deficit views undermine learning for those students with the most need. Deficit assumptions are well documented in the international literature and have been attributed to 'widespread and resilient logic[s] of practice' that restrict the likelihood of students encountering, or being supported to engage in, an intellectually challenging curriculum (Johnston & Hayes, 2008, p. 110).

Such logics delimit what can be achieved by students in places where deficit ways of thinking about them, their families and their communities infuse teachers' explanations of what they are capable of achieving at school. This is especially the case for those students with the most need for schooling to work for them, rather than the other way around.

Collectively, these conditions ensure the prevalence of low-level literacy demands in classrooms associated with 'deep disadvantage' (McLachlan, Gilfillan & Gordon, 2013; Perales *et al.*, 2014) that are experiencing existential pressures (Troman, 2000).

We draw attention to the bitter irony that *there is a prevalence of low-level literacy demands in the very contexts where just the opposite is required.* Rather than being enhanced by school improvement efforts, pedagogy can be impoverished. The irony here is that teachers shared a firm conviction that their job was to teach literacy. However, literacy was defined as a set of skills or 'basics', which, while necessary, are insufficient. The pressure on literacy assessment, and the faith placed by their school leaders in particular approaches, resulted in teachers focusing on these skills in a decontextualised way and not being 'distracted' by other opportunities to extend children's learning, confidence, participation, trust and so on.

The 'NAPLAN effect' is much more complex than teaching to the test and involves not only a repression of productive and engaging pedagogies, but also the production of literacy pedagogies that foreground the features of language as the primary purpose for teaching and learning, rather than assuming that literacy is for meaning-making. The fickle literacies that we describe in Chapter 5 are not limited to worksheets and rote learning; they also include learning tasks that have been designed in the name of concepts that now circulate in schools and that are mostly highly regarded, such as 'differentiation', 'genre pedagogy', 'explicit teaching', 'AL' and so on.

What gets done in the name of literacy learning has been a consistent theme throughout this book and we have demonstrated the importance of the frames of reference that are used in the interpretation and enactment of pedagogical practice. We do, however, strongly disavow claims that teachers are solely to blame for the prevalence of fickle literacies and acknowledge prior research that points to 'systematic deficit in quality precisely in the areas where a high quality education is needed most' (Lupton, 2005, p. 590). How can we say that teachers are not to blame for poor 'results' and teaching? The answer lies in our use of the notion of discourse.

We have argued throughout the book that there is a set of 'knowledge' problems related to the challenges of leading and teaching in schools serving high-poverty communities. We have suggested that there are 'truths' that circulate in schools about students and their communities. Such truths circulate as discourses, understood here as 'systems of thoughts composed of ideas, attitudes, courses of action, beliefs and practices that systematically construct the subjects and the worlds of which they speak' (Lessa, 2006, p. 285). Each school has its own specific 'regime of truth', understood as an historically constituted and rather informal 'system of thoughts'; it has a working local theory for informing how policy and practice is made local. As we have suggested, this 'vernacularisation' can have an ambivalent relationship to overarching systems policy discourses. Local discourses produce particular kinds of knowledge about children and their families. In the four schools we studied, there were contested regimes of truth about the students. Certainly the principals were working hard to unsettle deficit views, arguing instead for views that highlighted the learning assets that young people brought to school.

In Chapter 6, we provided a reading of how discourses work in schools. We followed a number of students over three years who were not performing at the same level as their peers in the later part of our fieldwork, all selected by teachers who were willing to share their perspectives on these students and we provided a reading of three of these students. We hope that our reading provides a nuanced account of how deficit views are normalised and naturalised in teacher talk, and the rather disturbing effects such discourses have on too many young people. We do not think that any of us are outside deficit discourses and certainly cannot make those claims for ourselves. But we argue that it is possible to trouble the ways in which discourse produces knowledge about teaching, students and literacy. This requires unsettling those truths that frame students from the outset by an overdetermined sense of lack, as in a lack of capacity to learn that leads to some predetermined socially stratified future.

Our analysis shows that too often the turn-around logic we have argued for in other parts of this book is not evident in school regimes of truth. This is particularly the case with the students who are either 'trouble' or 'not doing as well as' their peers. In the hectic life of schools, there is not often time to open up readings/analyses of those students – who may be a large cohort. Multiple versions or truths about students circulate in schools and these may include different versions by the classroom teacher and the principal. Parents too provide very different accounts when opportunities are provided. However, when there is little time for these accounts to be brought together, little time for critical reflection and debate, a culture of poverty logic often trumps the other options.

Often in schools, teachers and principals draw on psycho-pathological theories about young people – the 'problem' is an individual psychology that requires fixing. As a result, self-improvement and resilience interventions are provided. All that is required for such children is for them to think more positively to 'make their lives better'. Discourses of 'choice' are also prominent in schools and student behaviour can be understood as a matter of choice, something that could be controlled by each individual regardless of circumstance.

The story of Gus (Chapter 6) was particularly poignant. As we showed, Gus's behaviour was very different in the two schools he attended while we were following his progress. In one school he caused trouble, including violent and uncooperative behaviour that none of us would tolerate. But in another school, to quote that section: 'Gus neither disrupted the class nor engaged in inappropriate yard behaviour during the ten-week placement. For Andrea [Gus's teacher at Easton], what stood out was Gus's "lack of self-esteem and not trying because he was worried about failing, about failure". Nevertheless, Andrea felt that he "thrived" and she recalled "a few times where [Mum] had tears of happiness from some of the things that he was doing in class".' What is happening here when one child can demonstrate such wildly different behaviours in two different contexts? We suggest that it is the school that is different, not Gus.

Schools need to be understood as providing the conditions that either enable – or not – students to take up productive learning practices. Rather than blaming the students from the outset for not learning, we need to examine the 'interactive trouble' between schools and some young people. The different regimes of truth lead to different practices, which offer different affordances to young people, different opportunities for them to act, think, be and learn. Such an analysis suggests ways to re-mediate educative relationships.

Brendan's story, also in Chapter 6, exemplifies the ways in which parental versions of the truth about children are contested in schools and, in his case, mostly ignored. The truth games of school seemed institutionally deaf to the views and aspirations of the parent for their child and, in this case, the parent felt he had no choice but to take his child out of school. Brendan's early traumatic experiences still resonated through his life and contributed to the educational challenges that he faced. His is a complex story, and we recognise the efforts of two schools to mobilise their available resources to support Brendan's learning. The aspect of his story that we want to highlight here is how schooling discourses positioned Brendan's father Jeff. Like many parents, Jeff's own schooling experiences were cut short by circumstances beyond his control. Yet, his concern for his son, and his determination to ensure that opportunities were made available to Brendan that had been closed to him, were clearly visible in his words and actions. Despite Jeff's desire to be actively involved in decisions related to his son's learning, he was excluded from important conversations by inaccessible language and the assumption that he was part of the problem. A common feature of institutional discourses is that they are closed to outsiders, particularly those who are considered unqualified. In contrast, over the course of our research, early-childhood teacher Suzy's approach to welcoming parents and carers into her classroom reminded us of what is made possible when this discourse is disrupted. In Suzy's practice, parents and carers were recognised as resources in their children's learning – they provided Suzy with access to the everyday knowledge of the children's lives and Suzy harnessed their concern for their children by assisting them to learn ways they could support their literacy development at home. Suzy established a two-way relationship with the adults in her students' lives and disrupted prevailing relationships of power and knowledge that excluded them from schooling discourses.

These issues of truth highlighted above are also exacerbated by the resource limitations in the schools we studied. We heard, in every school, the ways in which resource allocation for student support was increasingly tightened. When options for alternative forms of support are seriously narrowed, schools have little real autonomy to make their own decisions in response to their actually existing challenges.

## Uncommon pedagogies: teachers supporting literacy learning

In this book, we have reported on both uncommon pedagogies in Chapter 4 and common pedagogies in Chapter 5. An important question that arises from these descriptions is how to support teachers to develop the kinds of classroom practices that we describe as uncommon. As Hayes *et al.* (2009) point out, schools serving disadvantaged neighbourhoods do have teachers who do make a difference; teachers whose pedagogies enable students to learn challenging relevant learning tasks that lead to success in the mainstream game of school. In a similar vein, there are examples of teachers whose professional development experiences have led to the sorts of 'turn-around' documented by Comber and Kamler (2005). This aspect of our book contributes to the growing archive of Australian (Comber, 2016; McInerney, 2004; Prosser, Lucas & Reid, 2010; Munns, Sawyer & Cole, 2013) and international (Apple & Beane, 1995; Chapman & Hobbel, 2010; Steinberg & Kincheloe, 1998; te Riele, 2009; Wrigley, 2012) research that takes up this insight and outlines a range of curriculum and pedagogical experiments that provide hopeful accounts of how educational leadership and teachers can contribute to advancing more socially just outcomes in schools. In discussing the practices of these teachers, we do not want to romanticise heroic teachers – and certainly those we represent here did not see themselves as extraordinary when we were in their classrooms. This archive invokes a range of metaphors, but for our purposes we have relied upon the notion of *uncommon pedagogies* to name practices that stood out substantially and were different to the common pedagogies – *fickle literacies* – we described above. Whilst it is not possible to provide a narrow set of characteristics to define uncommon pedagogies, the following features do provide a starting point:

- Classroom complexity was recast as a pedagogical challenge rather than an excuse for low expectations.
- Students were understood as having knowledge and experience that were valuable resources that could be connected to school learning.
- Classroom practices were actively and positively connected to families and communities.
- Learning tasks were designed that were open-ended and that demanded complex thinking and language.
- Students were engaged as active collaborators in co-constructing classroom learning and assessment.
- Popular culture was included into expanded literacy practices.
- Students were provided with opportunities to research place and history using primary sources and generating new knowledge.
- Deep knowledge about science, literature and/or language was utilised when developing and implementing classroom practices.
- Students were provided with opportunities to think about significant personal and social issues, such as loneliness, hope and relationships, by engaging with relevant texts.

- Teachers engaged in developing shared understandings of agreed collective literacy practices, through building trust and a genuine desire to learn from each other.
- Decoding and functional language skills were recontextualised and embedded within challenging learning tasks that included some degree of relevance and/or problem-solving.
- Students were able to exercise choice related to how and what they learnt and how they demonstrated their learning.
- Students were supported to develop a metalanguage for how language or texts work.

Perhaps most importantly though, teachers who demonstrated uncommon pedagogies were improvisers in the jazz sense of that term. They co-constructed the learning experience with the unique set of young people they were teaching. As such, they were not adopting those highly scripted performances we mentioned in previous chapters – pedagogies that predetermine too much of teaching practice before entering any classroom and hence close down important affordances for spontaneous moments of learning that appear in many lessons. Improvisation, based upon wide-range repertoires of pedagogical practice, also enabled teachers to set more interesting and intriguing learning tasks, connected to substantial issues in their students' lives and with the potential to engage students with their communities in productive and educative ways.

## Implications for practice

Through our research, we have attempted to contribute to a deeper understanding of what we have termed uncommon and common pedagogies. We have distinguished between these types of pedagogies by describing what teachers are doing in the classrooms in our study; how what they do matters and produces different effects; and the kinds of leadership and policies that give rise to these different pedagogical practices.

We recognise that the features of uncommon pedagogies that we listed earlier in this chapter are not easily translated into diverse and complex school contexts, but we did notice that the teachers whose classroom practices we drew upon to generate this list engaged in sustained observation and inquiry into their own practice. Their classrooms were places in which they experimented with ideas and approaches and assessed in an ongoing way the resulting effects on students' learning and their engagement in learning. As a result, their classroom practices were continually being modified and adapted according to their professional judgement of what was working, in terms of what was supporting or hindering learning.

Our research has also emphasised the importance of educational leaders and teachers interrogating the discursive frameworks they may take for granted. What assumptions underpin their understandings of their roles and those of parents and caregivers; the potential of their students to learn; and their collective capacity to support students' learning? These are challenging questions to ask, since they require an examination of how knowledge shapes relationships of power. Yet these are precisely the questions that might enable educational leaders and teachers to maximise opportunities for young people to learn, and sustain an enthusiasm for learning. This form of questioning is supported by open and honest relationships, conducted in an atmosphere of trust and respect.

We have drawn upon our own research, as well as relevant prior research, to argue in support of school-based enactment of a more expansive view of literacy to inform school planning, professional learning and curriculum design, including locally designed assessment and pedagogical practices. When informed by such an expansive view of literacy, we suggest the practices of educational leaders and teachers need to take into account the following:

1.  Contextualising views of literacy are enacted: Teaching of functional skills and the technical aspects of being literate need to be embedded in learning how to understand and compose meaningful texts of various kinds, using texts for multiple purposes, and critically analysing and transforming texts (see also Green, 1988; Luke & Freebody, 1999; Nixon, 2003).
2.  A shift towards multimodal literacies: Language-only views of literacy fail to account for the growing importance of other modalities of representation, especially the visual mode (semiotics). Being able to read and write the world now demands learning literate repertoires for multiple modes of representation and in multiple cultural contexts, and that often goes by the term 'multiliteracies' (Cope & Kalantzis, 2000; New London Group, 1996). Importantly, taking on a multiliteracies approach means 'creating a different kind of pedagogy, one in which language and other modes of learning are dynamic representational resources, constantly being remade by their users' (New London Group, 1996, p. 64).
3.  Young people's engagement with popular culture and new information and communication technologies (ICT) are taken seriously and utilised as resources: Young people now negotiate between real and virtual realities, live in media-saturated societies, and do much of their identity work through engagement with popular culture using ICT (Durrant & Green, 2000; Giroux, 1994; Goldfarb, 2002; Kress, 2003; Kress & Jewett, 2003; Lankshear & Knobel, 2003).

Again, translating these ideas into practice is never straightforward, but the educational leaders and classroom teachers that we observed who enacted an expanded view of literacy generally demonstrated a hopeful, modest confidence that they could support young people to learn, and to enjoy learning. Their practices reinforced that 'what works' locally to improve professional practice and students' learning cannot be determined from a distance or transported from elsewhere. Instead, they demonstrated the importance of supporting and resourcing their inquiries into the effects of their practice and their assessments of what works in their schools and classrooms.

A persistent theme in our book has been the need to think past deficit views of young people living in high-poverty communities. We have attempted to describe what this might mean practically for schools and to illustrate it through the practices of educational leaders and teachers we encountered. In all of the schools we studied, the principals attempted to change the school culture from one of complaint and deficit to a culture that focused instead on foregrounding the learning assets that young people bring to school and opening up debate on what curriculum and pedagogy could do to engage with those assets. If we are to take students' everyday experiences seriously in schools, then we need to develop much richer vocabularies about their lifeworlds to give what seems like an abstract idea some definite content and make this knowledge 'pedagogically viable' (Moll, 2005, p. 278). Roche (1987, p. 283) defines the lifeworld as 'the social world as subjectively experienced, and communicated, as acted in and acted upon'. Lifeworld knowledge may include community knowledge, local knowledge, personal experience, and media and popular-culture sources. Whilst not an exhaustive list, the following list indicates various aspects of students' lifeworlds that might provide themes for curriculum design:

- keywords in vernacular language;
- texts with currency;
- popular cultures;
- features of the local environment;
- young people's sense of place;
- places of learning for young people out-of-school;
- issues considered to be important by young people;
- young people's fears in the present and for their future;
- young people's hopes for the present and for the future;
- important relationships in young people's lives.

Luis Moll and colleagues (González, Moll & Amanti, 2005; Moll, Amanti, Neff & González, 1992) have developed, theoretically and practically, a 'funds of knowledge' approach as a counter-discourse to scripted and overdetermined curriculum designs. Alternatively, a local literacies approach advanced by Street (1994) and Luke, O'Brien & Comber (1994) proposes the need for access and validity in school settings for vernacular literacies (McLaughlin, 1996) closely associated with subcultures that are marginal, misrepresented or absent in mainstream institutions. And in a similar vein, the 'unofficial curriculum' of popular culture and out-of-school learning settings provides another productive site for ethnographies of vernacular, popular and subcultures that young people inhabit around and beyond school (Dimitriadis & Weis, 2001; Scherpf, 2001). More recently, there has been interest in 'place-based' education that argues for curriculum that enables 'students to connect what they are learning to their own lives, communities, and regions' (Smith, 2002). The multiliteracies project (New London Group, 1996), mentioned above, argues for 'situated practice', or that part of curriculum that aims to 'recruit learners' previous and current experiences, as well as their extra-school communities and discourses, as an integral part of the learning experience' (p. 85). In a similar vein, the *productive pedagogies* approach adopted by the Queensland Department of Education and Training proposes 'connectedness' as one of its four key elements – connectedness being defined in terms of knowledge integration, connecting with students' background knowledge, connecting with real-life contexts and engaging in problem-based curriculum tasks (Hayes, Mills, Christie & Lingard, 2006, pp. 53–60). Shor (1988) also refers to 'situated' pedagogy, which he defines in these terms: '[t]he course is … situated in the language, statements, issues and knowledge students bring to class. Their cognitive and social situation is the starting point, not my prefabricated syllabus' (p. 108). All of these approaches, in one way or another, pursue a theory and practice of teachers-as-ethnographers and students-as-researchers (Egan-Robertson & Bloom, 1998; Kincheloe & Steinberg, 1998; Thomson & Comber, 2003).

## Professional learning should focus on the existential classroom challenges of teachers

Unfortunately, too much professional learning in schools is driven by the demand to implement systems policy, which is very evident when reading School Improvement Plans. In which case, the problems being attended to have been named elsewhere than in schools and the purpose for professional learning is 'implementing' the policy. As a consequence, the problems and challenges of classroom teachers are marginalised or ignored in the tight scheduling of professional development time. But, as Hayes *et al.* (2009, p. 253) argue, 'the sticking point remains *practice*'. They point out the weakness of models of improving professional practice in schools in contexts of high poverty and difference that rely upon the faithful adoption of something shown to work elsewhere, since such approaches do not sufficiently take into account local knowledge about young people, their lifeworlds and learning needs. Instead, 'improvement relies upon being able to develop new knowledge about what is possible in these contexts and … this is primarily a pedagogical challenge associated with supporting the [local] professional learning of teachers and leaders' (Hayes *et al.*, 2009, p. 263). For the sake of clarity here, we are not arguing that schools ignore system policies or practice that is shown to work elsewhere, but we are arguing that school-based professional learning should be driven, in the first instance, by those existential challenges that teachers struggle with in their classrooms.

What Hayes and colleagues point to is the need to support action research-driven, professional learning opportunities for teachers, which we think have the greatest potential for supporting teachers' engagement in the process of redesigning pedagogy (see Luke & Freebody, 1999). Collaborative and participatory action research has growing influence internationally and in Australian educational research, contributing to teacher capacity-building and professional renewal in local settings (Hattam, Zipin, Brennan & Comber, 2009; Somekh, 2006; Somekh &

Zeichner, 2009). Such methodologies enable the systematic examination of the redesigning of pedagogic practice by teachers.

### Resist buying in the solution without due diligence

We were not surprised to observe similar pedagogical practices across our study schools, since they were operating according to literacy agreements, discussed in Chapter 2, which detailed what would be taught and assessed in order to 'raise literacy standards'. Although these documents were locally negotiated, they included a number of agreements that were common to all the schools about what counted as good literacy pedagogy. Hence, common features of the agreements included structural arrangements, such as the Literacy Block; and the adoption of commercially available resources, such as Jolly Phonics, Lexile reading levels, the teaching of genres and so on. The retreat of systems-led curriculum and professional development during the past 20 years or so now means that many educational leaders look for commercial products that might provide solutions to their problems. In which case, schools are now prey to all manner of educational entrepreneurs selling their wares (Au & Ferrare, 2015; Ball, 2012; Ball & Junemann, 2012; Junemann & Ball, 2015; Reckow, 2013). In the words of Hogan (2016):

> A pervasive neoliberal imaginary has been working to recast education policy-making in specific ways, where contemporary policy settings now encourage the privatisation of education as a key means to improve school effectiveness and the quality of student outcomes. Such an approach to education has challenged the ideology of the traditional state-centred public provision of schooling, opening it instead to market-based processes of reform. Here not only does the state adopt neoliberal policy principles that encourage the discourses of accountability, competition and choice in education, but the state also works to open public policy processes to private sector participation.
>
> (pp. 93–4)

As we have argued earlier, we are not against commercial products *per se*, but our research revealed that too often the simple adoption of such material and models means that classroom practice gets dumbed down. These resources can lead to overdetermined ritual performance by teachers, which in turn undermines the opportunities for learning that connect with the unique children in every classroom.

### Implications for policy

Education system policies must enable the highest-quality teaching and learning to take place where it is needed most – in schools like the ones in our study. In order for this to be achieved, school funding has to be redistributed in ways that redresses the residualisation that has occurred due to past and current funding policies in schools primarily serving children from disadvantaged families. It is not just a problem of funding but also a problem of testing – since, as we have argued, standardised tests are likely to result in a more narrow view of literacy in places where young people need more support to match the levels of literacy achieved by their peers in less residualised settings.

School funding in Australia is internationally unusual because of the extent to which government funds private schooling (Nous Group, 2011, p. 5). However, the majority of schools serving children living in poverty are part of the public school system and evidence is mounting that the residualisation of public schooling is now a serious policy problem for Australian state and federal governments (Bonnor & Shepherd, 2016). In his report, *From Opportunity to Outcomes*, Teese (2011, p. 20) describes the changing role of national funding arrangements and the pattern of residualisation it generates:

> In poor urban areas, public schools 'over-reflect' the social profile of the area. They have a disproportionate share of the poorest families, but also of children who are most educationally disadvantaged (not necessarily by socioeconomic status). Local community after local community displays a characteristic pattern in which nongovernment schools – whether Catholic or private non-Catholic – 'under-reflect' the social profile of the area, though not invariably. They recruit a disproportionate share of socially and also academically advantaged children …
>
> The result is a pattern of residualisation in poorer communities, and an intensification of the stress experienced in public schools in more socially mixed areas. The division of labour between schools works in such a way as to create more socially blended environments in the private sector and more complex and manifold disadvantage in the public sector.
>
> *(Teese, 2011, p. vii)*

Kenway (2013) refers to the problem as educational ghettoisation that exists in many urban suburbs: 'ghettos of luxury, praise and prospects at one end of the spectrum and ghettos of necessity, stagnation and denigration at the other' (p. 300). But there is little evidence that any jurisdiction is taking this seriously, other than an attempt by the Federal Labor party to support increasing levels of funding for public school in the 2016 federal election. What is clear, however, is that residualisation of public schooling is created by systemic policy failures and a lack of will by government to intervene in the politics of school funding in Australia. In Kenway's terms, no government seems 'willing to take on the extraordinary lobbying power of the non-government sector' (p. 297). Either way, we suggest that policy-makers review the rationale for policy, especially the ways that parental choice logic works, or not, as the case may be. There is no level playing field when most parents do not have a choice, and public schools decline whilst the elite schools are able to use public funding to further differentiate themselves on the basis of superior school infrastructure, lower class sizes and so on.

Central to our concerns are the ways in which the problem of 'equity' and 'inequity' has been refashioned in recent years. Equity can now mean that everyone should be treated the same; and inequity now means not making a contribution to the schooling of all children, even when some come from families with the means to provide them with a well-resourced education without the need for public funding. Under such logics, redistribution is rendered inequitable and parents living in high-poverty communities are blamed for not having enough economic capital to pay for private schooling. Kenway argues that funding arrangements in Australia show subtle but important relationships between different sectors of schooling. The principle of funding all students across sectors means that 'advantage can be built from disadvantage' (Kenway, 2013, p. 306). For Kenway, a failure to acknowledge these relationships lets the 'elite schools in all sectors … off the hook with no expectation on them to seriously consider, let alone attend to, their social responsibilities to less fortunate students and schools' (p. 306).

Approaches to policy-making need to support and enable the leadership and pedagogical practices that we have set out in this chapter. This means, for example, that one-size-fits-all policy logics are unlikely to support educational leaders and teachers to inquire into their local contexts and develop the kinds of practices that are needed to support their students' learning. These inquiry processes require educational leaders who are focused on improving teachers' professional practice and the capacity of schooling processes to respond to local needs. Whereas, different kinds of leadership are required to ensure compliance with externally imposed standards of professional practice and assessments of the needs of students. Current education policy requires educational leaders to attend to both of these demands, while providing limited support to achieve either one of them.

## Further research

We are reluctant to end the book with implications for research, because what really matters is how the schooling of children living in poverty can be improved. But we also believe that the detailed research that has led to this book has demonstrated the continued value of school ethnographies in illuminating the practices of educational leaders and teachers, which is too often masked in high-level policy prescriptions. Research, especially if it can be done alongside teachers and leaders, has an important role to play. Thus we suggest that there is a need for further national multisited ethnographies of educational leadership; and, in the context of global testing mechanisms, these should be extended to international studies. Such approaches are particularly suited to investigating important issues raised in our research about the impact of educational, economic and social policies on schools in high-poverty contexts. We suggest that there is an ongoing need to examine the effects of the intensification of poverty and the increasing cultural diversity of communities on schools, leadership and pedagogy.

One of the methodological themes we have attempted to develop in this book has been the requirement to be more attentive to the local school-level rationality when examining policy effects. We think that too much policy sociology laminates over important school-level realities and then provides overdetermined accounts of systemic policy and its effects. In which case, we need to be developing theoretical frames for accounting for local school logics and how these get developed, sustained and enacted. Our research points to all manner of local rationalities that significantly affected leadership practices, curriculum, pedagogy and student learning that did not come from outside of the school, or at least not in the recent past. For us, a frontier for policy effect studies is to be giving accounts of the relationships between systems policy and the local rationality of schools and how this plays out in defining school structures, school culture and pedagogical change.

Future research could further investigate the promising pedagogies of Suzy, Alicia, Jason, Carrie and others, especially the ways in which they communicate with students, negotiate high-expectations curriculum, and design enabling and worthwhile tasks. It would also document how school leaders can support such work and provide opportunities for it to flourish beyond individual classrooms. How and when might their peers engage in collegial learning? And what of their students? As researchers, we could see the high levels of demonstrable student engagement in these classrooms; future studies would document the ways in which different students were able to learn in these classrooms over time. To what extent do they equip students with durable and varied repertoires of literate practices? To what extent might several years in Andrea's classroom play out for Gus? How might Jeff's insights about his child's learning experiences inform what happens in the school? Such inquiries would involve extended research partnerships between school- and university-based educators working together to make a difference.

## References

Apple, M., & Beane, J. (eds.). (1995). *Democratic Schools*. Alexandria, Virginia: Association for Supervision and Curriculum Development.

Ashurst, F., & Venn, C. (2014). *Inequality, Poverty, Education: A political economy of school exclusion*. Basingstoke, Hampshire: Palgrave Macmillan.

Au, W. (2009). *Unequal by Design: High stakes testing and the standardization of inequality*. New York: Routledge.

Au, W., & Ferrare, J. (eds.). (2015). *Mapping Corporate Education Reform*. New York: Routledge.

Ball, S. (1997). 'Good school/bad school: Paradox and fabrication'. *British Educational Research Journal*, *18*(3), 317–36.

Ball, S. (2012). *Global Education Inc: New policy networks and the neoliberal social imaginary*. London: Routledge.

Ball, S., & Junemann, C. (2012). *Networks, New Governance and Education*. Bristol, UK: The Policy Press.

Bonnor, C., & Shepherd, B. (2016). *Uneven Playing Field: The state of Australia's schools*. Sydney, New South Wales: Centre for Policy Development. Retrieved 13 July 2016 from http://cpd.org.au/category/publications/policy-papers/.

Brown, W. (2015). *Undoing the Demos: Neoliberalism's stealth revolution*. New York: Zone Books.

Chapman, T., & Hobbel, N. (2010). *Social Justice Pedagogy Across the Curriculum: The practice of freedom*. London: Routledge.

Comber, B. (2016). 'Poverty, place and pedagogy in education: Research stories from front-line workers'. *Australian Educational Researcher, 43*(4), 393–417.

Comber, B., & Kamler, B. (eds.) (2005). *Turn-around Pedagogies: Literacy interventions for at-risk students*. Newtown: Primary English Teaching Association.

Cope, B., & Kalantzis, M. (eds.) (2000). *Multiliteracies: Literacy learning and the design of social futures*. Melbourne, Victoria: Macmillan.

Dimitriadis, G., & Weis, L. (2001). 'Imagining possibilities with and for contemporary youth: (Re)writing and (re)visioning education today'. *Qualitative Research, 1*(2), 223–40.

Duggan, L. (2003). *The Twilight of Equality? Neoliberalism, cultural politics and the attack on democracy*. Boston: Beacon Press.

Durrant, C. & Green, B. (2000). 'Literacy and the new technologies in school education: Meeting the l(IT)eracy challenge'. *Australian Journal of Language and Literacy, 23*(2), 89–108.

Egan-Robertson, A., & Bloom, D. (eds.) (1998). *Students as Researchers of Culture in Their Own Communities*. Cresskill, NJ: Hampton Press.

Fitzgerald, R. T. (1976). *Poverty and Education in Australia: Commission of inquiry into poverty*. 5th Main Report. Canberra: Australian Government Publishing Service (AGPS).

Freebody, P. (1992). 'A sociocultural approach: Resourcing the four roles as a literacy learner'. In A. Watson & A. Badenhope (eds.), *Prevention of Reading Failure* (pp. 48–60). Sydney: Ashton Scholastic.

Freebody, P., & Luke, A. (1990). 'Literacies programs: Debates and demands in cultural context'. *Prospect: Australian Journal of TESOL, 5*(7), 7–16.

Giroux, H. (1994). *Disturbing Pleasures: Learning popular culture*. New York: Routledge.

Goldfarb, B. (2002). *Visual Pedagogy: Media cultures in and beyond the classroom*. Durham and London: Duke University Press.

González, N., Moll, L., & Amanti, C. (2005). *Funds of Knowledge: Theorising practices in households, communities, and classrooms*. Mahwah, NJ, Lawrence Erlbaum Associates.

Green, B. (1988). 'Subject-specific literacy and school learning: A focus on writing'. *Australian Journal of Education, 32*(2), 156–179.

Griffith, A., & Smith, D. (eds.) (2014). *Under New Public Management: Institutional ethnographies of changing front-line work*. Toronto: University of Toronto Press, Scholarly Publishing Division.

Gunter, H. (2012). *Leadership and the Reform of Education*. Bristol, UK: The Policy Press.

Gutiérrez, K., Morales, P. Z., & Martinez, D. (2009). 'Re-mediating literacy: Culture, difference, and learning for students from nondominant communities'. *Review of Research in Education, 33*, 212–45.

Hacking, I. (1986). 'Making up people'. In T. Heller, M. Sosna & D. Wellbery (eds.), *Reconstructing Individualism* (pp. 222–36). Stanford: Stanford University Press.

Hattam, R. (2010). '"Listen to me I'm still leaving": Young people's perspectives on school'. In T. Stehlik & J. Patterson (eds.), *Changing the Paradigm: Education as the key to a socially inclusive future*. Mt. Gravatt, Qld: PostPressed.

Hattam, R., Zipin, L., Brennan, M., & Comber, B. (2009). 'Researching for social justice: Contextual, conceptual and methodological challenges'. *Discourse: Studies in the Cultural Politics of Education, 30*(3), 303–16.

Hayes, D., Johnston, K., & King, A. (2009). 'Creating enabling classroom practices in high poverty contexts: The disruptive possiiblities of looking in classrooms'. *Pedagogy, Culture & Society, 17*(3), 251–64.

Hayes, D., Mills, M., Christie, P., & Lingard, B. (2006). *Teachers and Schooling. Making a Difference: Productive pedagogies and assessment.* Sydney: Allen & Unwin.

Hogan, A. (2016). 'NAPLAN and the role of edu-business: New governance, new privatisations and new partnerships in Australian education policy'. *Australian Educational Researcher, 43*(1), 93–110.

Johnston, K., & Hayes, D. (2008). '"This is as good as it gets": Classroom lessons and learning in challenging circumstances'. *Australian Journal of Language and Literacy, 31*(2), 109–27.

Junemann, C., & Ball, S. (2015). *Pearson and PALF: The mutating giant.* Brussels: Education International.

Kenway, J. (2013). 'Challenging inequality in Australian schools: Gonski and beyond'. *Discourse: Studies in the Cultural Politics of Education, 34*(2), 286–308.

Kerkham, L., & Comber, B. (2016). 'Literacy leadership and accountability: Holding onto ethics in ways that count'. In B. Lingard, G. Thompson & S. Sellar (eds.), *Testing in Schools: An Australian assessment* (pp. 86–97). London and New York: Routledge.

Kerkham, L., & Nixon, H. (2014). 'Literacy assessment that counts: Mediating, interpreting and contesting translocal policy in a primary school'. *Ethnography and Education, 9*(3), 343–58. doi:10.1080/17457823.2014.917592.

Kincheloe, J., & Steinberg, S. (eds.) (1998). *Unauthorized Methods: Strategies for critical teaching.* New York: Routledge.

Kress, G. (2003). *Literacy in the New Media Age.* London: Routledge.

Kress, G., & Jewett, C. (eds.) (2003). *Multimodal Literacy.* New York: Peter Lang.

Lankshear, C., & Knobel, M. (2003). *New Literacies: Changing knowledge and classroom learning.* Buckingham: Open University Press.

Lessa, L. (2006). 'Discursive struggles within social welfare'. *British Journal of Social Work, 36*(2), 283–98.

Lingard, B. (2007). 'Pedagogies of indifference'. *International Journal of Inclusive Education, 11*(3), 245–66.

Lipman, P. (1998). *Race, Class and Power in School Restructuring.* New York: SUNY Press.

Luke, A., O'Brien, J., & Comber, B. (1994). 'Making community texts objects of study'. *Australian Journal of Language and Literacy, 17*(2), 139–49.

Luke, A., & Freebody, P. (1999). 'A map of possible practices: Further notes on the four resources model'. *Practically Primary, 4*(2), 5–8.

Lupton, R. (2005). 'Social justice and school improvement: Improving the quality of schooling in the poorest neighbourhoods'. *British Educational Research Journal, 31*(5), 589–604.

McInerney, P. (2004). *Making Hope Practical: School reform for social justice.* Flaxton, Qld.: Post Pressed.

McLachlan, R., Gilfillan, G., & Gordon, J. (2013). *Deep and Persistent Disadvantage in Australia.* Canberra: Productivity Commission Staff Working Paper.

McLaughlin, T. (1996). *Street Smarts and Critical Theory: Listening to the vernacular.* Madison, WI: University of Wisconsin Press.

Moll, L. (2005). 'Reflection and possibilities'. In L. Moll, N. González & C. Amanti (eds.), *Funds of Knowledge: Theorizing practices in households, communities and classrooms.* Mahwah, New Jersey: Lawrence Erlbaum.

Moll, L., Amanti, C., Neff, D., & González, N. (1992). 'Funds of knowledge for teaching: Using a qualitative approach to connect homes and classrooms'. *Theory into Practice, 31*(2), 132–41.

Munns, G., Sawyer, W., & Cole, B. (eds.) (2013). *Exemplary Teachers of Students in Poverty: The fair go team.* London: Routledge.

New London Group (1996). 'A pedagogy of multiliteracies: Designing social futures'. *Harvard Educational Review, 66*(1), 60–92.

Nixon, H. (2003). 'New research literacies for contemporary research into literacy and new media?' *Reading Research Quarterly, 38*(4), 407–13.

Nous Group (2011). *Schooling Challenges and Opportunities: A report for the review of funding for schooling panel.* Melbourne: Melbourne Graduate School of Education.

Peel, M. (2003). *The Lowest Rung: Voices of Australian poverty.* Cambridge, UK: Cambridge University Press.

Perales, F., Higginson, A., Baxter, J., Western, M., Zubrick, S., & Mitrou, F. (2014). *Intergenerational Welfare Dependency in Australia: A review of the literature.* LCC Working Paper Series. Life Course Centre, Institute for Social Science Research, The University of Queensland.

Prosser, B., Lucas, B., & Reid, A. (eds.). (2010). *Connecting Lives and Learning: Renewing pedagogy in the middle years.* Kent Town, South Australia: Wakefield Press.

Reckow, S. (2013). *Follow the Money: How foundation dollars change public school politics.* New York: Oxford University Press.

Roche, M. (1987). 'Social theory and the lifeworld'. *British Journal of Sociology, 38*(2), 283–87.

Rose, N. (1999). *Powers of Freedom: Reframing Political Thought.* Cambridge, UK: Cambridge University Press.

Scherpf, S. (2001). 'Rap pedagogy: The potential for democratization'. *The Review of Education/Pedagogy/Cultural Studies, 23*(1), 73–110.

Shor, I. (1988). 'Working hands and critical minds: A Paulo Freire model for job training'. *Journal of Education, 170*(2), 102–21.

Simons, S., & Masschelein, J. (2008). '"It makes us believe that it's about our freedom": Notes on the irony of the learning apparatus'. In S. Smeyers & M. Depaepe (eds.), *Eductional Research: The educationalization of social problems.* Dordrecht, Netherlands: Springer.

Smith, D. (2006). 'Incorporating texts into ethnographic practice'. *Institutional Ethnography as Practice* (pp. 65–88). Lanham, Maryland: Rowman & Littlefield Publishers.

Smith, G. (2002). 'Place-based education: Learning to be where we are'. *Phi Delta Kappan, 83*(8), 584–94.

Smyth, J., & Hattam, R. (2004). *'Dropping Out', Drifting Off, Being Excluded: Becoming somebody without school.* New York: Peter Lang.

Somekh, B. (2006). *Action Research: A methodology for change and development.* Maidenhead, Berkshire: Open University Press.

Somekh, B., & Zeichner, K. (2009). 'Action research for educational reform: Remodelling action research theories and practices in local contexts'. *Educational Action Research, 17*(1), 5–21.

Steinberg, S., & Kincheloe, J. (1998). *Students as Researchers: Creating classrooms that matter.* London: Falmer.

Street, B. (1994). 'What is meant by local literacies?' *Language and Education, 8*(1/2), 9–17.

Sullivan, A., Johnson, B., & Lucas, B. (2016). *Challenging Dominant Views of Student Behaviour in Schools: Answering back.* Dordrecht, Netherlands: Springer.

te Riele, K. (ed.) (2009). *Making Schools Different: Alternative approaches to educating young people.* London: Sage.

Teese, R. (2011). *From Opportunity to Outcomes. The changing role of public schooling in Australia and national funding arrangements.* Melbourne University: Centre for Research on Education Systems.

Thomson, P. (1998). 'Thoroughly modern management and a cruel accounting: The effects of public sector reform on public education'. In A. Reid (ed.), *Education Policy and Public*

*Education in Australia* (pp. 37–46). Deakin West, Canberra: Australian Curriculum Studies Association.

Thomson, P., & Comber, B. (2003). 'Deficient "disadvantaged students" or media-savvy meaning makers? Engaging new metaphors for redesigning classrooms and pedagogies'. *McGill Journal of Education, 38*(2), 305–28.

Troman, G. (2000). 'Teacher stress in the low-trust society'. *British Journal of Sociology of Education, 21*(3), 331–53.

Willmott, H. (1993). 'Strength is ignorance; slavery is freedom: Managing culture in modern organisations'. *Journal of Management Studies, 30*(4), 515–52.

Wrigley, T. (2012). 'Rethinking school effectiveness and improvement: A question of paradigms'. *Discourse: Studies in the Cultural Politics of Education, 34*(1), 31–47. doi:10.1080/0 1596306.2012.698862.

# APPENDIX

It is clearly stated on the National Assessment Programme Literacy and Numeracy (NAPLAN) website that NAPLAN is not a test of content. Rather, it 'tests the types of skills that are essential for every child to progress through school and life. The tests cover skills in reading, writing, spelling, grammar and punctuation, and numeracy' (Australian Curriculum Assessment and Reporting Authority, 2016). NAPLAN is a 'census test' (Lingard, Thompson & Sellar, 2016, p. 4) and participation is mandated for all Australian schools that receive funding from the federal government. Because it is a 'census test' the data it generates can be used to monitor and compare individual students, schools and even teachers, although that is not our purview here.

The NAPLAN data we present is a selection of data that is publicly available on the *My School* website (Australian Curriculum Assessment and Reporting Authority, 2014). *My School* displays cumulative data from 2008–15, making it possible to track the schools' performances over seven years. Data in the form of graphs, numbers, bands and student gain are displayed for each literacy domain (reading, writing, grammar and punctuation, and spelling).

The visual impact of the tables of 'results in numbers' deserves comment before we turn to a brief discussion of the results. For each domain and year level, the score for the school is recorded in a box, beneath which are two columns – one where the average score for 'like schools' is recorded, and one where the average for 'all schools' is recorded. The colour coding is associated with these last two scores. A red square below the school's test score indicates that the scores are substantially below the average of schools serving 'students from similar socio-educational backgrounds' and the average of all Australian schools; a pink square indicates that test scores are below these averages; a white square indicates that the scores are close to the averages; a light green square indicates above the averages; and a dark green square indicates that the scores are substantially above the averages. The NAPLAN tables included use the following key for shading to represent the colours:

Substantially below the average of similar schools

Below the average of similar schools

Close to the average of similar schools

Above the average of similar schools

Substantially above the average of similar schools

In the following sections, we briefly discuss the NAPLAN data for each of the schools in our study, focusing on bands and 'results in numbers' for 2008–14.

## Riverview NAPLAN results

NAPLAN results for 2008–14 show that almost 90 per cent of student scores for each of the literacy tests fall into the lower two NAPLAN bands, and that while there were significantly fewer in the lowest quarter in 2012, the improvement was not sustainable. Over the seven years, the number of students achieving in the top quarter is minimal and overall improvement fluctuates (Figure A.1).

The visual display on the *My School* website, and the reports that are sent to the school, show NAPLAN scores becoming 'lighter', indicating that students were performing as well as or better than students with 'similar socio-educational backgrounds' or 'like schools' (Australian Curriculum Assessment and Reporting Authority, 2014).

In 2008 scores for each component were 'dark grey', substantially below 'like schools' and 'all schools'. In 2011, Year 3 persuasive writing was above scores for 'like schools' (light diagonal). In 2013 the school was ranked in the top 25 schools across Australia for improvement in NAPLAN scores, with 63 per cent of Year 5 students achieving above the national average in the writing test (see also Bond, 2013). In 2014, except for Year 7 persuasive writing and grammar and punctuation (both light diagonal) all other component scores were close to those of 'like schools' (white), while being below (light grey) or well below (dark grey) 'all schools' (Figure A.2).

| Year | Bottom quarter | Middle quarters | | Top quarter |
|------|----------------|-----------------|------|-------------|
| 2008 | 75% | 23% | 2% | 0 |
| 2009 | Data not reported | | | |
| 2010 | 71% | 19% | 9% | 2% |
| 2011 | 62% | 29% | 10% | 0 |
| 2012 | 47% | 39% | 14% | 0 |
| 2013 | 59% | 30% | 10% | 2% |
| 2014 | 67% | 23% | 9% | 1% |

**FIGURE A.1**   Riverview NAPLAN data by quarters.

| | Reading | | Narrative writing | | Spelling | | Grammar & punctuation | |
|---|---|---|---|---|---|---|---|---|
| **Yr. 3** | **331** 312–350 | | **368** 352–384 | | **313** 296–330 | | **316** 296–336 | |
| | SIM **363** 354–372 | ALL **400** | SIM **384** 376–392 | ALL 414 | SIM **367** 358–376 | ALL **400** | SIM **361** 351–371 | ALL **403** |
| **Yr. 5** | **413** 393–433 | | **413** 394–432 | | **405** 387–423 | | **427** 405–449 | |
| | SIM **450** 441–459 | ALL **484** | SIM **455** 447–463 | ALL **486** | SIM **455** 447–463 | ALL **484** | SIM **456** 447–465 | ALL **496** |
| **Yr. 7** | **468** 450–486 | | **480** 460–500 | | **453** 434–472 | | **452** 432–472 | |
| | SIM **503** 496–510 | ALL **536** | SIM **498** 489–507 | ALL **534** | SIM **509** 501–517 | ALL **539** | SIM **491** 482–500 | ALL **529** |

**FIGURE A.2a** Riverview NAPLAN results in numbers for 2008.

| | Reading | | Persuasive writing | | Spelling | | Grammar & punctuation | |
|---|---|---|---|---|---|---|---|---|
| **Yr. 3** | **405** 380–431 | | **397** 375–418 | | **389** 366–412 | | **407** 380–434 | |
| | SIM **380** 371–389 | ALL **419** | SIM **378** 370–386 | ALL **416** | SIM **372** 363–380 | ALL **411** | SIM **386** 376–396 | ALL **428** |
| **Yr. 5** | **467** 437–498 | | **431** 406–445 | | **440** 415–464 | | **449** 421–477 | |
| | SIM **469** 461–478 | ALL **502** | SIM **439** 431–447 | ALL **478** | SIM **458** 450–466 | ALL **494** | SIM **460** 450–469 | ALL **501** |
| **Yr. 7** | **496** 475–518 | | **437** 413–461 | | **485** 463–507 | | **487** 462–511 | |
| | SIM **504** 496–511 | ALL **541** | SIM **475** 467–484 | ALL **517** | SIM **512** 504–519 | ALL **549** | SIM **492** 483–500 | ALL **535** |

**FIGURE A.2b** Riverview NAPLAN results in numbers for 2013.

| | Reading | | Persuasive writing | | Spelling | | Grammar & punctuation | |
|---|---|---|---|---|---|---|---|---|
| **Yr. 3** | **365** 340–391 | | **367** 346–388 | | **357** 334–380 | | **361** 334–388 | |
| | SIM | ALL | SIM | ALL | SIM | ALL | SIM | ALL |
| | **367** 358–376 | **418** | **358** 350–366 | **402** | **364** 356–373 | **412** | **368** 358–378 | **426** |
| **Yr. 5** | **441** 418–465 | | **433** 411–455 | | **452** 430–473 | | **442** 417–468 | |
| | SIM | ALL | SIM | ALL | SIM | ALL | SIM | ALL |
| | **454** 445–462 | **501** | **425** 417–433 | **468** | **456** 448–464 | **498** | **453** 443–462 | **504** |
| **Yr. 7** | **506** 485–527 | | **483** 459–507 | | **502** 480–524 | | **517** 493–541 | |
| | SIM | ALL | SIM | ALL | SIM | ALL | SIM | ALL |
| | **503** 496–510 | **546** | **462** 453–470 | **512** | **501** 494–509 | **545** | **496** 487–505 | **543** |

**FIGURE A.2c**  Riverview NAPLAN results in numbers for 2014.

## Sandford NAPLAN results

In 2011 NAPLAN results 'hadn't been fantastic apart from reading in year 3' according to the principal, although running[1] records and other school-based assessment had shown improvements. NAPLAN results for 2011-14[2] show that almost all student scores for each of the literacy tests fall into the lower two NAPLAN bands, although small improvements in reading are being achieved each year (Table A.1). The writing test scores, however, show a continuing downward trend, especially for Year 7 students.

It is difficult to make definitive statements about the scores and what might be attributable to any improvement or lack thereof. As is the case in all three city schools, the student population is highly transient and only about half the students at any given year level sit consecutive tests. The concept of 'student gain' at cohort level in a school is somewhat problematic for that reason.

**TABLE A.1** Sandford NAPLAN data in quarters

| Year | Bottom quarter | Middle quarters | | Top quarter |
|---|---|---|---|---|
| 2011 | 40% | 60% | 0 | 0 |
| 2012 | 83% | 15% | 2% | 0 |
| 2013 | 72% | 20% | 7% | 1% |
| 2014 | 70% | 21% | 8% | 2% |

In 2011, except for the Year 7 results which were similar to 'like schools' in each domain, Sandford's scores are either below (light grey) or substantially below (dark grey) 'like schools' and the national average. In 2014, except for Year 7, the actual scores in each domain improved in each domain and in all year levels. However, the test scores are either below or substantially below 'like schools' and 'all schools' (Figure A.3).

## Easton NAPLAN results

Between 2008 and 2014 the percentage of students achieving the lowest quarter dropped significantly, except for 2012 when there was an increase to 80 per cent. The percentage of students achieving the second quarter improved from 0 per cent (2 per cent achieved the third quarter) in 2008 to 31 per cent in 2010 but has declined in the following years. Overall Easton's results suggest gains across the years, with 4 per cent of students achieving the top quarter in 2013 and 2014.

Because the number of students sitting consecutive tests is almost two-thirds higher at Easton than the other two city schools, it may be possible to draw some tentative conclusions about the work teachers are doing in relation to aligning their analysis of data with focused literacy teaching. It is apparent in Table A.2 that there has been overall steady improvement in NAPLAN results, notably the percentage of students performing in the middle quarters.

|  | Reading | | Persuasive writing | | Spelling | | Grammar & punctuation | |
|---|---|---|---|---|---|---|---|---|
| Yr. 3 | **316** 291–342 | | **316** 295–337 | | **293** 270–316 | | **291** 264–318 | |
|  | SIM **370** 361–379 | ALL **416** | SIM **378** 370–386 | ALL **416** | SIM **367** 358–375 | ALL **406** | SIM **371** 361–381 | ALL **421** |
| Yr. 5 | **396** 374–418 | | **406** 386–426 | | **415** 395–435 | | **389** 366–412 | |
|  | SIM **449** 440–457 | ALL **488** | SIM **443** 435–451 | ALL **483** | SIM **448** 440–456 | ALL **484** | SIM **454** 445–463 | ALL**499** |
| Yr. 7 | **491** 472–510 | | **489** 465–513 | | **516** 496–536 | | **486** 464–508 | |
|  | SIM **503** 496–511 | ALL **540** | SIM **489** 481–498 | ALL **529** | SIM **504** 496–512 | ALL **538** | SIM **491** 483–500 | ALL **532** |

**FIGURE A.3a** Sandford NAPLAN results in numbers for 2011.

| | Reading | | Persuasive writing | | Spelling | | Grammar & punctuation | |
|---|---|---|---|---|---|---|---|---|
| | **365** 340–391 | | **367** 346–388 | | **357** 334–380 | | **361** 334–388 | |
| **Yr. 3** | SIM | ALL | SIM | ALL | SIM | ALL | SIM | ALL |
| | **367** 358–376 | **418** | **358** 350–366 | **402** | **364** 356–373 | **412** | **368** 358–378 | **426** |
| | **441** 418–465 | | **433** 411–455 | | **452** 430–473 | | **442** 417–468 | |
| **Yr. 5** | SIM | ALL | SIM | ALL | SIM | ALL | SIM | ALL |
| | **454** 445–462 | **501** | **425** 417–433 | **468** | **456** 448–464 | **498** | **453** 443–462 | **504** |
| | **506** 485–527 | | **483** 459–507 | | **502** 480–524 | | **517** 493–541 | |
| **Yr. 7** | SIM | ALL | SIM | ALL | SIM | ALL | SIM | ALL |
| | **503** 496–510 | **546** | **462** 453–470 | **512** | **501** 494–509 | **545** | **496** 487–505 | **543** |

**FIGURE A.3b**  Sandford NAPLAN results in numbers for 2014.

**TABLE A.2**  Easton NAPLAN results by quarters

| Year | Bottom quarter | Middle quarters | | Top quarter |
|---|---|---|---|---|
| 2008 | 98% | 0 | 2% | 0 |
| 2009 | 98% | 0 | 2% | 0 |
| 2010 | 58% | 31% | 8% | 3% |
| 2011 | 59% | 30% | 7% | 4% |
| 2012 | 80% | 9% | 10% | 1% |
| 2013 | 56% | 28% | 12% | 4% |
| 2014 | 54% | 29% | 13% | 4% |

In 2008, Year 3 students performed substantially better (dark diagonal) than students in similar schools on reading, spelling and punctuation and grammar. In comparison to similar schools, Year 3 and Year 7 students scored above the average for narrative writing, although lower than average compared to students across Australia.

In 2014 scores for reading and for grammar and punctuation for each year level are on a par with 'like schools'. Despite scores for persuasive writing for Year 3 and Year 7, which were above 'like schools', Easton students at each year level are below or well below the national average in three of the four domains: reading, spelling, and punctuation and grammar (Figure A.4).

| | Reading | | Narrative writing | | Spelling | | Grammar & punctuation | |
|---|---|---|---|---|---|---|---|---|
| Yr. 3 | **407** 390–424 | | **399** 384–414 | | **405** 389–421 | | **389** 371–407 | |
| | SIM **349** 340–358 | ALL **400** | SIM **372** 364–380 | ALL **414** | SIM **355** 346–364 | ALL **400** | SIM **345** 335–355 | ALL **403** |
| Yr. 5 | **439** 422–456 | | **452** 436–468 | | **445** 430–460 | | **435** 417–453 | |
| | SIM **437** 428–446 | ALL **484** | SIM **443** 435–451 | ALL **486** | SIM **445** 437–453 | ALL **484** | SIM **441** 432–450 | ALL **496** |
| Yr. 7 | **497** 481–513 | | **511** 493–529 | | **510** 494–526 | | **487** 469–505 | |
| | SIM **492** 485–499 | ALL **536** | SIM **485** 476–494 | ALL **534** | SIM **498** 490–506 | ALL **539** | SIM **477** 468–486 | ALL **529** |

**FIGURE A.4a**  Easton NAPLAN results in numbers for 2008.

| | Reading | | Persuasive writing | | Spelling | | Grammar & punctuation | |
|---|---|---|---|---|---|---|---|---|
| Yr. 3 | **394** 376–412 | | **388** 373–404 | | **388** 371–405 | | **391** 372–410 | |
| | SIM **382** 373–391 | ALL **418** | SIM **372** 364–380 | ALL **402** | SIM **377** 369–386 | ALL **412** | SIM **385** 375–395 | ALL **426** |
| Yr. 5 | **454** 436–472 | | **428** 411–445 | | **469** 453–485 | | **457** 438–476 | |
| | SIM **467** 459–476 | ALL **501** | SIM **438** 430–446 | ALL **468** | SIM **467** 459–475 | ALL **498** | SIM **467** 458–476 | ALL **504** |
| Yr. 7 | **518** 501–535 | | **499** 480–517 | | **529** 512–547 | | **519** 500–538 | |
| | SIM **514** 507–521 | ALL **546** | SIM **476** 468–485 | ALL **512** | SIM **512** 505–520 | ALL **545** | SIM **508** 500–517 | ALL **543** |

**FIGURE A.4b**  Easton NAPLAN results in numbers for 2014.

## Highfield NAPLAN results

Like Easton, Highfield has seen improvement overall in the percentage of students achieving the middle quarters.

Table A.3 indicates a sudden improvement in NAPLAN results in 2011, an improvement that was sustained for the two following years. NAPLAN scores in 2014 show only a slight decline. On average, half the students sit consecutive tests so, as with Sandford, it is difficult to know what might be making a difference to the literacy achievement that is measured by the test.

Despite the consistent predominance of dark grey and light grey shading, indicating results at least below national scores for all year levels and all literacy domains,

**TABLE A.3**  Highfield NAPLAN results by quarters

| Year | Bottom quarter | Middle quarters | | Top quarter |
|------|---------------|-----------------|----|-------------|
| 2008 | 99% | 1% | 0 | 0 |
| 2009 | 99% | 1% | 0 | 0 |
| 2010 | 97% | 3% | 0 | 0 |
| 2011 | 67% | 27% | 7% | 0 |
| 2012 | 63% | 33% | 4% | 0 |
| 2013 | 63% | 23% | 11% | 3% |
| 2014 | 69% | 21% | 9% | 2% |

| | Reading | | Narrative writing | | Spelling | | Grammar & punctuation | |
|---|---|---|---|---|---|---|---|---|
| | **351** 323–380 | | **297** 273–320 | | **292** 266–317 | | **276** 245–306 | |
| Yr. 3 | SIM **375** 366–384 | ALL **419** | SIM **372** 364–380 | ALL **416** | SIM **367** 358–375 | ALL **411** | SIM **380** 370–390 | ALL **428** |
| | **437** 411–464 | | **338** 313–362 | | **415** 391–439 | | **411** 383–439 | |
| Yr. 5 | SIM **465** 456–473 | ALL **502** | SIM **433** 425–442 | ALL **478** | SIM **453** 445–461 | ALL **494** | SIM **454** 445–463 | ALL **501** |
| | **492** 468–515 | | **455** 428–481 | | **490** 465–515 | | **499** 472–526 | |
| Yr. 7 | SIM **499** 491–506 | ALL **541** | SIM **469** 461–478 | ALL **517** | SIM **507** 499–514 | ALL **549** | SIM **486** 477–494 | ALL **535** |

**FIGURE A.5a**  Highfield NAPLAN results in numbers for 2008.

| | | Reading | | Persuasive writing | | Spelling | | Grammar & punctuation | |
|---|---|---|---|---|---|---|---|---|---|
| **Yr. 3** | | **342** 314–371 | | **338** 314–361 | | **345** 319–371 | | **336** 306–366 | |
| | | SIM **365** 356–374 | ALL **418** | SIM **357** 349–365 | ALL **402** | SIM **363** 355–372 | ALL **412** | SIM **367** 357–377 | ALL **426** |
| **Yr. 5** | | **411** 381–441 | | **371** 342–399 | | **407** 379–435 | | **378** 346–410 | |
| | | SIM **453** 444–461 | ALL **501** | SIM **424** 416–432 | ALL **468** | SIM **455** 447–463 | ALL **498** | SIM **451** 442–461 | ALL **504** |
| **Yr. 7** | | **489** 462–517 | | **475** 444–506 | | **458** 429–486 | | **476** 445–507 | |
| | | SIM **502** 495–509 | ALL **546** | SIM **461** 452–469 | ALL **512** | SIM **500** 493–508 | ALL **545** | SIM **495** 486–504 | ALL **543** |

**FIGURE A.5b** Highfield NAPLAN results in numbers for 2014.

there is some improvement in the numerical test scores over time. The results for Year 7 reading suggest that those students are performing as well as Year 7 students in 'like schools', although still well below 'all schools'.

It is not surprising, given this pattern of results in the context of the high-stakes nature of NAPLAN, that teachers might be demoralised, as Kathryn the principal at Highfield observed in an early interview. Despite their best efforts and the gains being tracked at the school level through a range of assessments such as running records, Waddington's Reading and Spelling tests (Waddington, 2000), and Westwood Spelling tests (Westwood, 2005), the NAPLAN scores seem to indicate little improvement (Figure A.5).

## Notes

1   Running records are used to document students' reading behaviours as they read aloud from a book that approximates their reading level; quantitative scores are calculated on the basis of errors and self-corrections. Level 26 indicates independent reading.
2   There were 2 schools on the site until 2010 when they were amalgamated as Sandford Primary. Results are available for this school only for the years 2011–2014.

## References

Australian Curriculum Assessment and Reporting Authority (2014). *My School*. Retrieved 3 March 2015 from http://www.myschool.edu.au.

Australian Curriculum Assessment and Reporting Authority (2016). *National Assessment Program*. Retrieved 25 June 2016 from http://www.nap.edu.au/about.

Bond, A. (2013, 9/4/13). Top results for Pirie West in NAPLAN improvement *Port Pirie Recorder*. Retrieved 12 April 2013 from http://www.portpirierecorder.com.au/story/1616958/top-results-for-pirie-west-in-naplan-improvement/.

Lingard, B., Thompson, G. & Sellar, S. (eds.) (2016). *Testing in Schools: An Australian assessment* (pp. 86–97). London and New York: Routledge.

Waddington, Neil (2000). *Diagnostic Standard and Advanced Reading and Spelling Tests 1 & 2* 2 edition Adelaide: Waddington Educational Resources Pty Ltd.

Westwood, P. (2005). *Spelling: Approaches to teaching and assessment*, Second edition, Camberwell, Victoria: ACER Press.

# INDEX